SHIPWRECK ™

WARREN ELLIS

PHIL HESTER

ERIC GAPSTUR

MARK ENGLERT

MARSHALL DILLON

AFTERSHOCK ™

S H I P

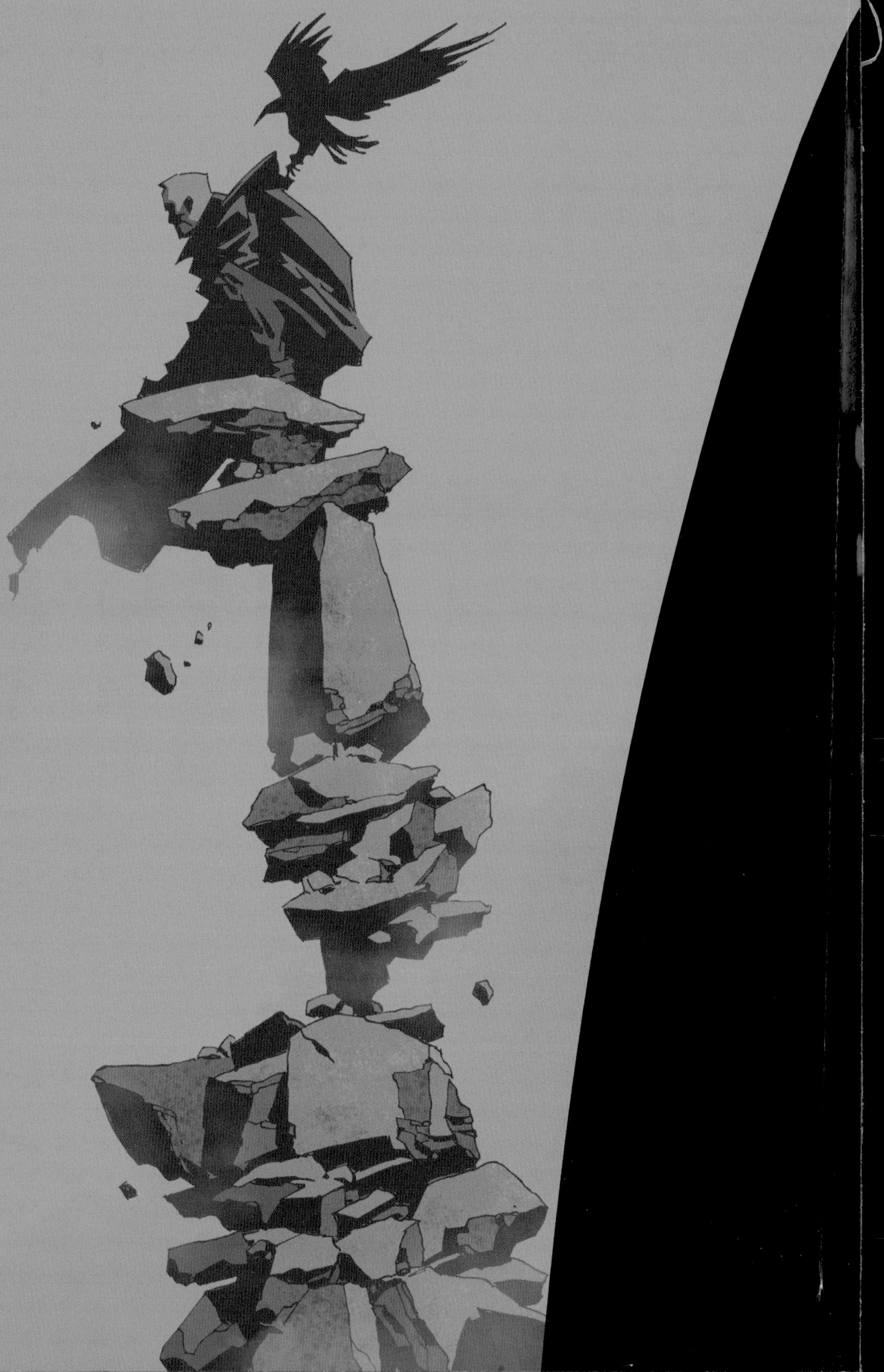

MARK ENGLERT colorist

MARSHALL DILLON letterer

PHIL HESTER front & original covers

JOHN McCREA, PHIL HESTER w/ MARK ENGLERT, DECLAN SHALVEY w/ JORDIE BELLAIRE & ELIZABETH TORQUE variant covers

COREY BREEN book designer

JOHN J. HILL logo designer

MIKE MARTS editor

AFTERSHOCK™

MIKE MARTS - Editor-in-Chief • JOE PRUETT - Publisher/ Chief Creative Officer • LEE KRAMER - President
JON KRAMER - Chief Executive Officer • MIKE ZAGARI - SVP, Brand • LISA Y. WU - Retailer/Fan Relations Manager
CHRISTINA HARRINGTON - Managing Editor • JAY BEHLING - Chief Financial Officer • JAWAD QURESHI - SVP, Investor Relations
AARON MARION - Publicist • CHRIS LA TORRE - Sales Associate • KIM PAGNOTTA - Sales Associate • LISA MOODY - Finance
CHARLES PRITCHETT - Comics Production • COREY BREEN - Collections Production • TEDDY LEO - Editorial Assistant
SIMON WHITE - Proofreader

AfterShock Trade Dress and Interior Design by JOHN J. HILL • AfterShock Logo Design by COMICRAFT
Publicity: contact AARON MARION (aaron@publichausagency.com) & RYAN CROY (ryan@publichausagency.com) at PUBLICHAUS
Special thanks to: IRA KURGEN, STEPHAN NILSON, JULIE PIFHER and SARAH PRUETT

SHIPWRECK VOL.1 Published by AfterShock Comics, LLC, 15300 Ventura Boulevard Suite 507, Sherman Oaks, CA 91403. Originally published as Shipwreck #1-6. PRINTED IN KOREA.
First Printing: June 2018. 10 9 8 7 6 5 4 3 2 1

AFTERSHOCKCOMICS.COM Follow us on social media

INTRODUCTION

Who is Shipwright? Or is it Ship*wreck*? And *where* the hell is he? Or is he *in hell*? Or is it all just the strange science dream of a wandering mad man?

I love a mystery. Nothing fires the imagination more than a good mystery. Well, *almost* nothing. A *Warren Ellis mystery* certainly does. It takes the imagination to all sorts of dark, weird places you never knew you wanted to go, but are sure glad you did. And SHIPWRECK is just that—dark, weird and full of imagination.

But, here is confession number one...there is also a big part of me that never wants a good mystery to end. Which is why I have not read the last issue of SHIPWRECK yet. Let me clarify, at the time of writing this, I do have Mr. Ellis' final script on my desktop, I just *refuse* to read it. You see, I don't want SHIPWRECK to ever end.

Here is confession number two: As much as I have admired Warren Ellis' work over the last three decades, and as much as he has inspired me to make comics, it was not Warren Ellis who got me to pick up SHIPWRECK #1 last year when it first came out. It was Phil Hester.

I have admired Phil's work for a long time, too. I remember first seeing his stuff on *Swamp Thing* in the 90s. He's drawn a *lot* of comics since then, but for my money, SHIPWRECK is his absolutely finest work. There is just something about the way Phil and his amazing inker, Eric Gapstur, draw Shipwright's worn, haunted face, and shroud his entire strange odyssey in blacks, and the way they lay the whole thing out with angular overlapping panels that I love so damn much. But Mark Englert may be the real hero. His slightly surreal, impressionistic use of color keeps everything beautifully off kilter and adds to the mystery Mr. Ellis is laying out in bizarre and unexpected ways.

Now back to Mr. Ellis and the story you now hold in your hands. It is a trip. A real journey. You feel that you are being guided by a master every step of the way. This is Warren Ellis' world, and he's the only one with the map. Now it's up to you, and poor Shipwright, to find your way without it.

So if you see me at a convention, don't tell me how it ends. I'll get there myself eventually, when I'm ready to finally read the ending. And I know I'll probably start right over and read it again when I do. That is the sign of a really good story. A really good comic book. SHIPWRECK is a lot of things, but it is first and foremost...a really, really good story. So strap in. Apporting begins in 5...4...3...2...

JEFF LEMIRE
May 2018

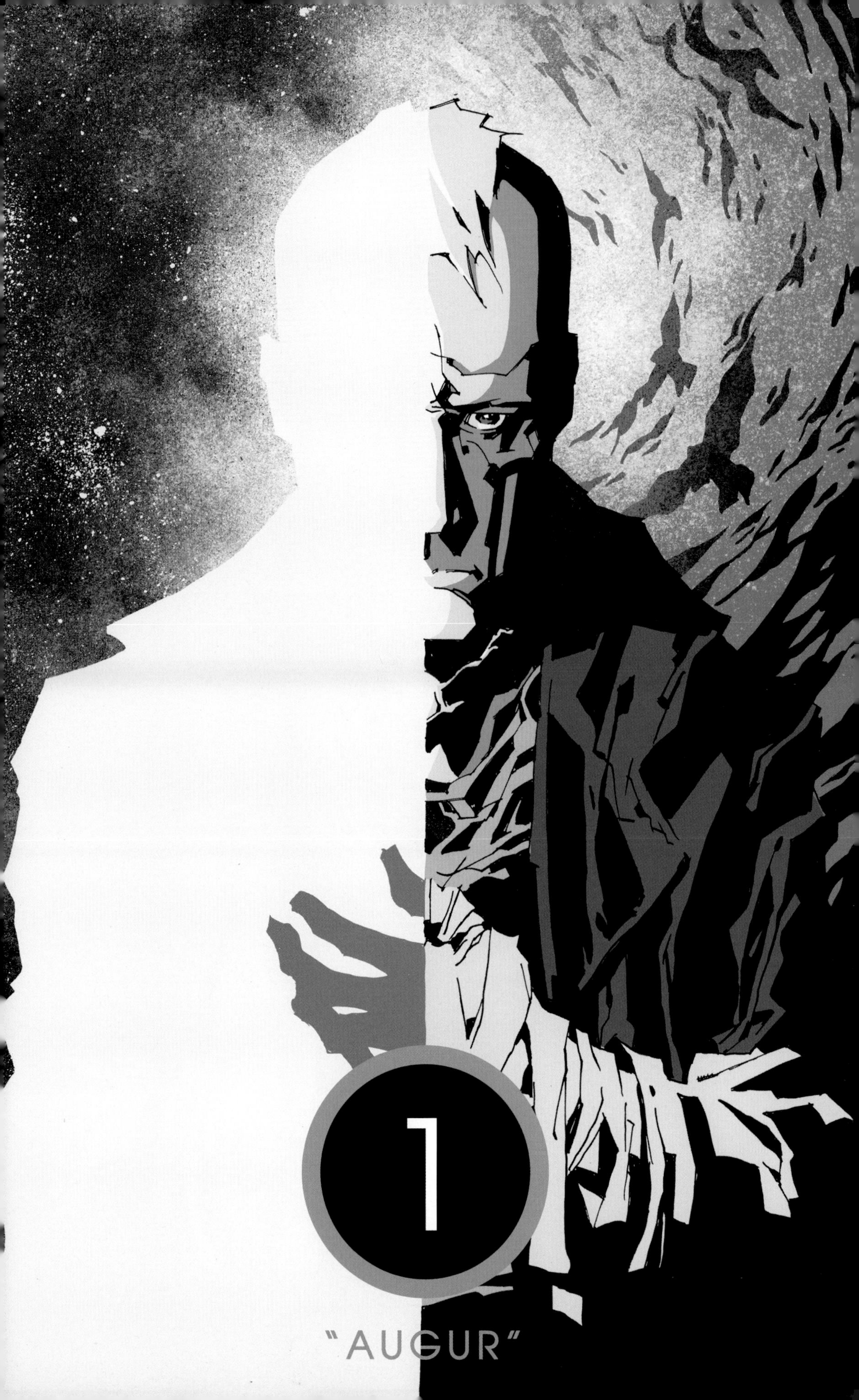
1
"AUGUR"

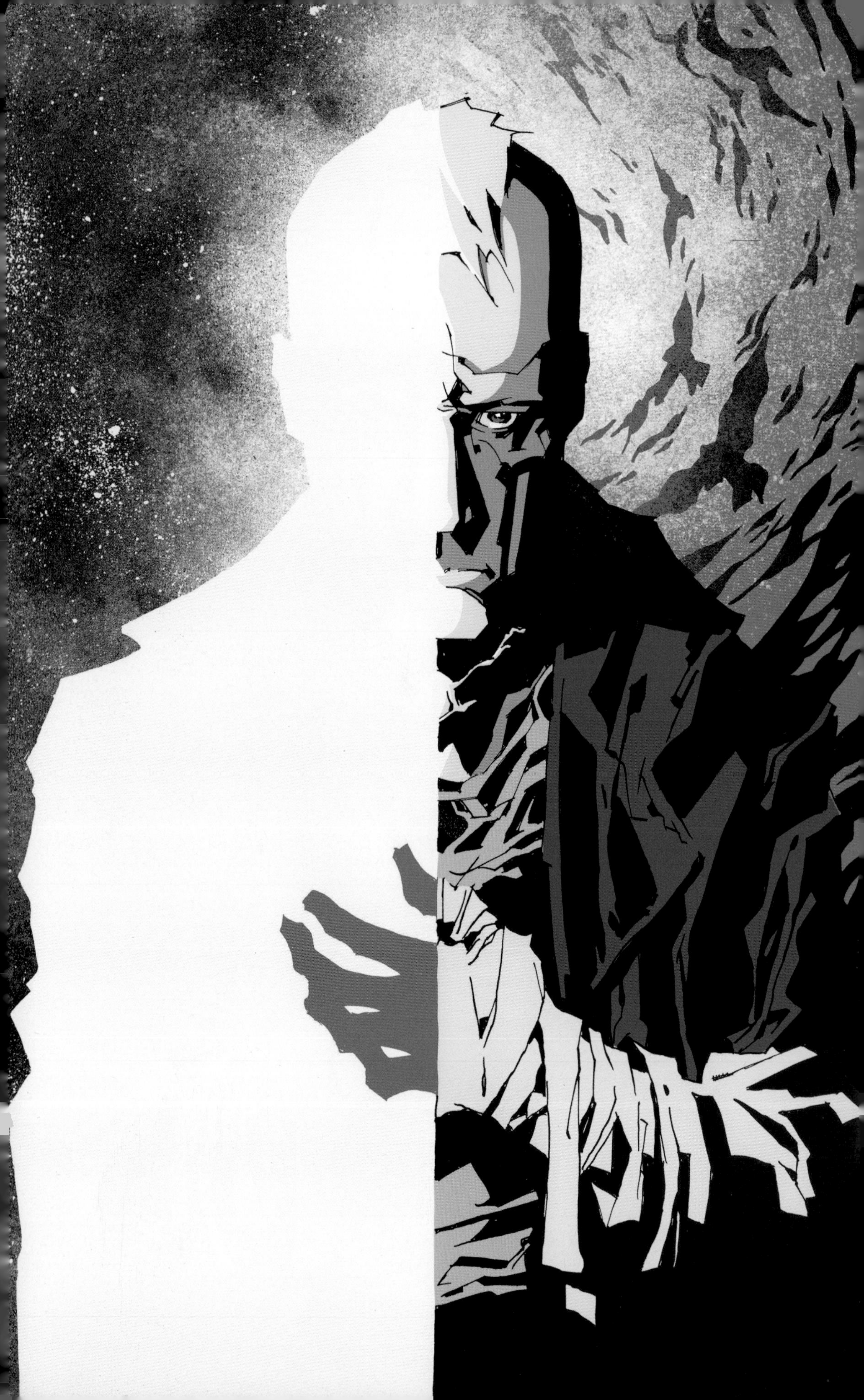

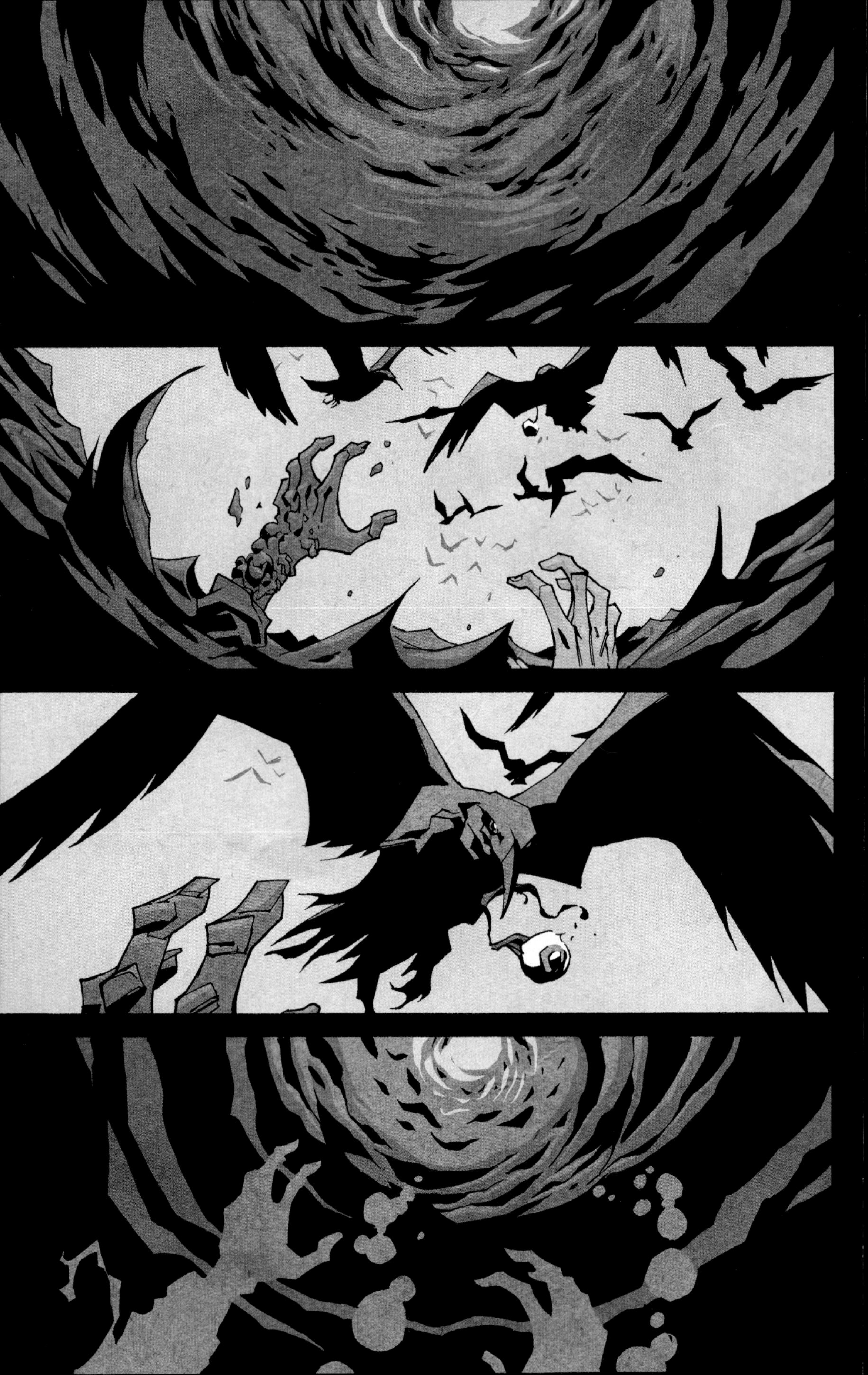

Shipwreck

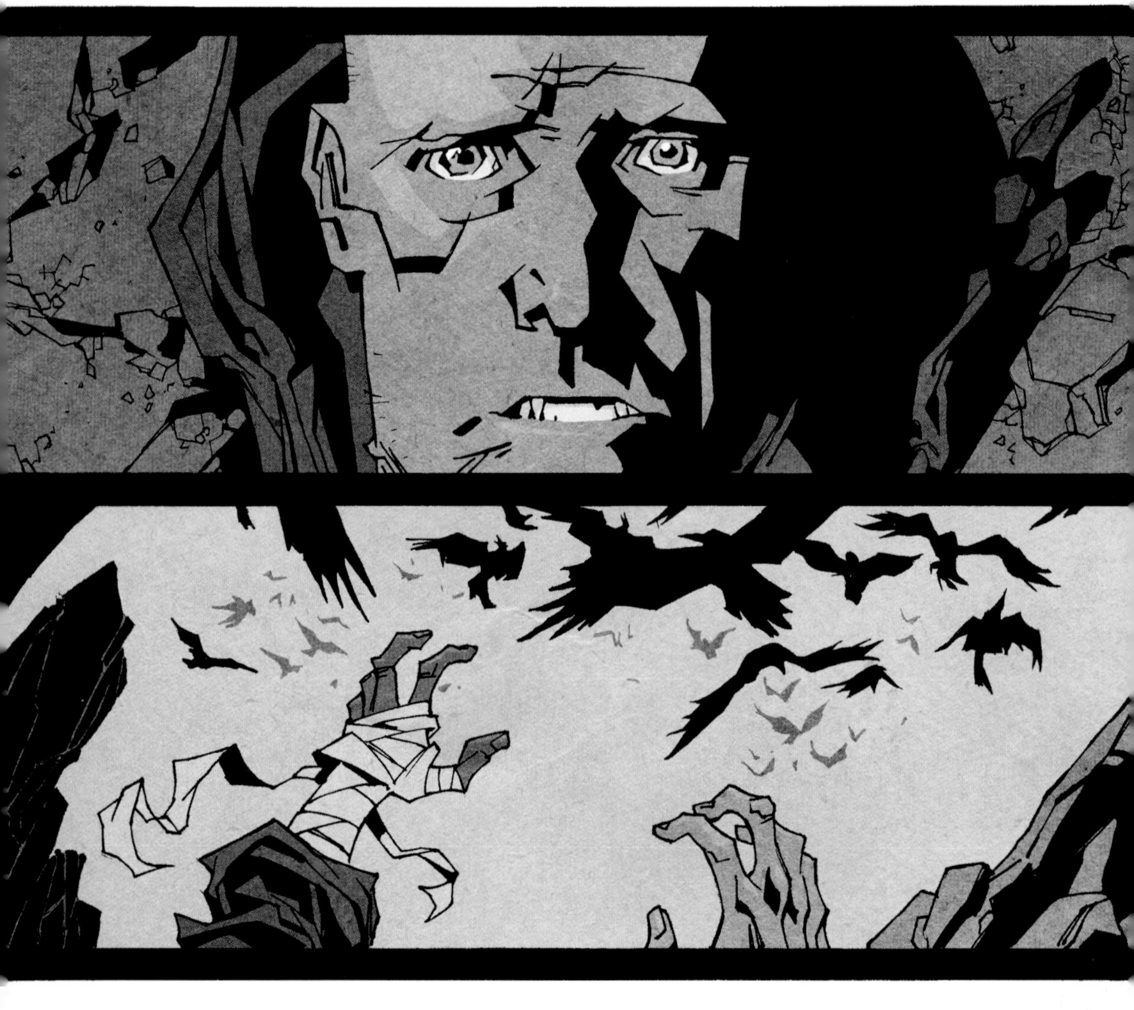

1. Augur

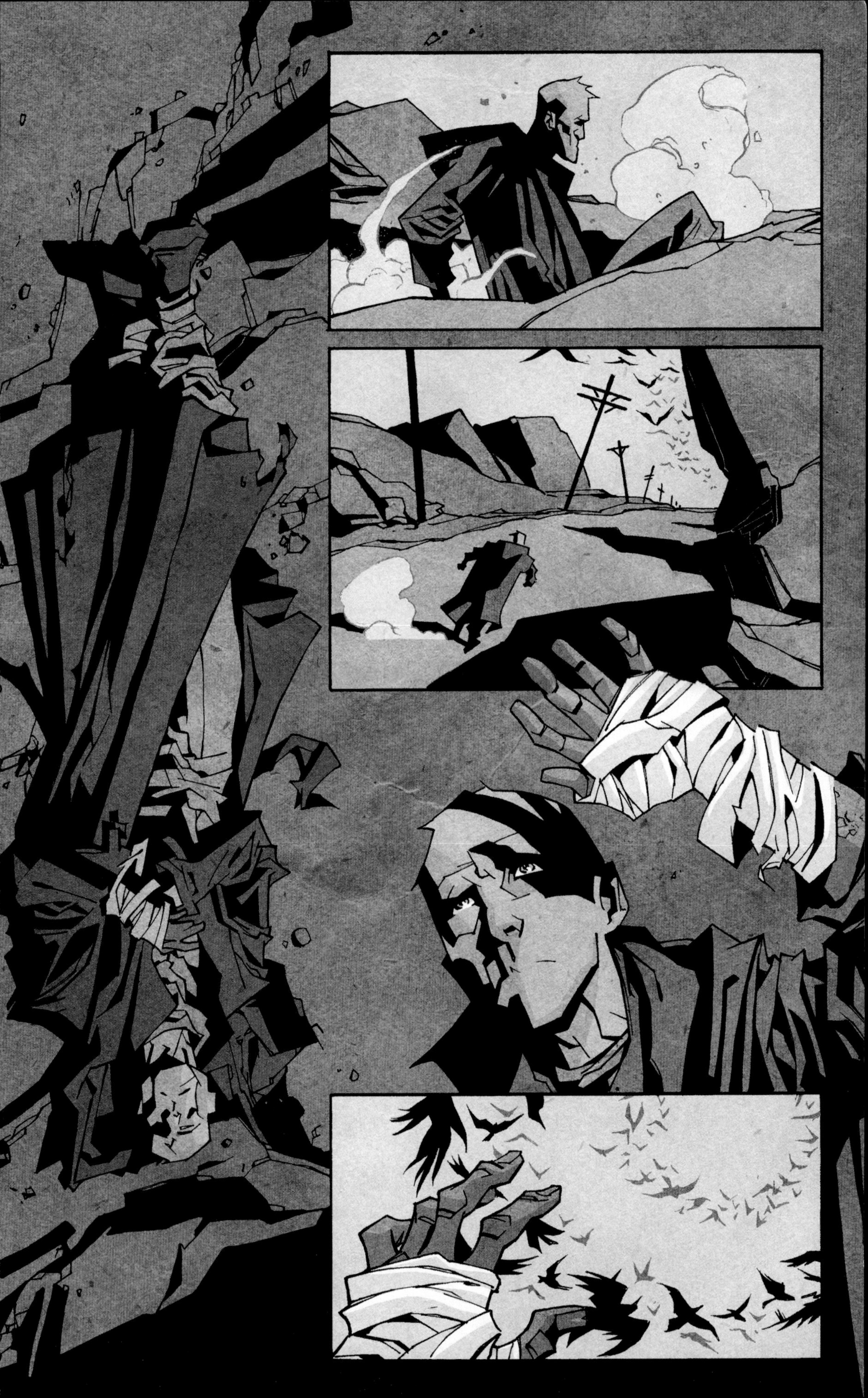

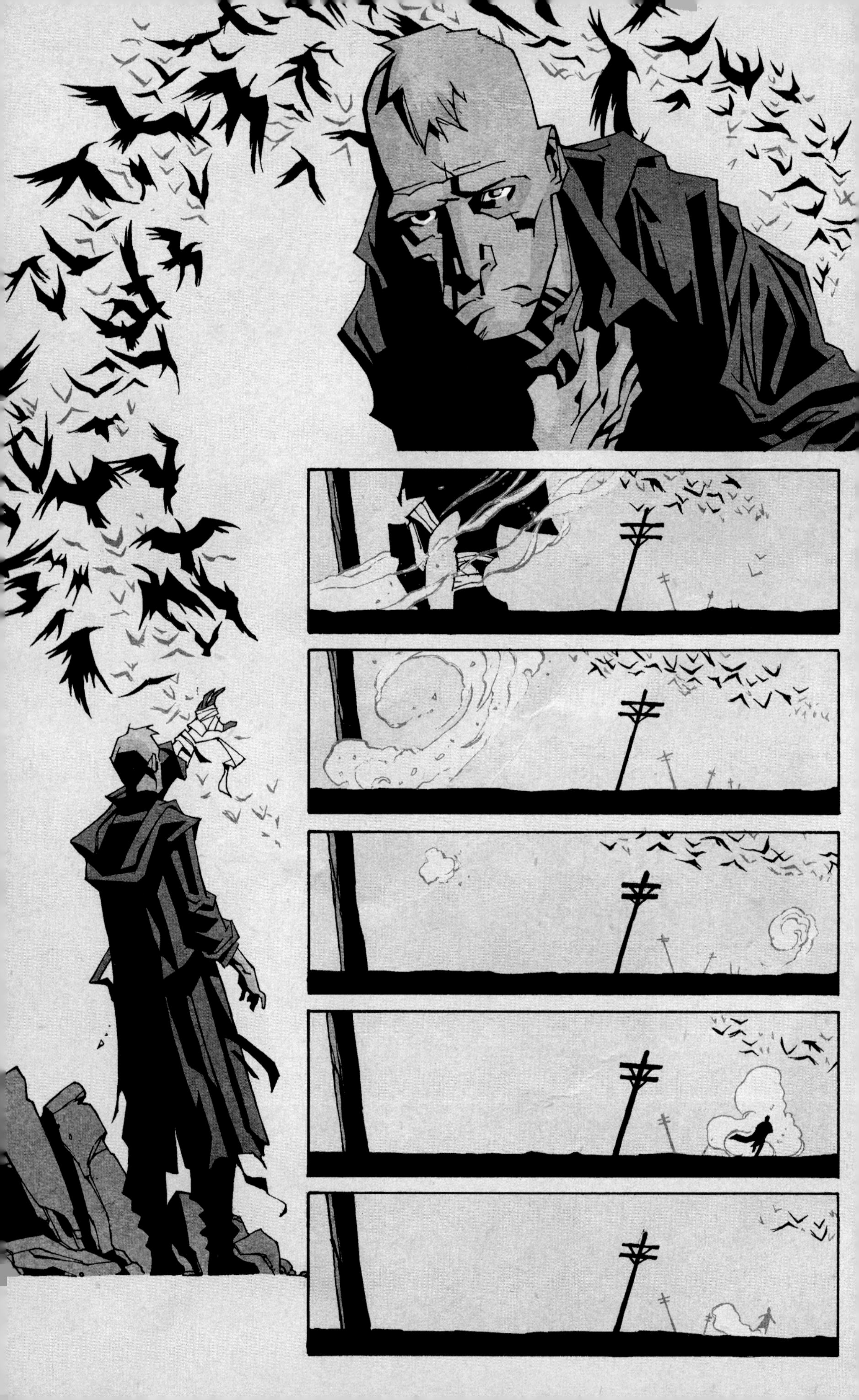

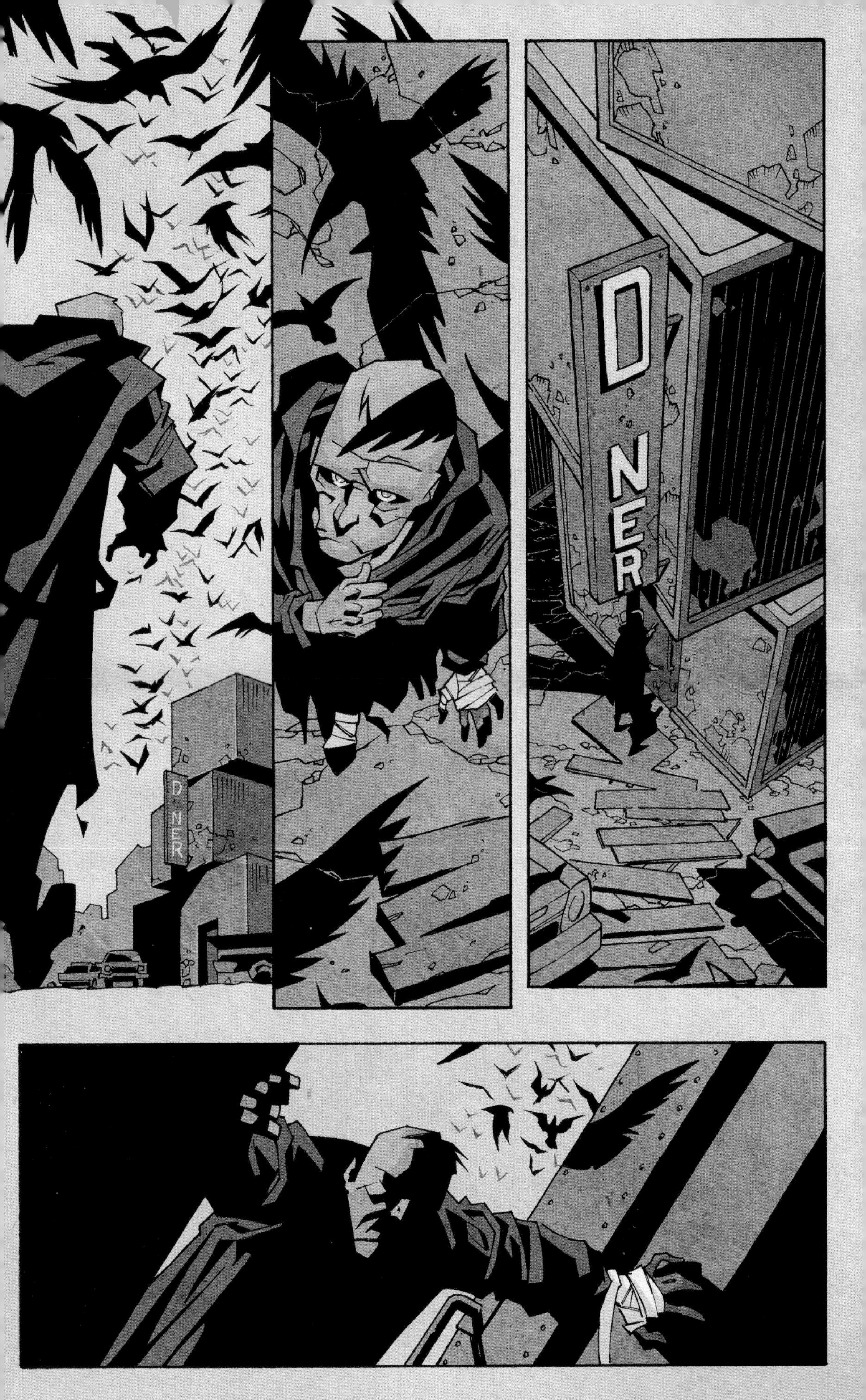
D NER
D NER

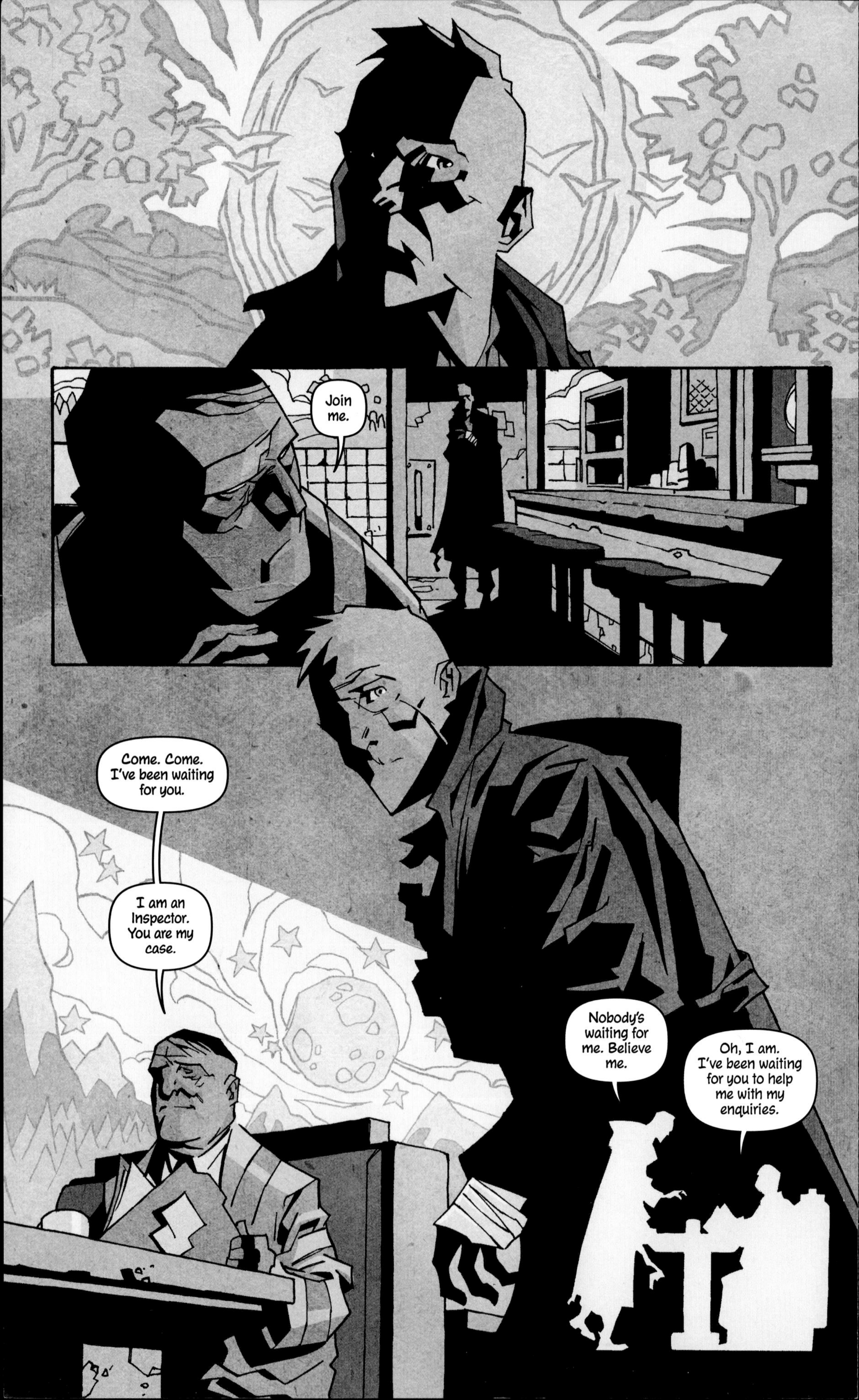
Join me.
Come. Come. I've been waiting for you.
I am an Inspector. You are my case.
Nobody's waiting for me. Believe me.
Oh, I am. I've been waiting for you to help me with my enquiries.

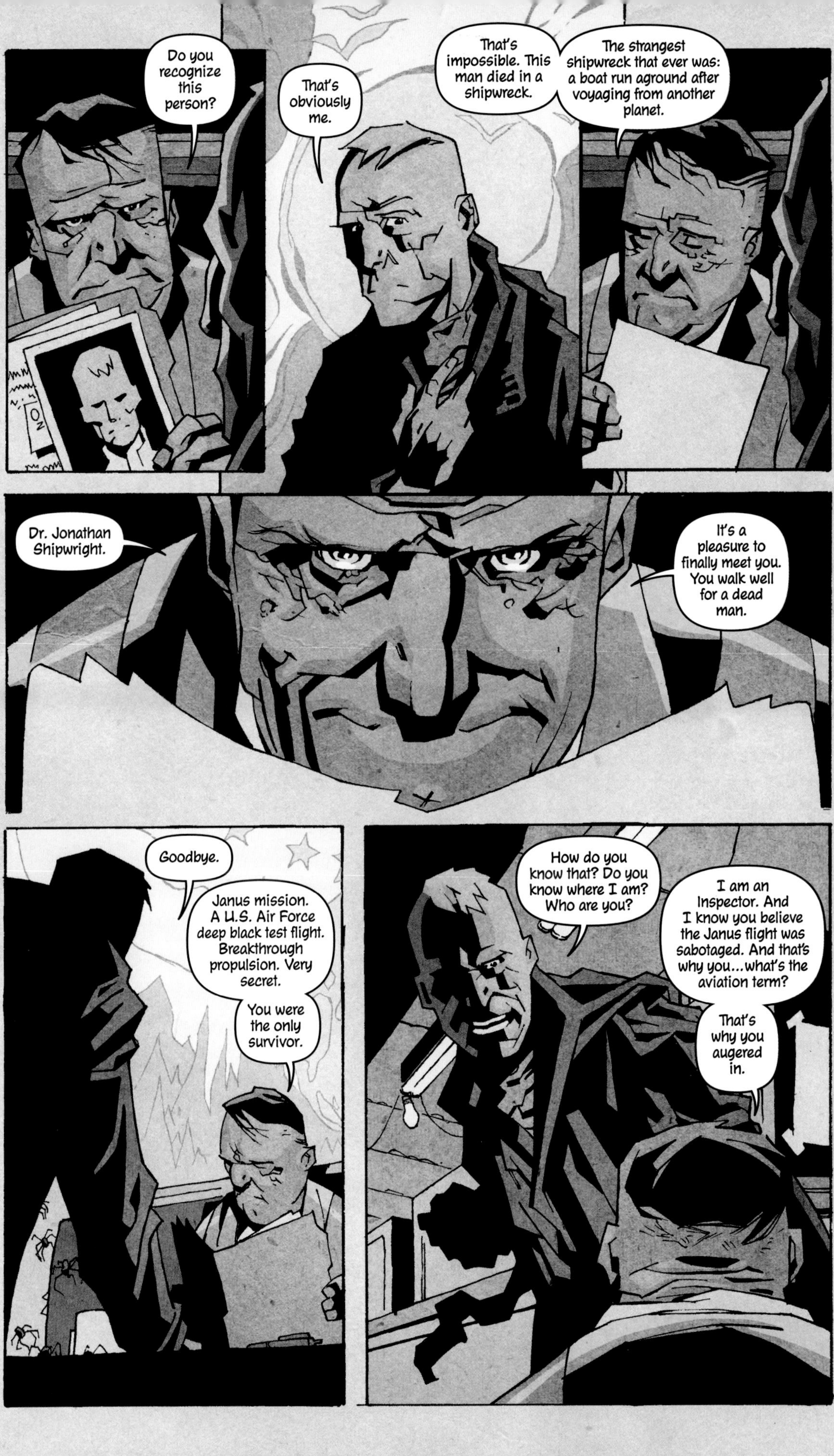

Do you recognize this person?
That's obviously me.
That's impossible. This man died in a shipwreck.
The strangest shipwreck that ever was: a boat run aground after voyaging from another planet.
Dr. Jonathan Shipwright.
It's a pleasure to finally meet you. You walk well for a dead man.
Goodbye.
Janus mission. A U.S. Air Force deep black test flight. Breakthrough propulsion. Very secret.
You were the only survivor.
How do you know that? Do you know where I am? Who are you?
I am an Inspector. And I know you believe the Janus flight was sabotaged. And that's why you...what's the aviation term?
That's why you augered in.

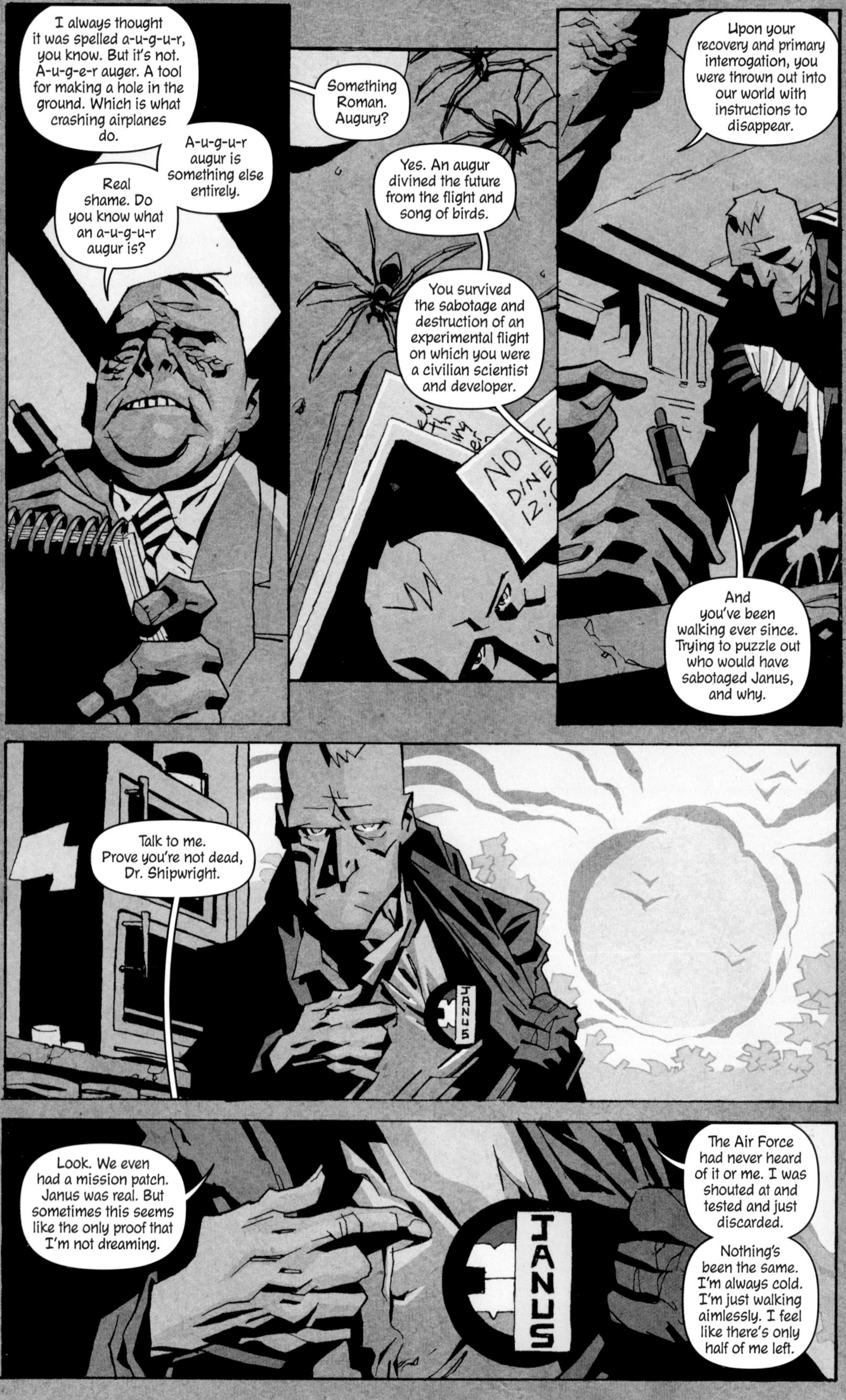
I always thought it was spelled a-u-g-u-r, you know. But it's not. A-u-g-e-r auger. A tool for making a hole in the ground. Which is what crashing airplanes do.
Real shame. Do you know what an a-u-g-u-r augur is?
A-u-g-u-r augur is something else entirely.
Something Roman. Augury?
Yes. An augur divined the future from the flight and song of birds.
You survived the sabotage and destruction of an experimental flight on which you were a civilian scientist and developer.
NO
Upon your recovery and primary interrogation, you were thrown out into our world with instructions to disappear.
And you've been walking ever since. Trying to puzzle out who would have sabotaged Janus, and why.
Talk to me. Prove you're not dead, Dr. Shipwright.
JANUS
Look. We even had a mission patch. Janus was real. But sometimes this seems like the only proof that I'm not dreaming.
JANUS
The Air Force had never heard of it or me. I was shouted at and tested and just discarded.
Nothing's been the same. I'm always cold. I'm just walking aimlessly. I feel like there's only half of me left.

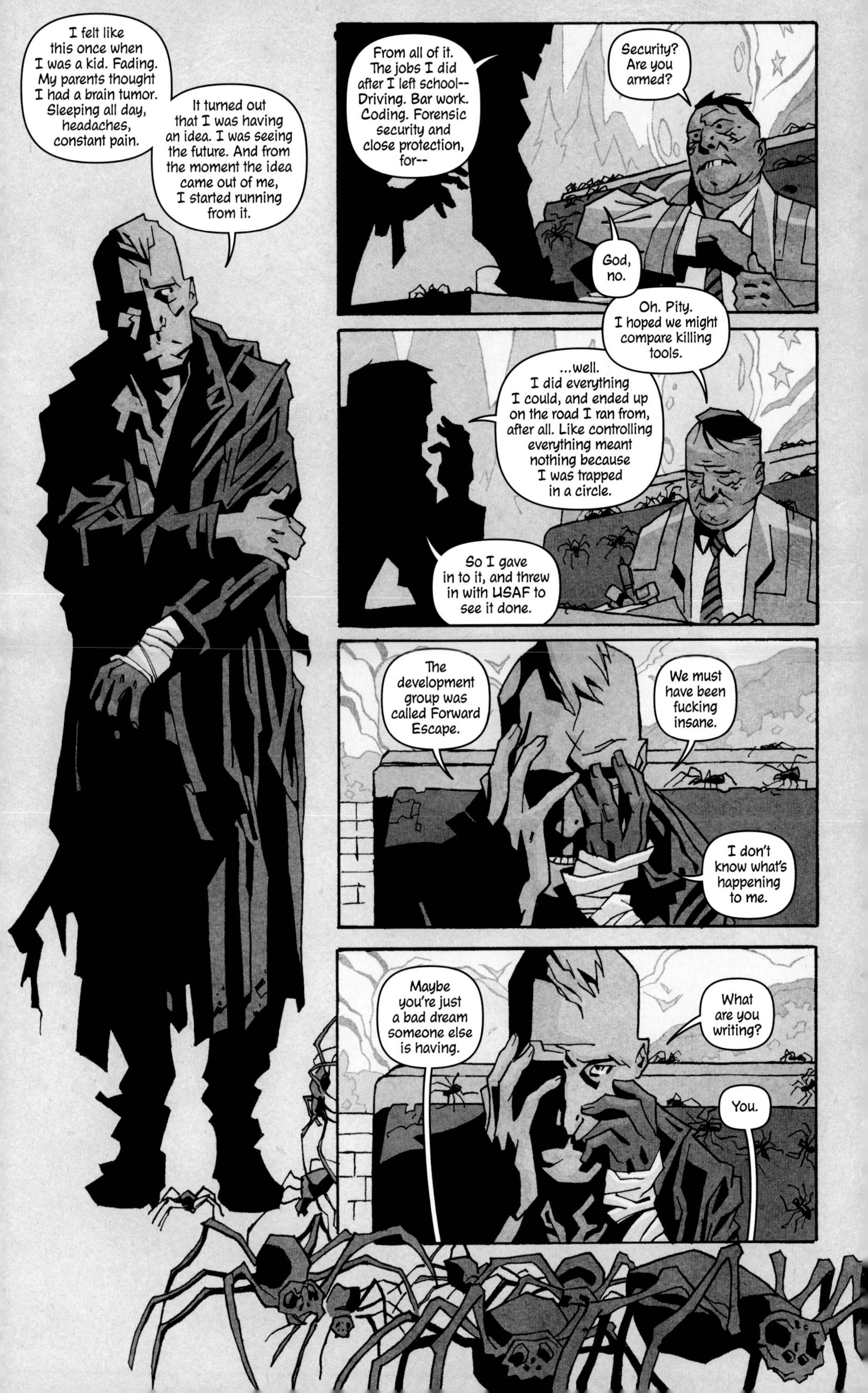
I felt like this once when I was a kid. Fading. My parents thought I had a brain tumor. Sleeping all day, headaches, constant pain.
It turned out that I was having an idea. I was seeing the future. And from the moment the idea came out of me, I started running from it.
From all of it. The jobs I did after I left school-- Driving. Bar work. Coding. Forensic security and close protection, for--
Security? Are you armed?
God, no.
Oh. Pity. I hoped we might compare killing tools.
...well. I did everything I could, and ended up on the road I ran from, after all. Like controlling everything meant nothing because I was trapped in a circle.
So I gave in to it, and threw in with USAF to see it done.
The development group was called Forward Escape.
We must have been fucking insane.
I don't know what's happening to me.
Maybe you're just a bad dream someone else is having.
What are you writing?
You.

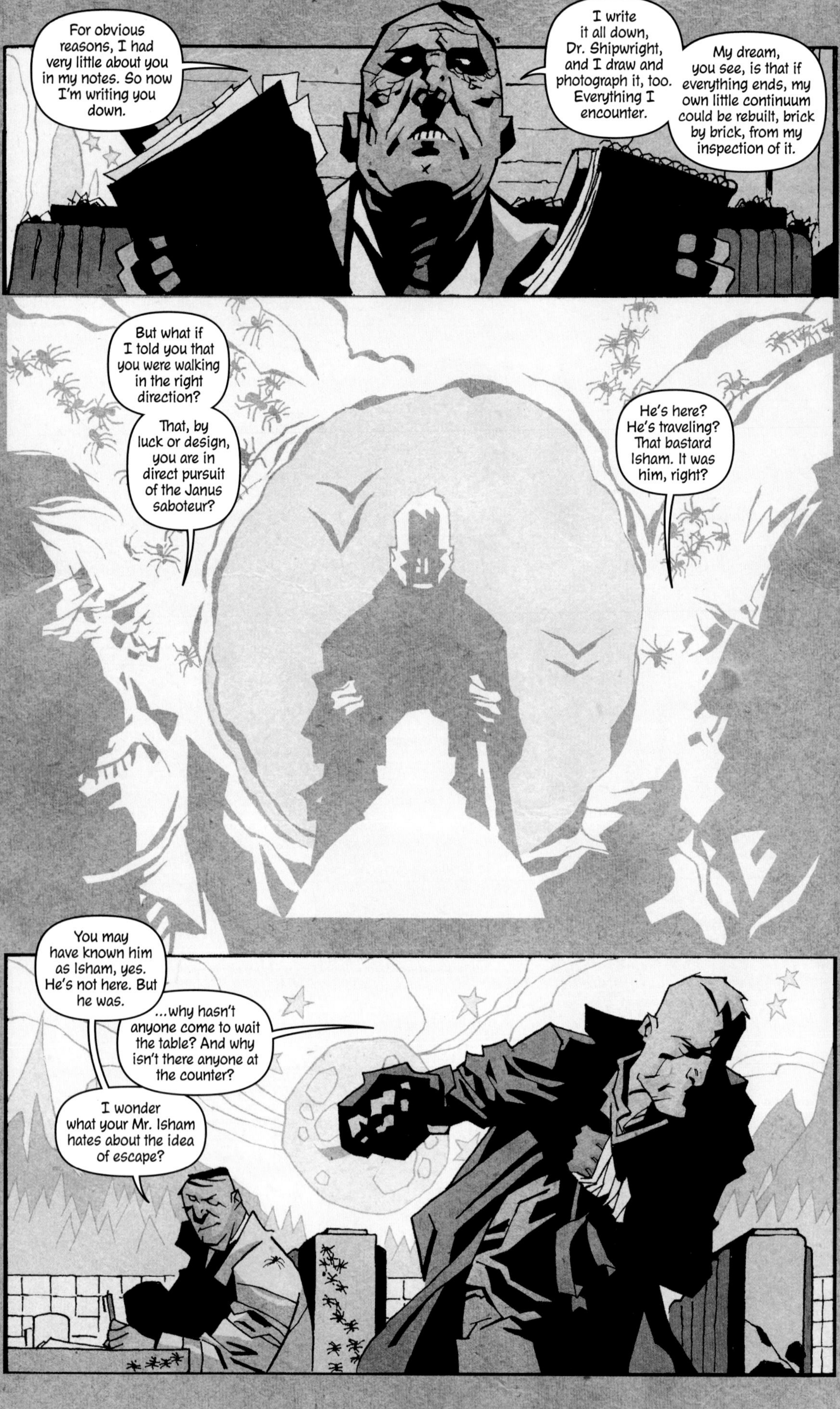
For obvious reasons, I had very little about you in my notes. So now I'm writing you down.
I write it all down, Dr. Shipwright, and I draw and photograph it, too. Everything I encounter.
My dream, you see, is that if everything ends, my own little continuum could be rebuilt, brick by brick, from my inspection of it.
But what if I told you that you were walking in the right direction?
That, by luck or design, you are in direct pursuit of the Janus saboteur?
He's here? He's traveling? That bastard Isham. It was him, right?
You may have known him as Isham, yes. He's not here. But he was.
...why hasn't anyone come to wait the table? And why isn't there anyone at the counter?
I wonder what your Mr. Isham hates about the idea of escape?

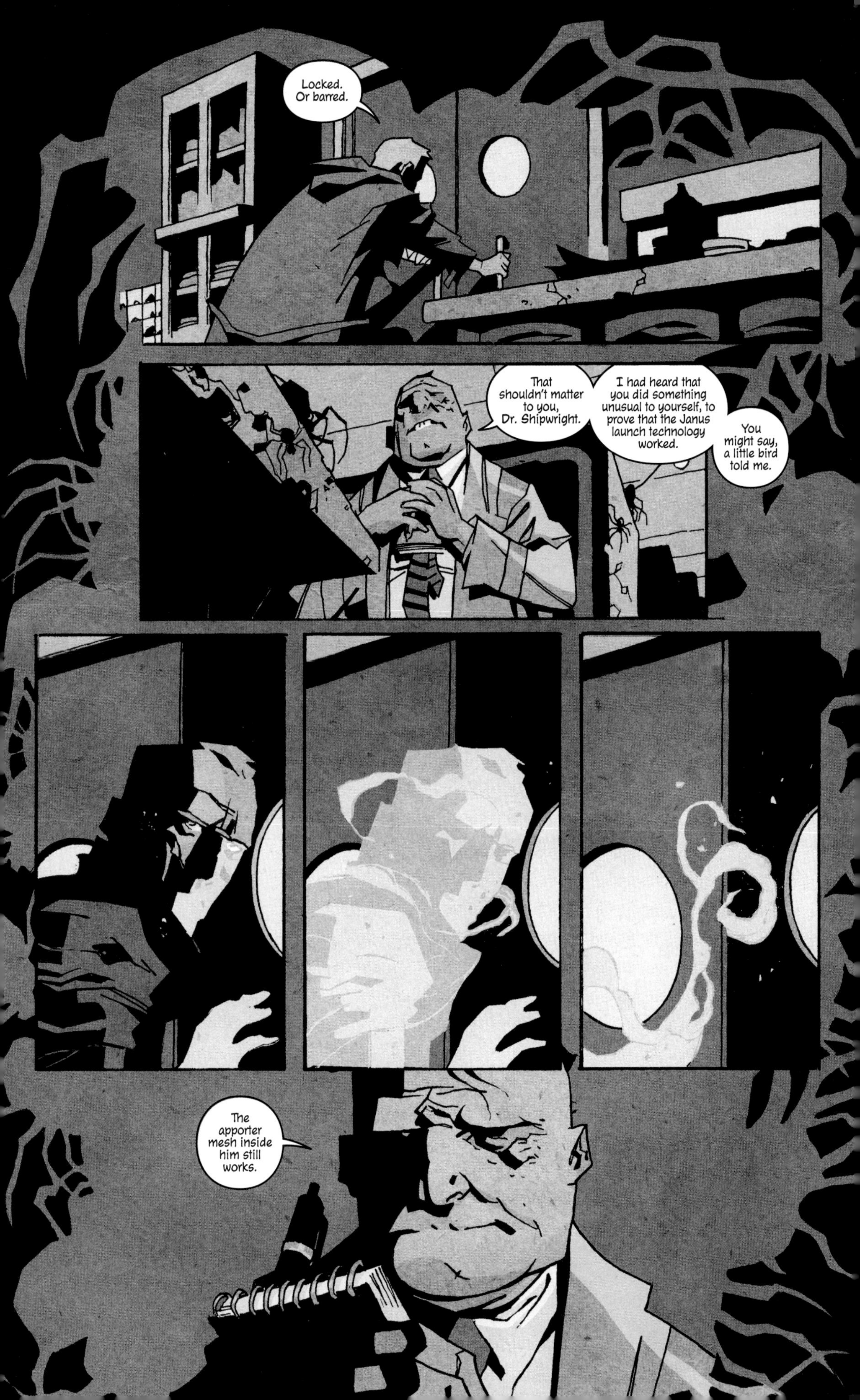
Locked.
Or barred.
That shouldn't matter to you, Dr. Shipwright.
I had heard that you did something unusual to yourself, to prove that the Janus launch technology worked.
You might say, a little bird told me.
The apporter mesh inside him still works.

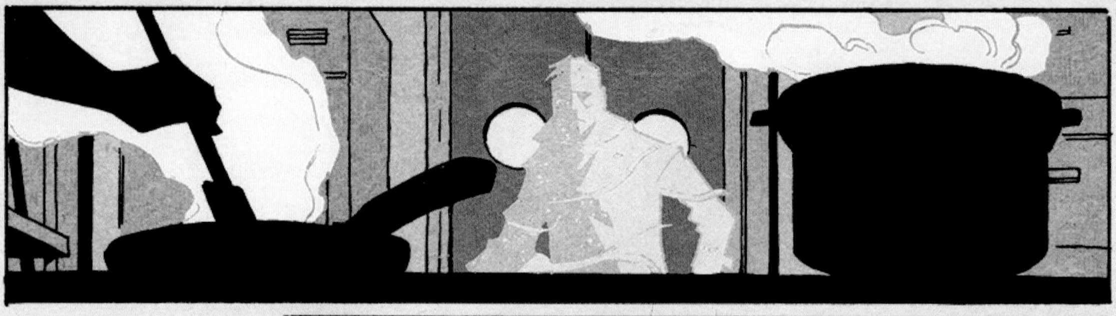

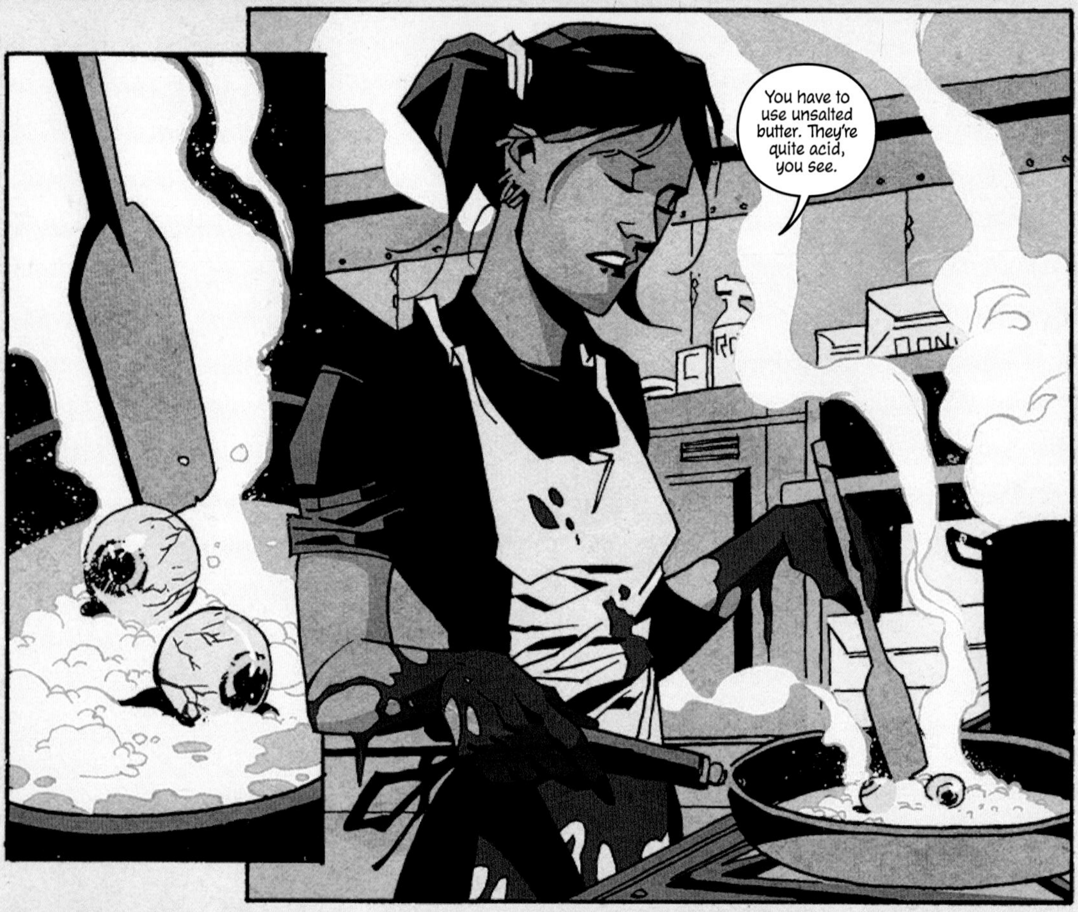
You have to use unsalted butter. They're quite acid, you see.

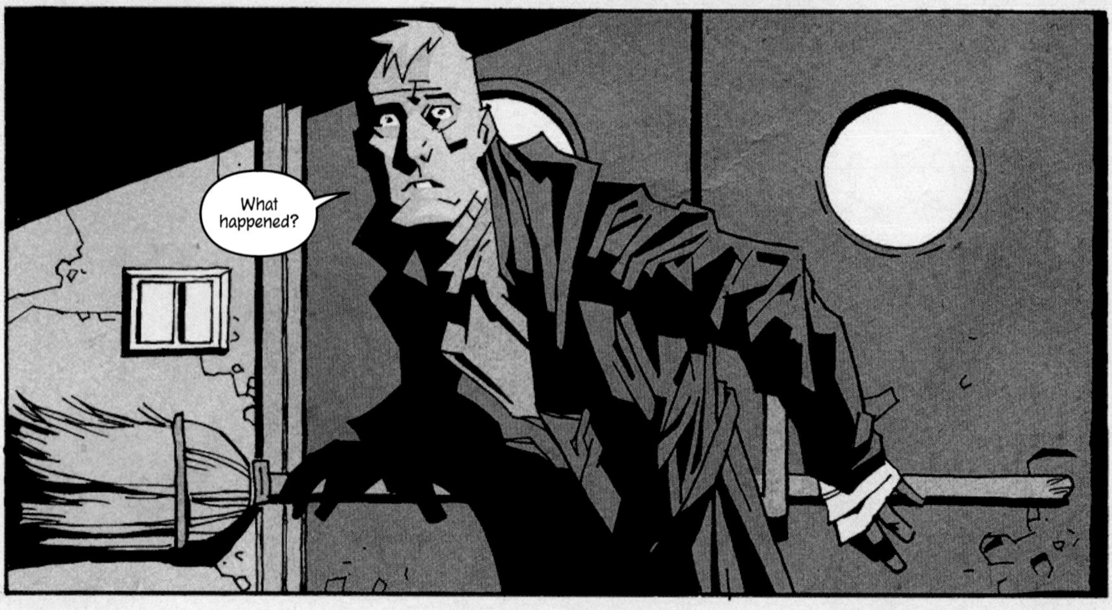
What happened?

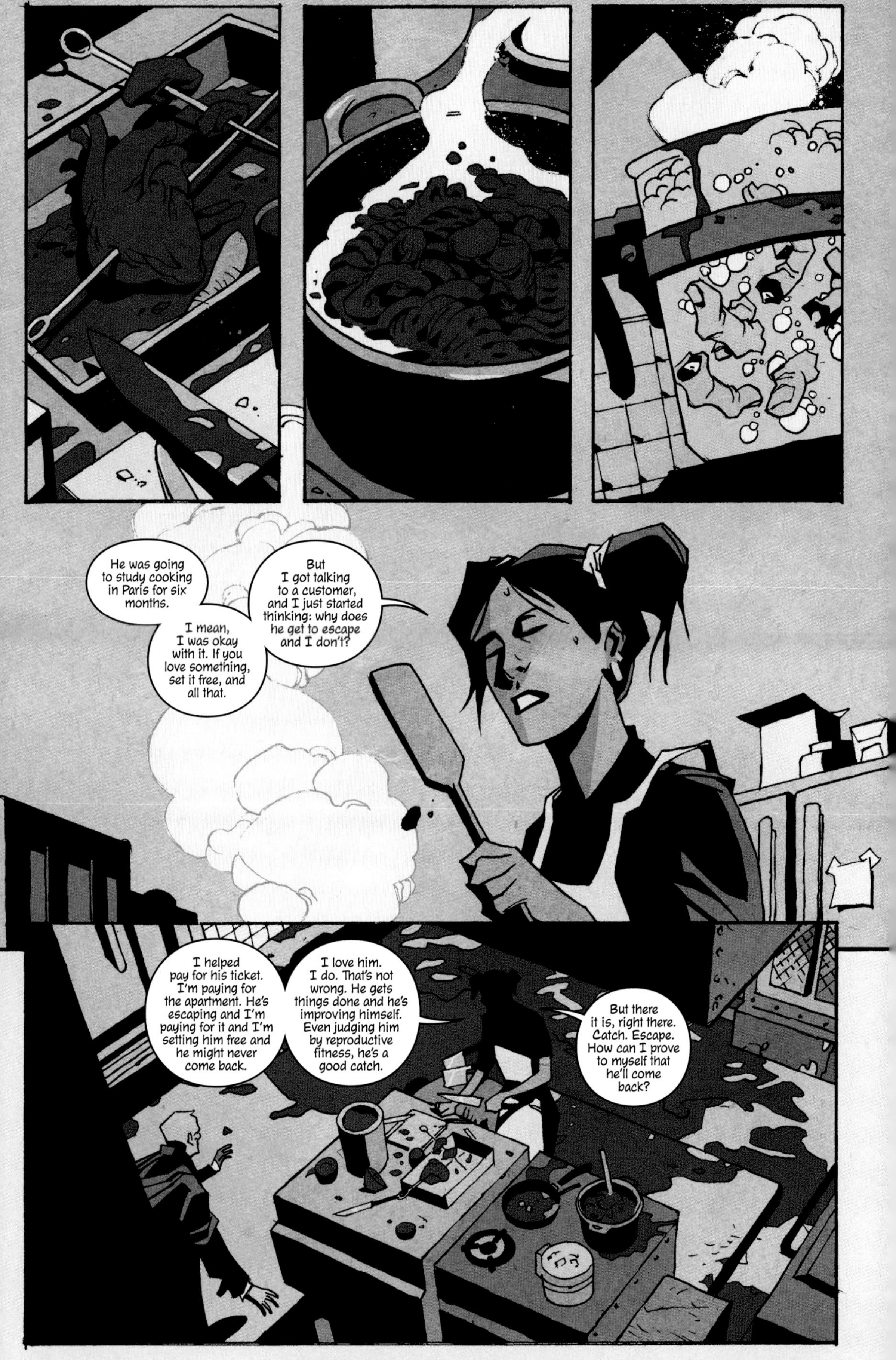
He was going to study cooking in Paris for six months.
I mean, I was okay with it. If you love something, set it free, and all that.
But I got talking to a customer, and I just started thinking: why does he get to escape and I don't?
I helped pay for his ticket. I'm paying for the apartment. He's escaping and I'm paying for it and I'm setting him free and he might never come back.
I love him. I do. That's not wrong. He gets things done and he's improving himself. Even judging him by reproductive fitness, he's a good catch.
But there it is, right there. Catch. Escape. How can I prove to myself that he'll come back?

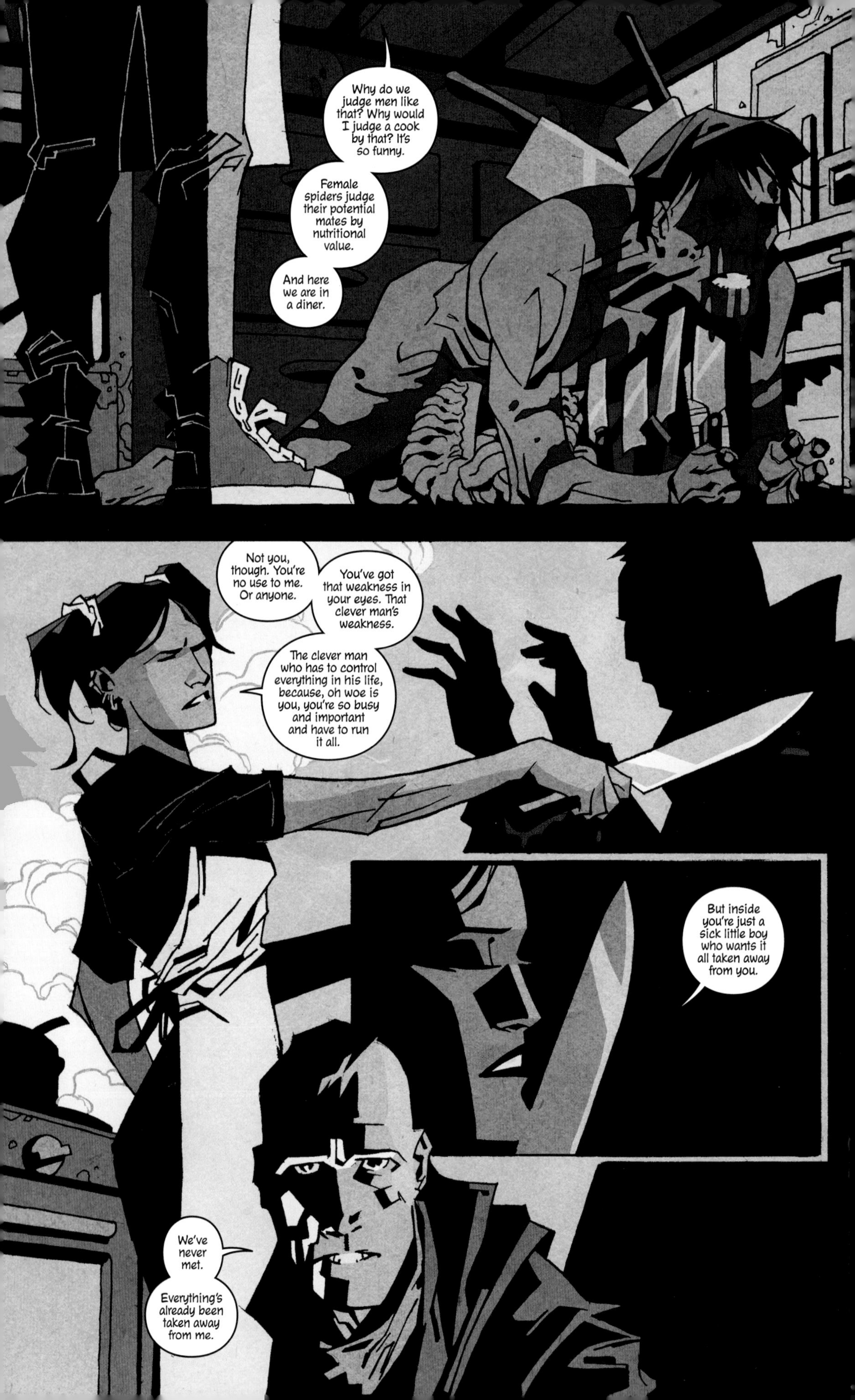
Why do we judge men like that? Why would I judge a cook by that? It's so funny.
Female spiders judge their potential mates by nutritional value.
And here we are in a diner.
Not you, though. You're no use to me. Or anyone.
You've got that weakness in your eyes. That clever man's weakness.
The clever man who has to control everything in his life, because, oh woe is you, you're so busy and important and have to run it all.
But inside you're just a sick little boy who wants it all taken away from you.
We've never met.
Everything's already been taken away from me.

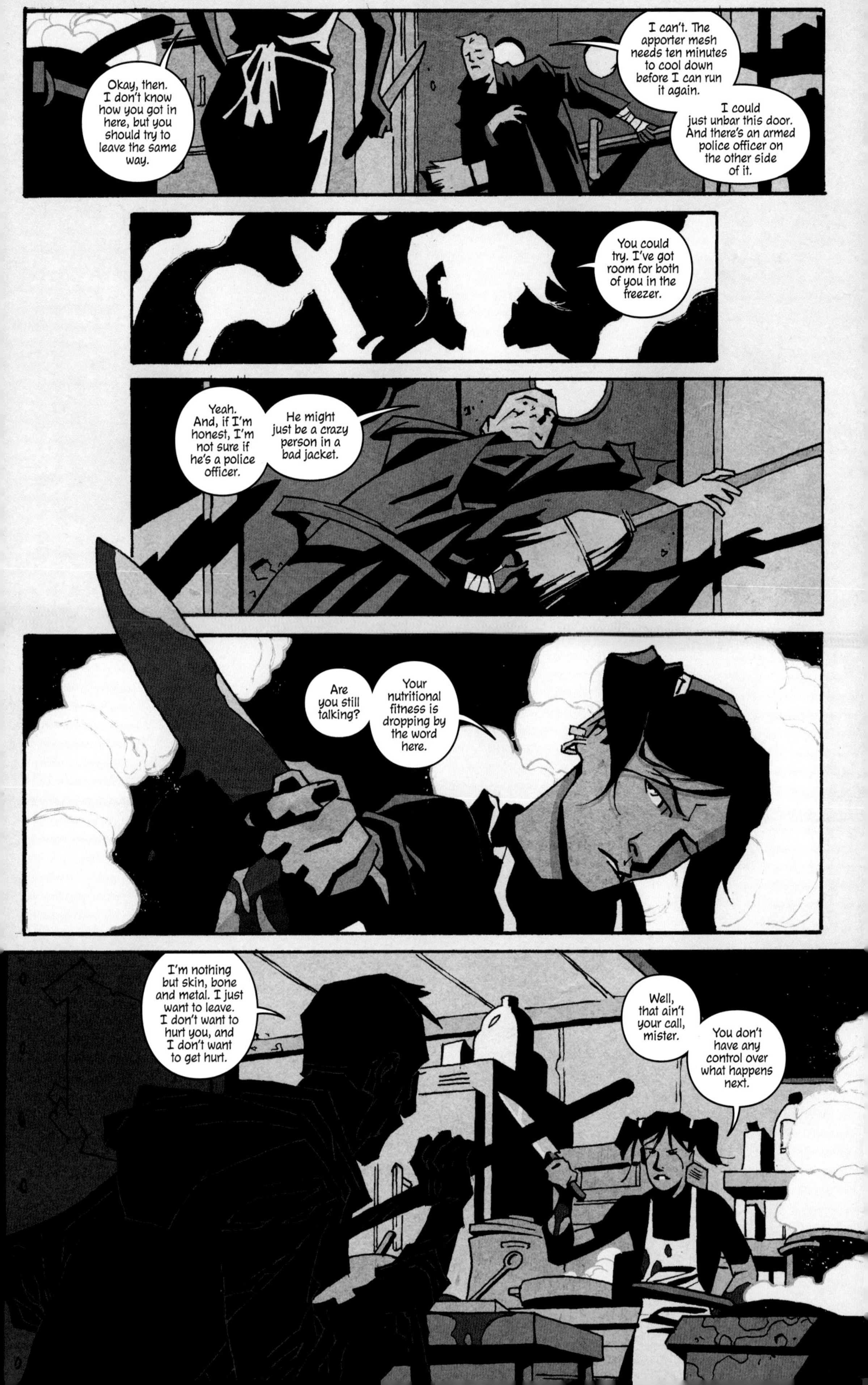
Okay, then. I don't know how you got in here, but you should try to leave the same way.
I can't. The apporter mesh needs ten minutes to cool down before I can run it again.
I could just unbar this door. And there's an armed police officer on the other side of it.
You could try. I've got room for both of you in the freezer.
Yeah. And, if I'm honest, I'm not sure if he's a police officer.
He might just be a crazy person in a bad jacket.
Are you still talking?
Your nutritional fitness is dropping by the word here.
I'm nothing but skin, bone and metal. I just want to leave. I don't want to hurt you, and I don't want to get hurt.
Well, that ain't your call, mister.
You don't have any control over what happens next.

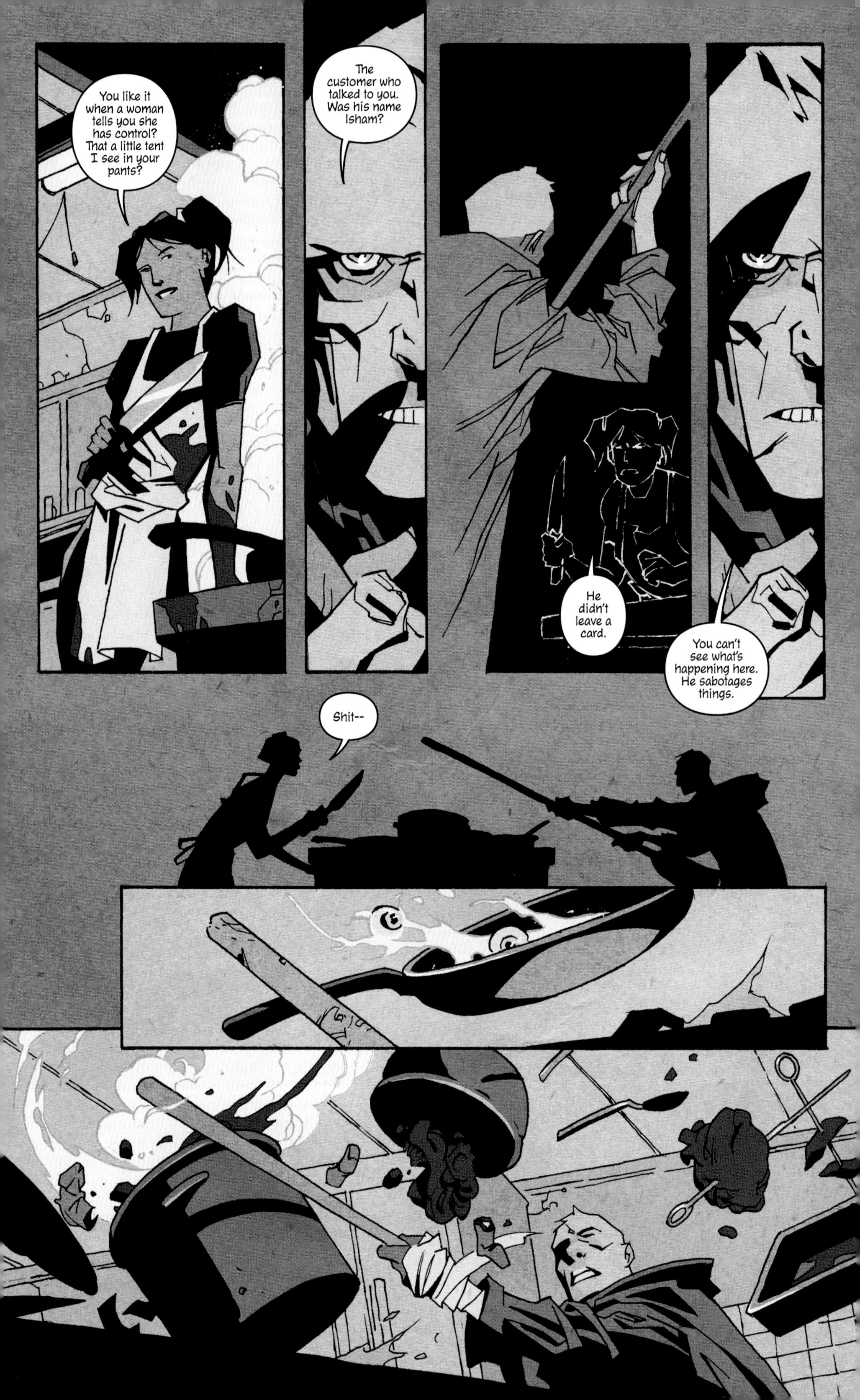
You like it when a woman tells you she has control? That a little tent I see in your pants?
The customer who talked to you. Was his name Isham?
He didn't leave a card.
You can't see what's happening here. He sabotages things.
Shit--

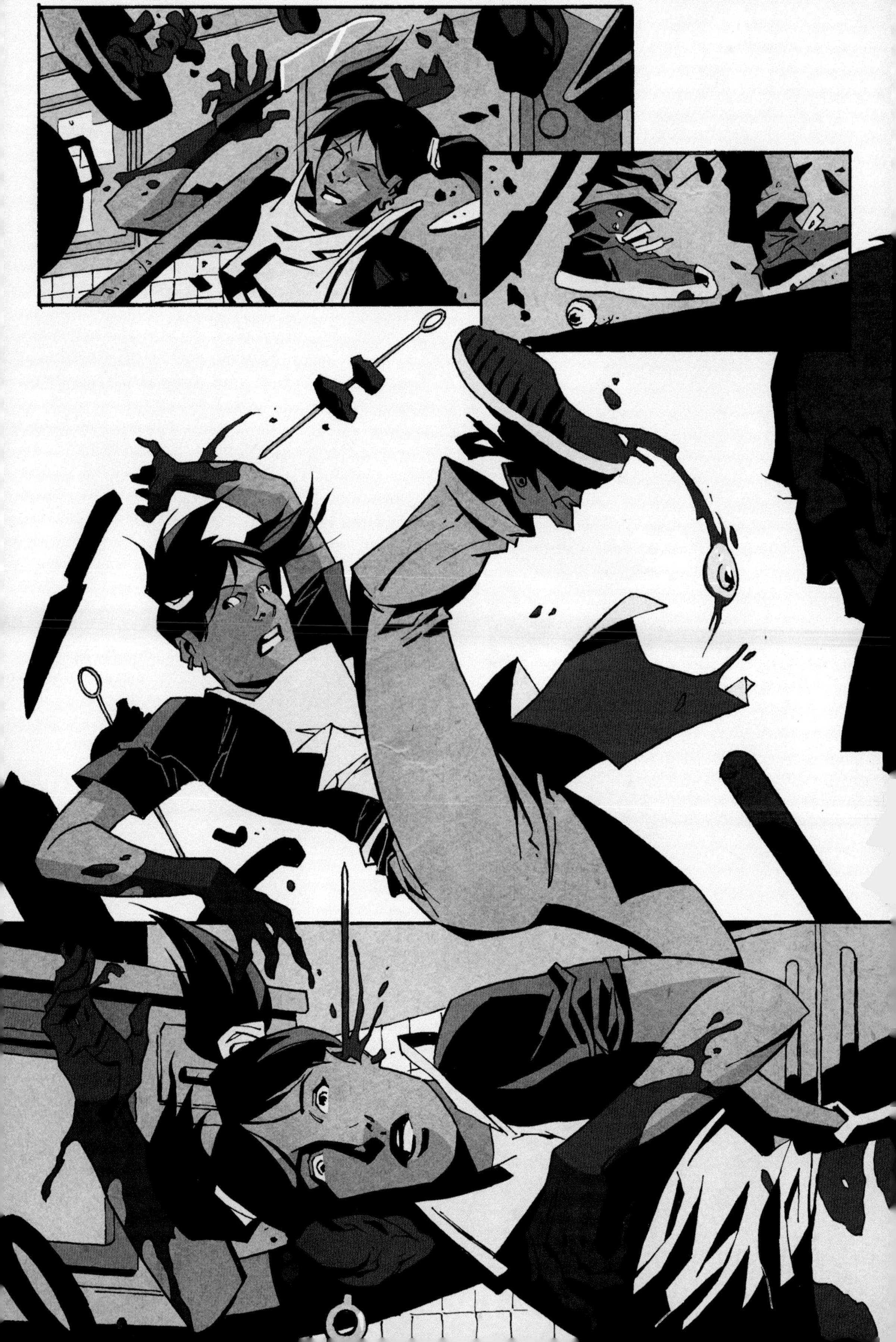

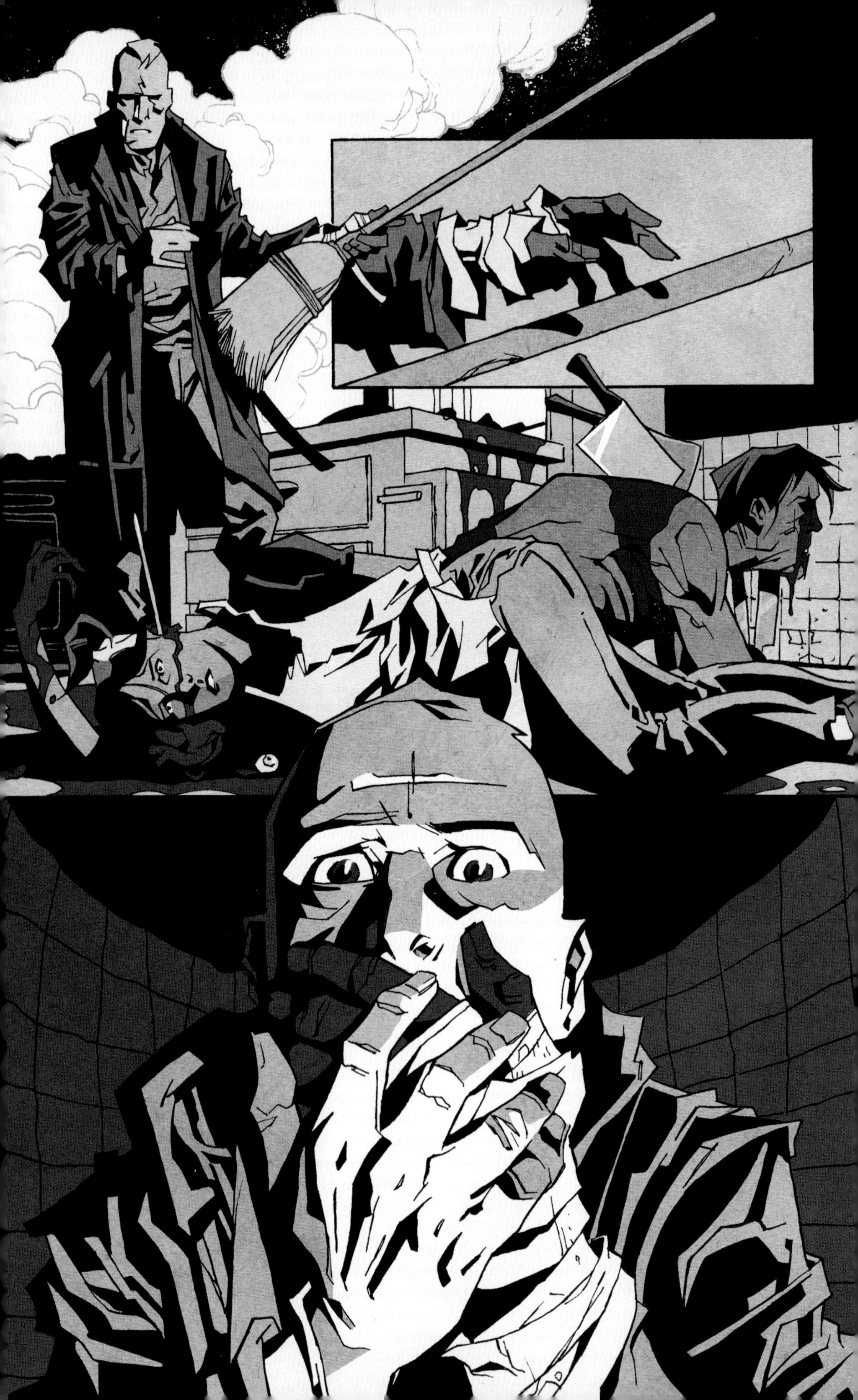

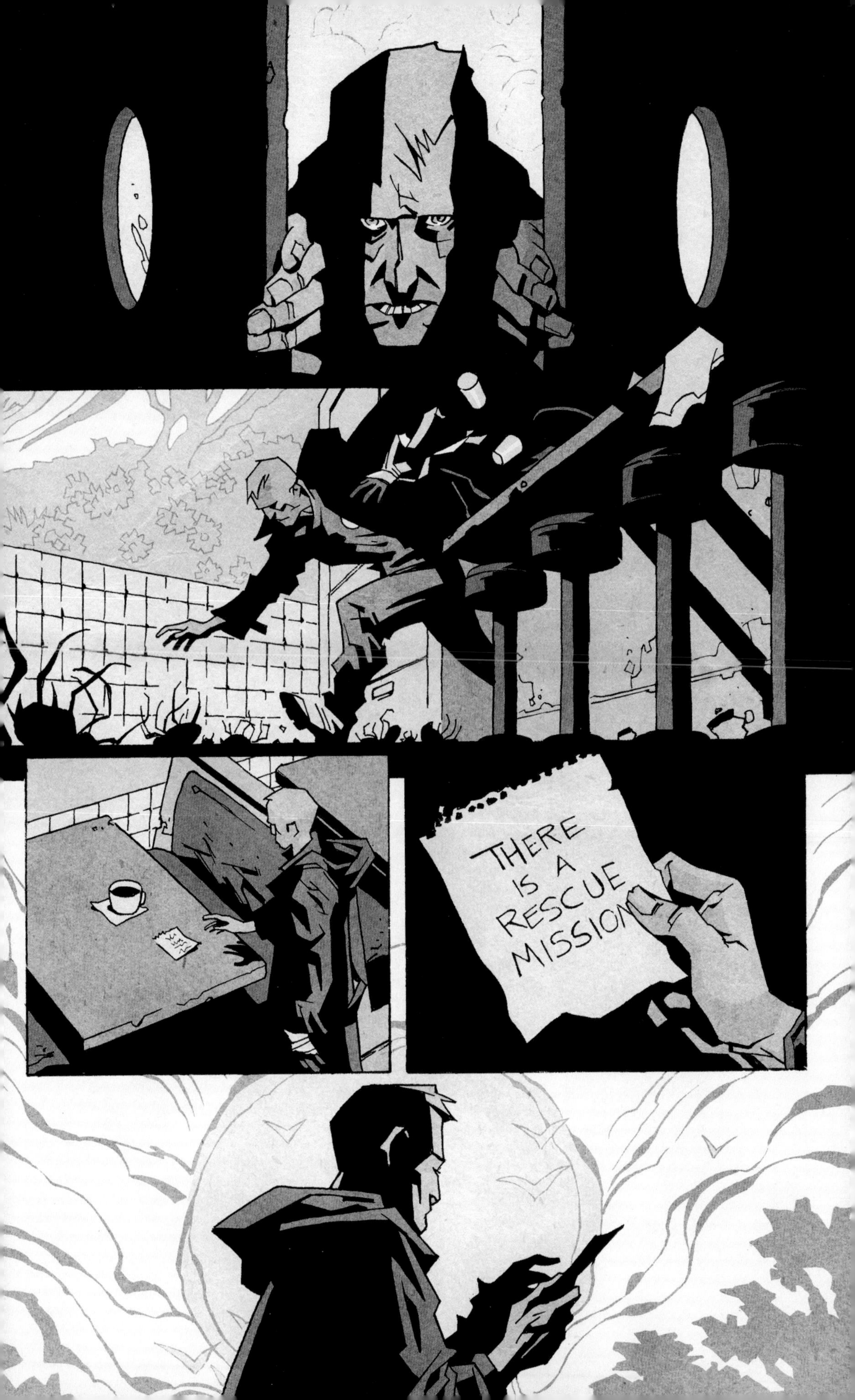
THERE IS A RESCUE MISSION

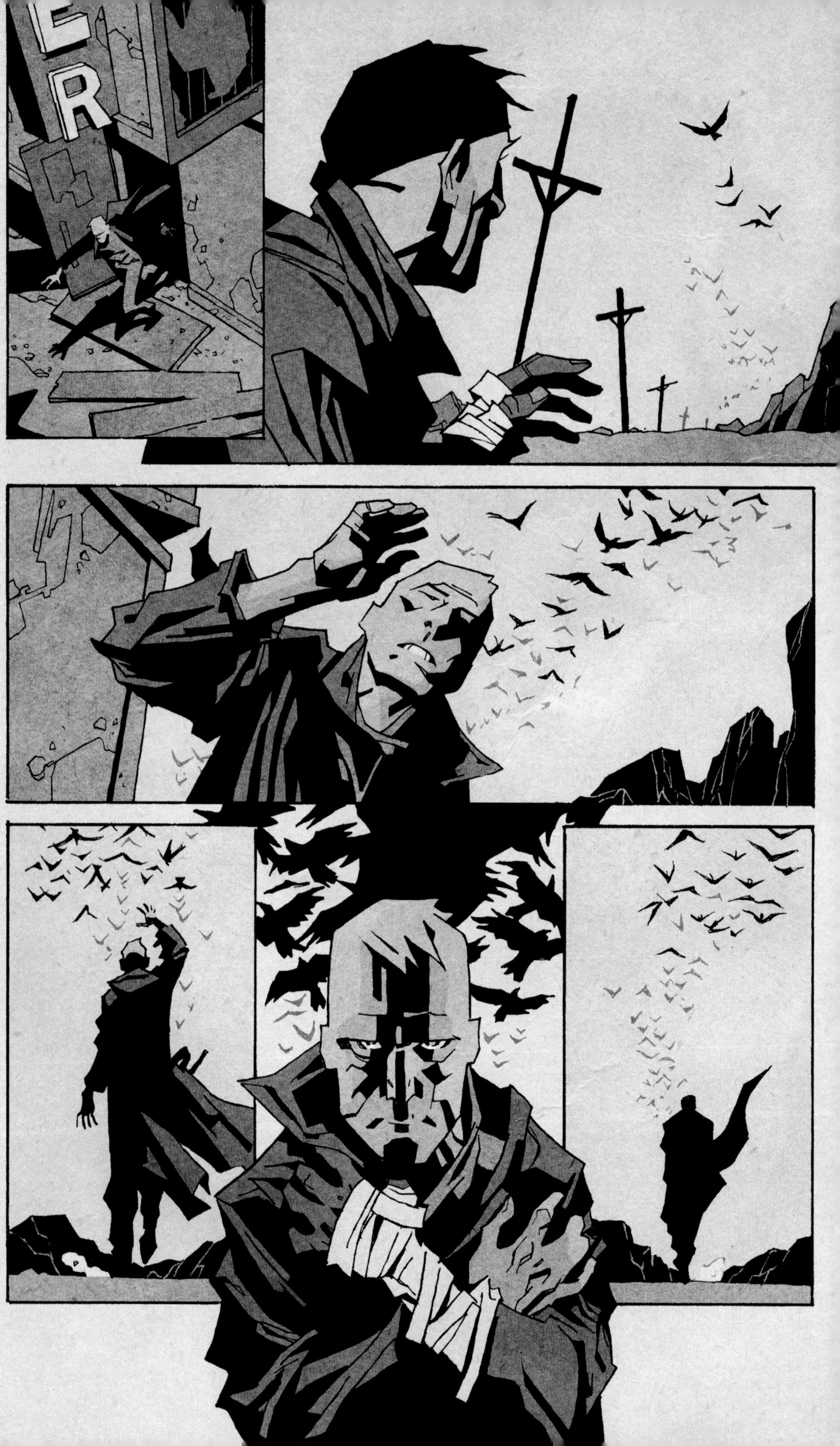

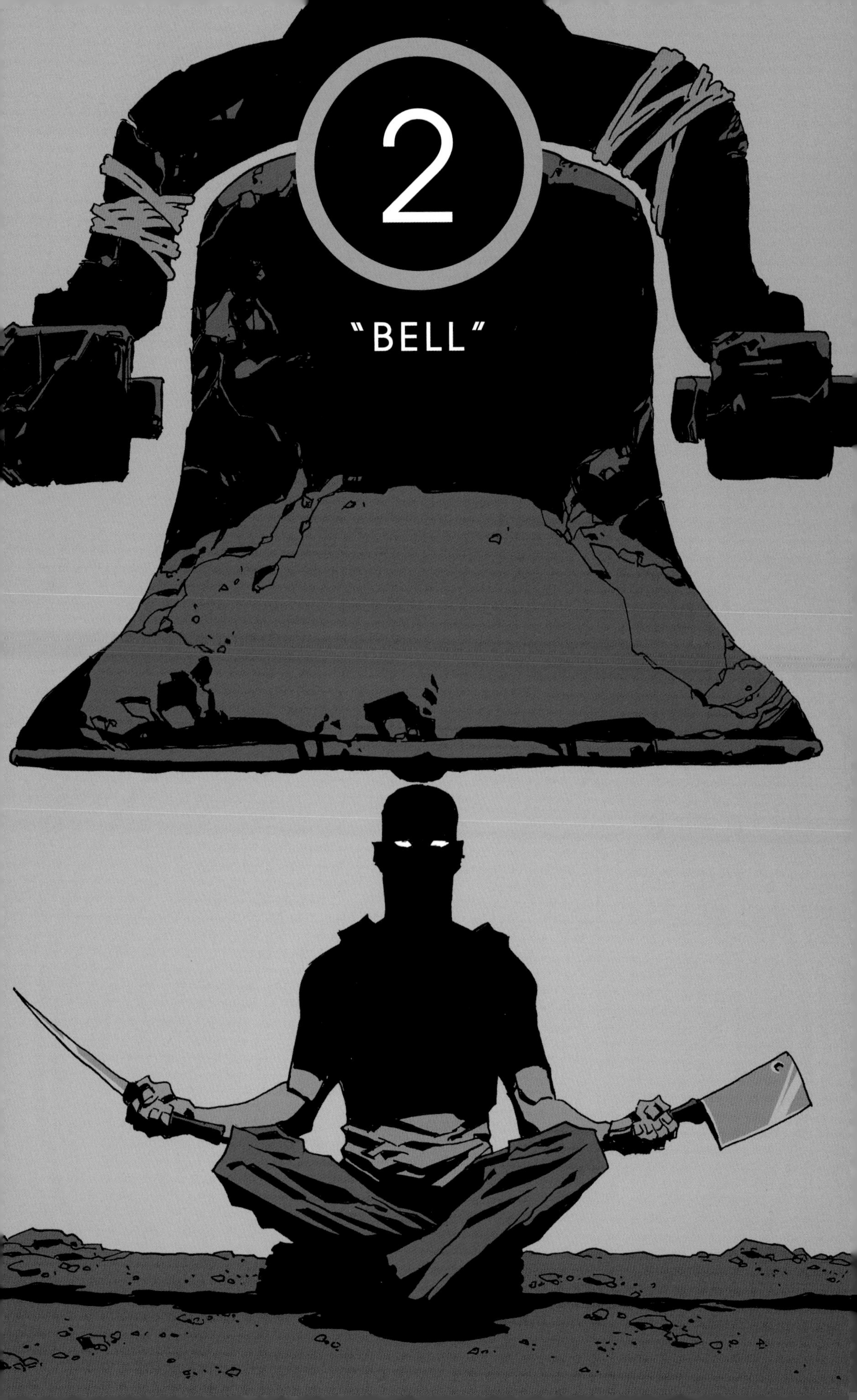
2
"BELL"

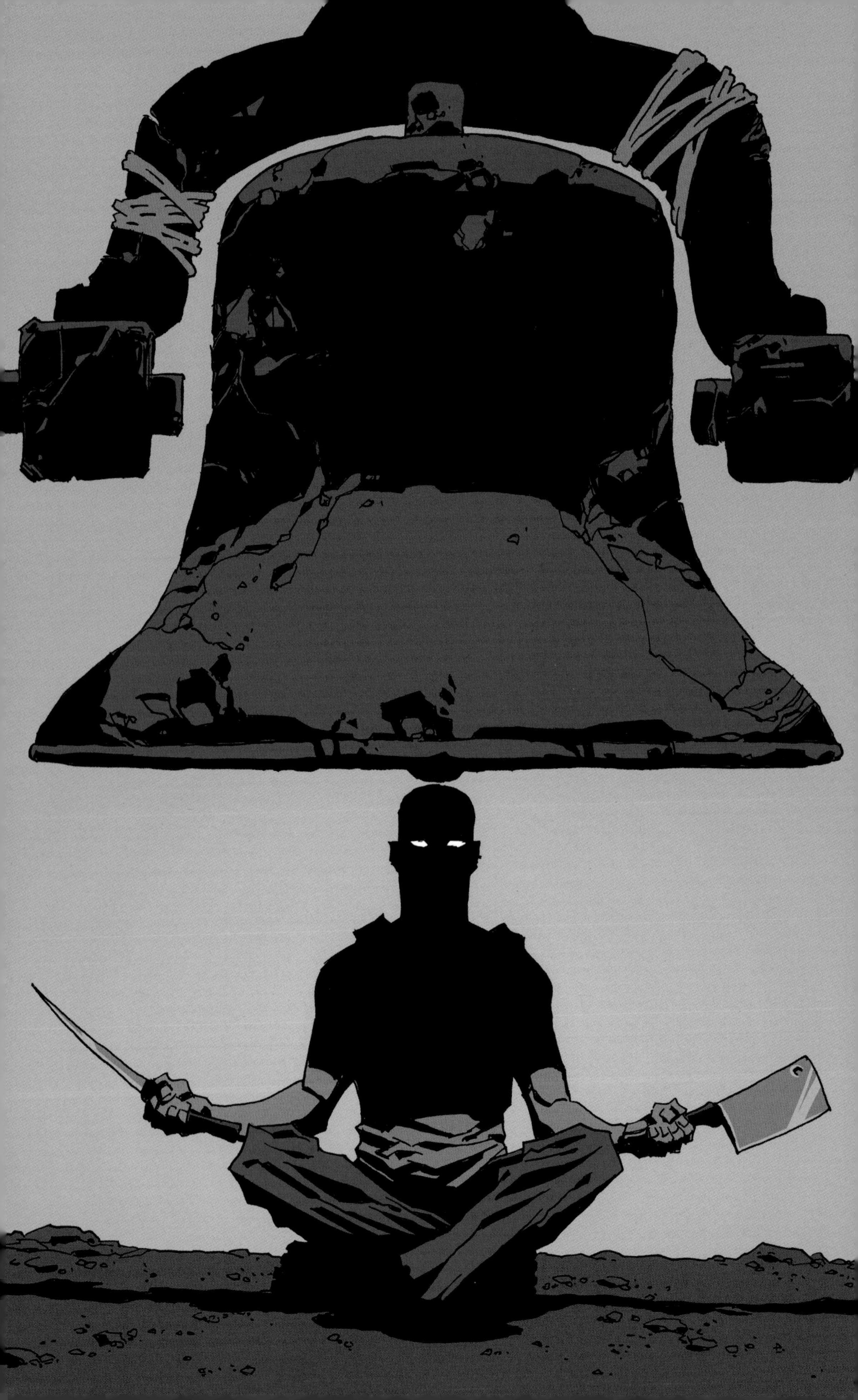

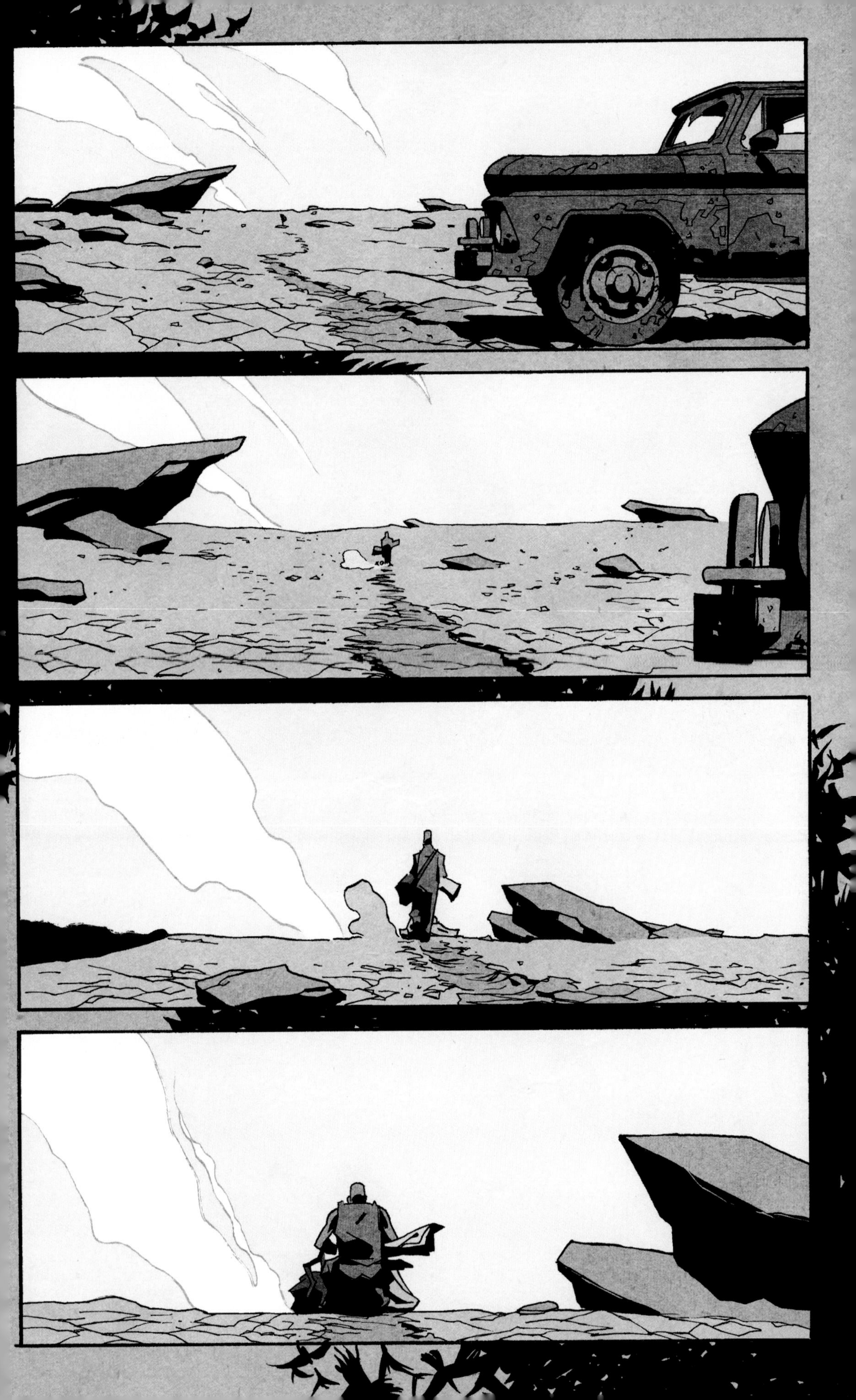

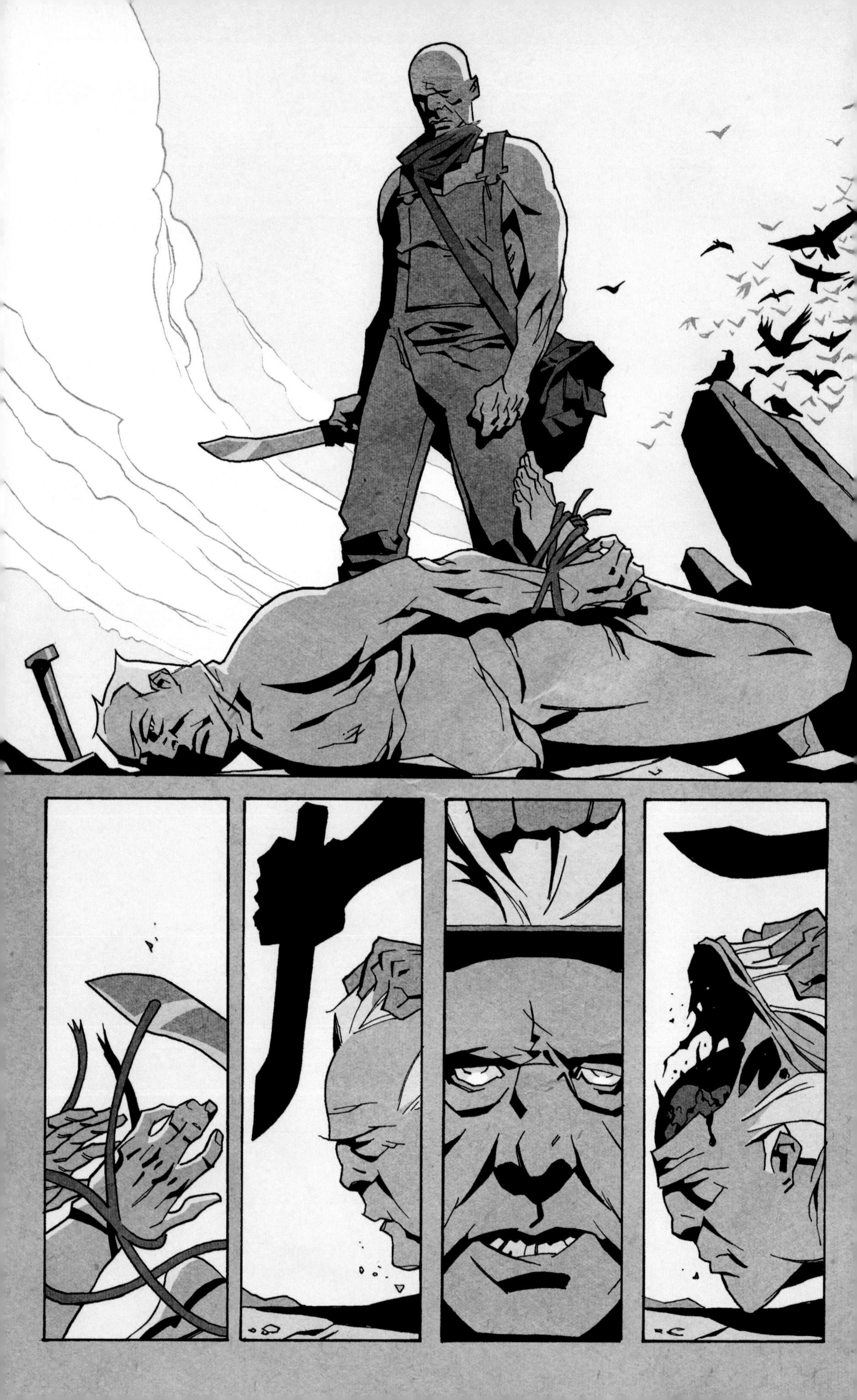

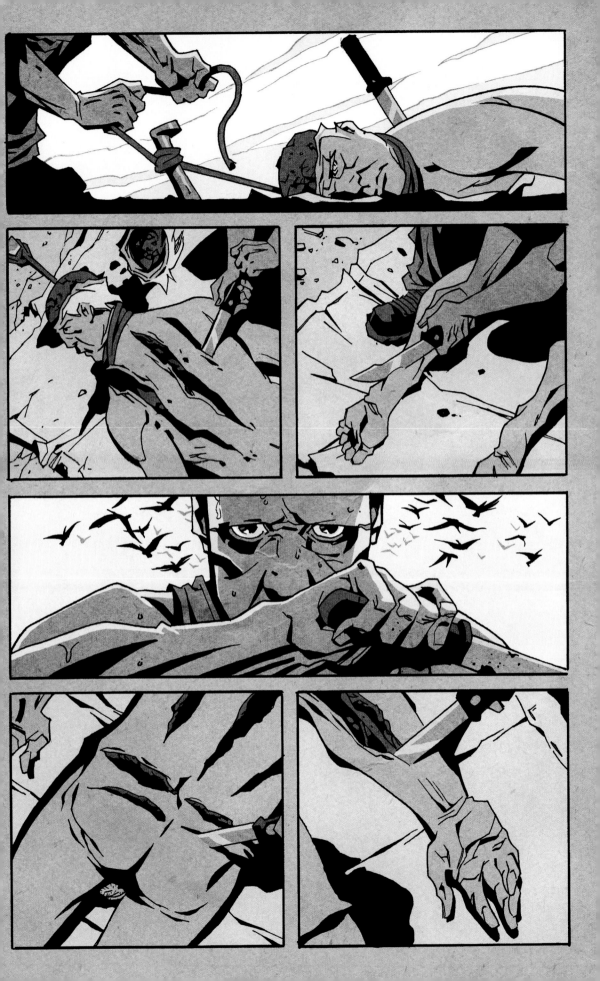

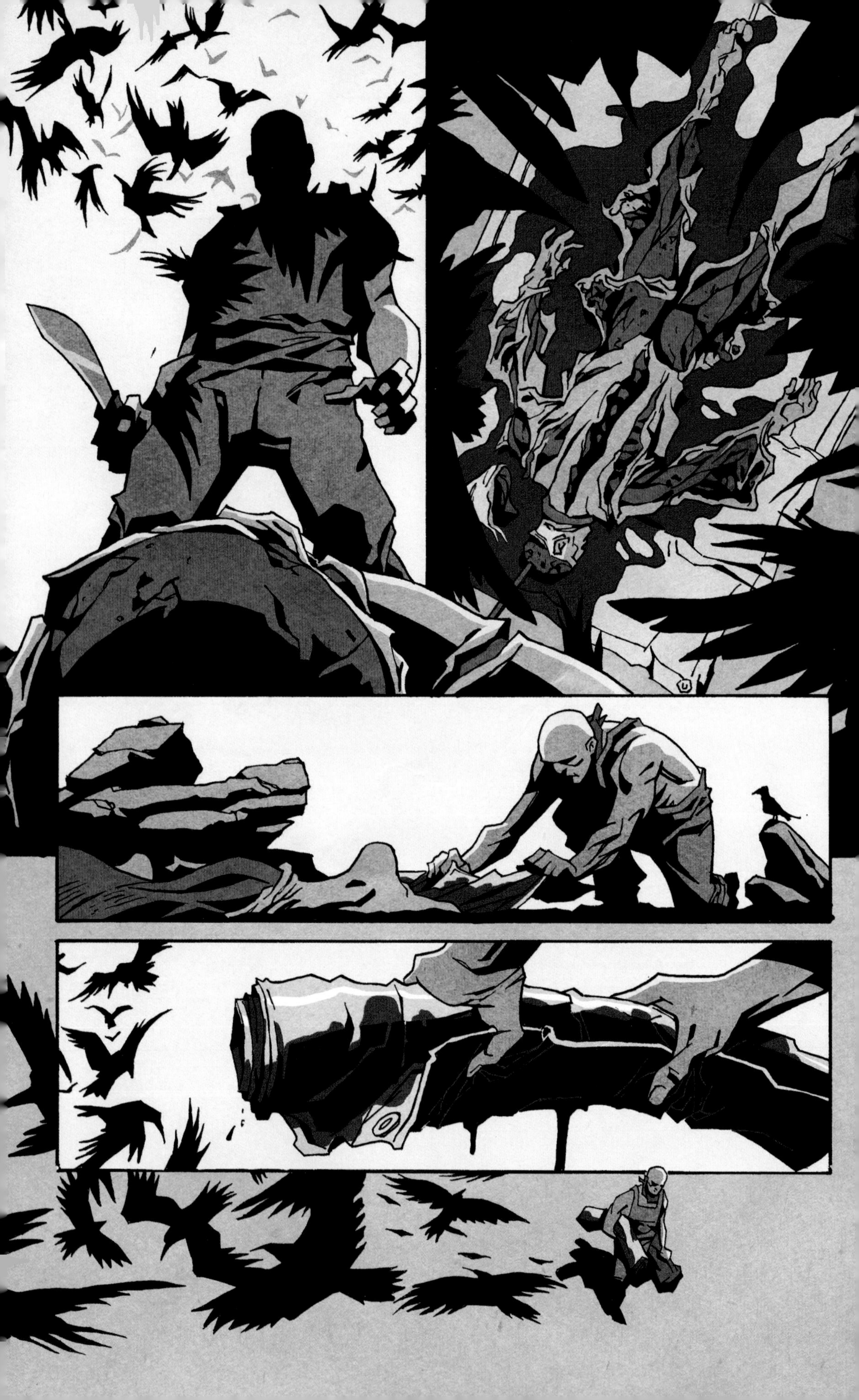

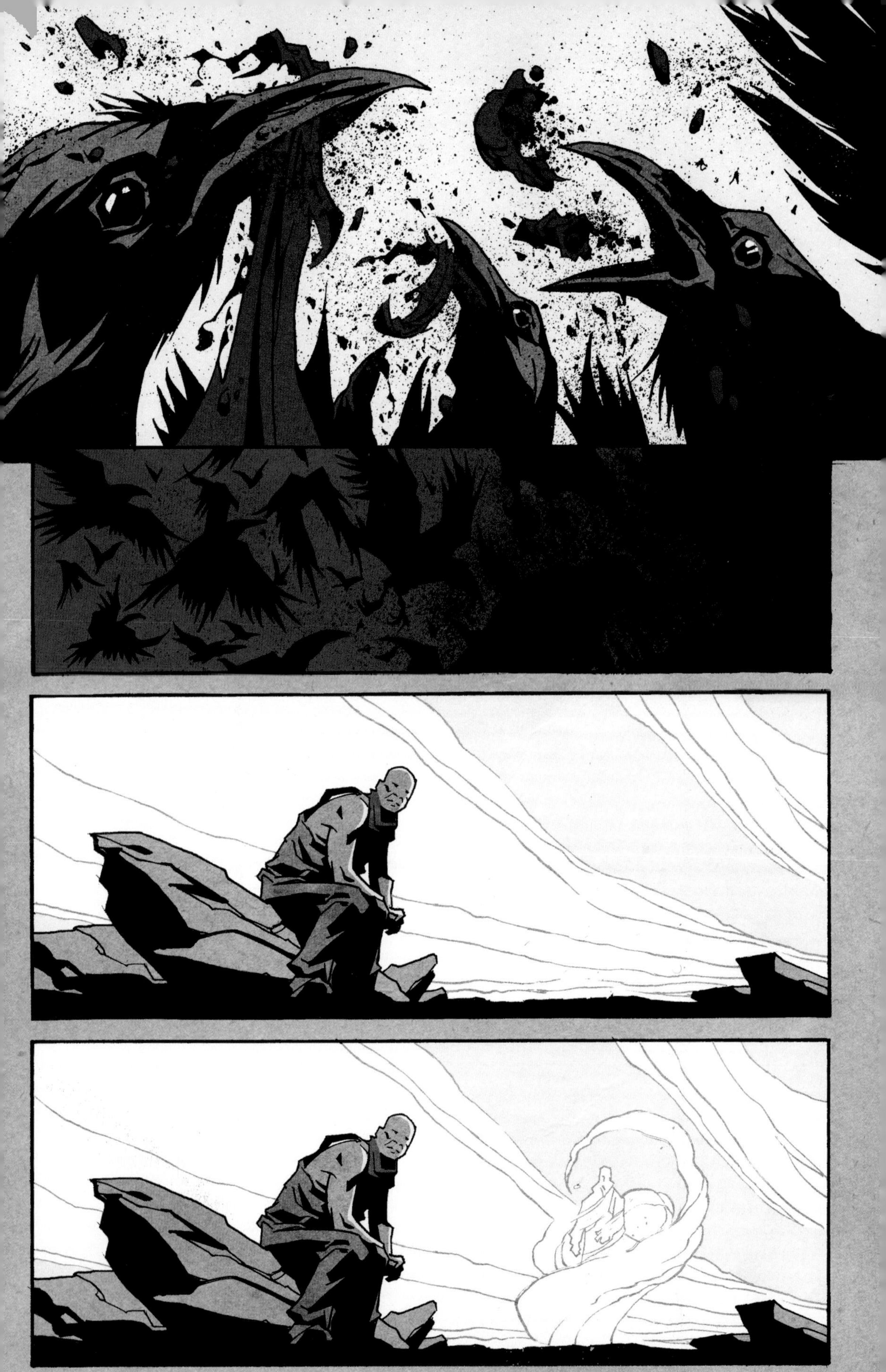

Shipwreck

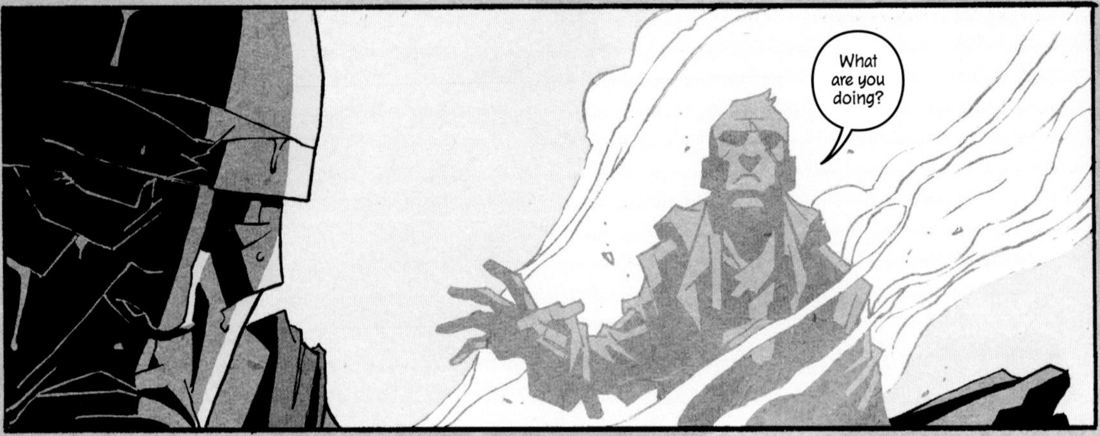
What are you doing?

2. Bell

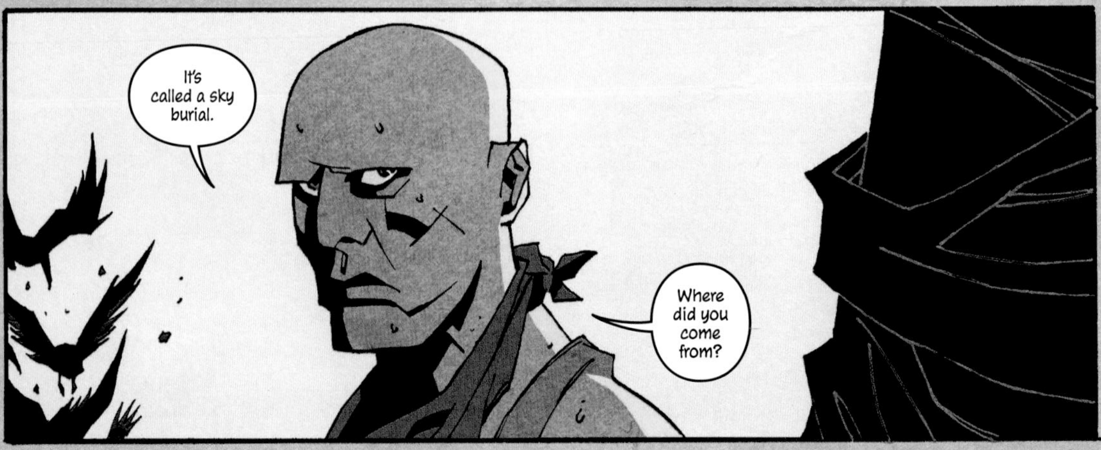
It's called a sky burial.
Where did you come from?

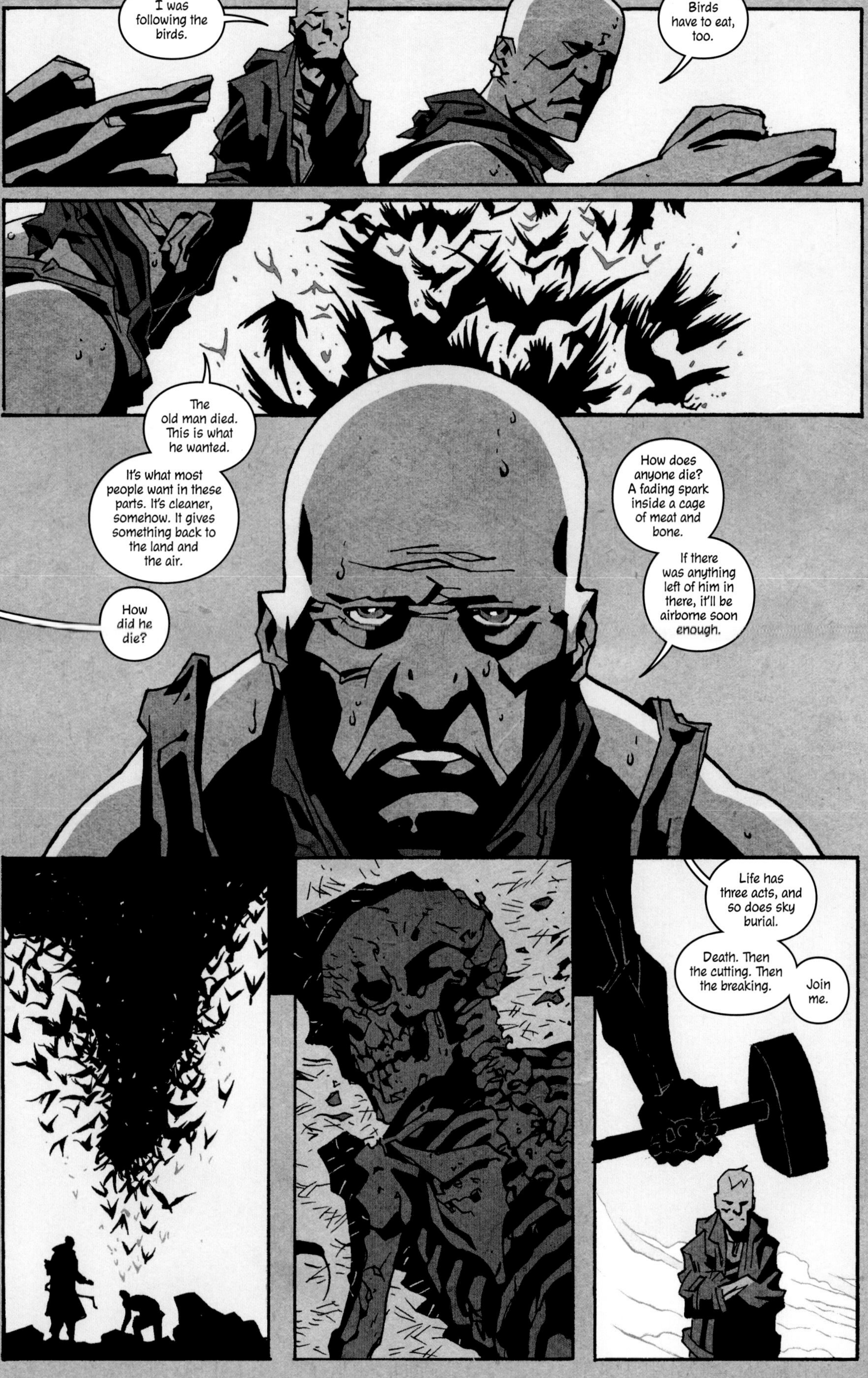
I was following the birds.
Birds have to eat, too.
The old man died. This is what he wanted.
It's what most people want in these parts. It's cleaner, somehow. It gives something back to the land and the air.
How did he die?
How does anyone die? A fading spark inside a cage of meat and bone.
If there was anything left of him in there, it'll be airborne soon enough.
Life has three acts, and so does sky burial.
Death. Then the cutting. Then the breaking.
Join me.

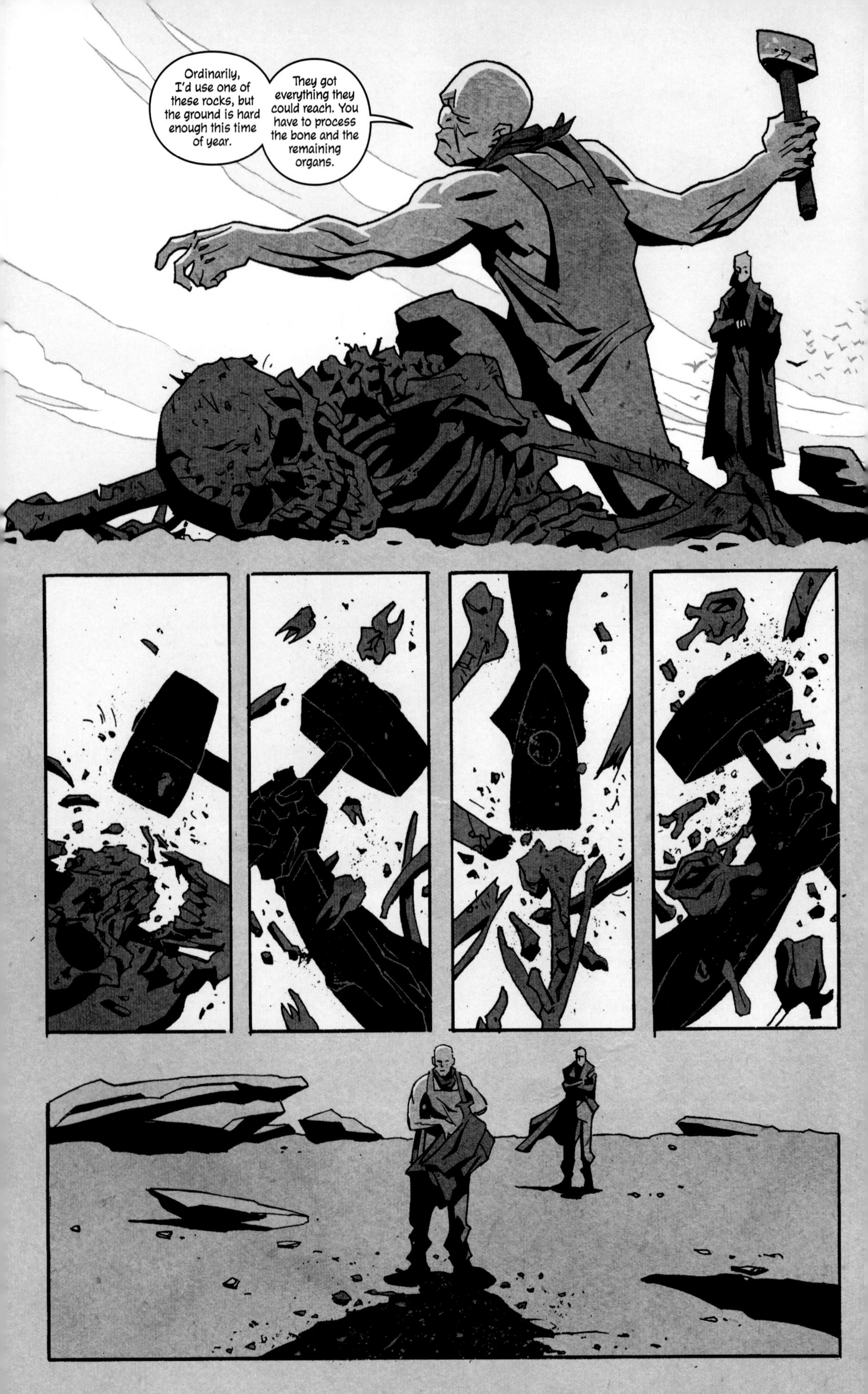

Ordinarily, I'd use one of these rocks, but the ground is hard enough this time of year.
They got everything they could reach. You have to process the bone and the remaining organs.

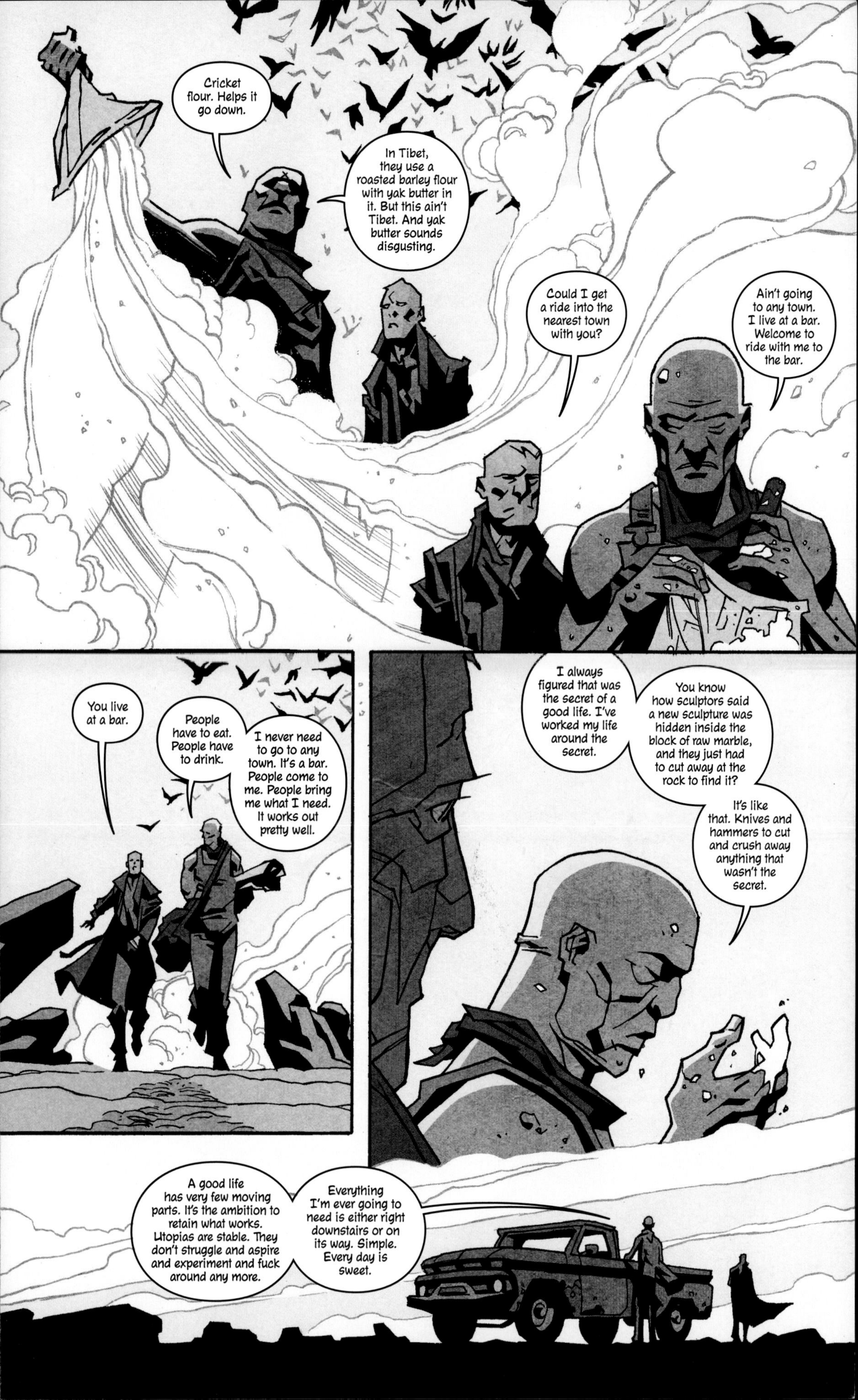
Cricket flour. Helps it go down.
In Tibet, they use a roasted barley flour with yak butter in it. But this ain't Tibet. And yak butter sounds disgusting.
Could I get a ride into the nearest town with you?
Ain't going to any town. I live at a bar. Welcome to ride with me to the bar.
You live at a bar.
People have to eat. People have to drink.
I never need to go to any town. It's a bar. People come to me. People bring me what I need. It works out pretty well.
I always figured that was the secret of a good life. I've worked my life around the secret.
You know how sculptors said a new sculpture was hidden inside the block of raw marble, and they just had to cut away at the rock to find it?
It's like that. Knives and hammers to cut and crush away anything that wasn't the secret.
A good life has very few moving parts. It's the ambition to retain what works. Utopias are stable. They don't struggle and aspire and experiment and fuck around any more.
Everything I'm ever going to need is either right downstairs or on its way. Simple. Every day is sweet.

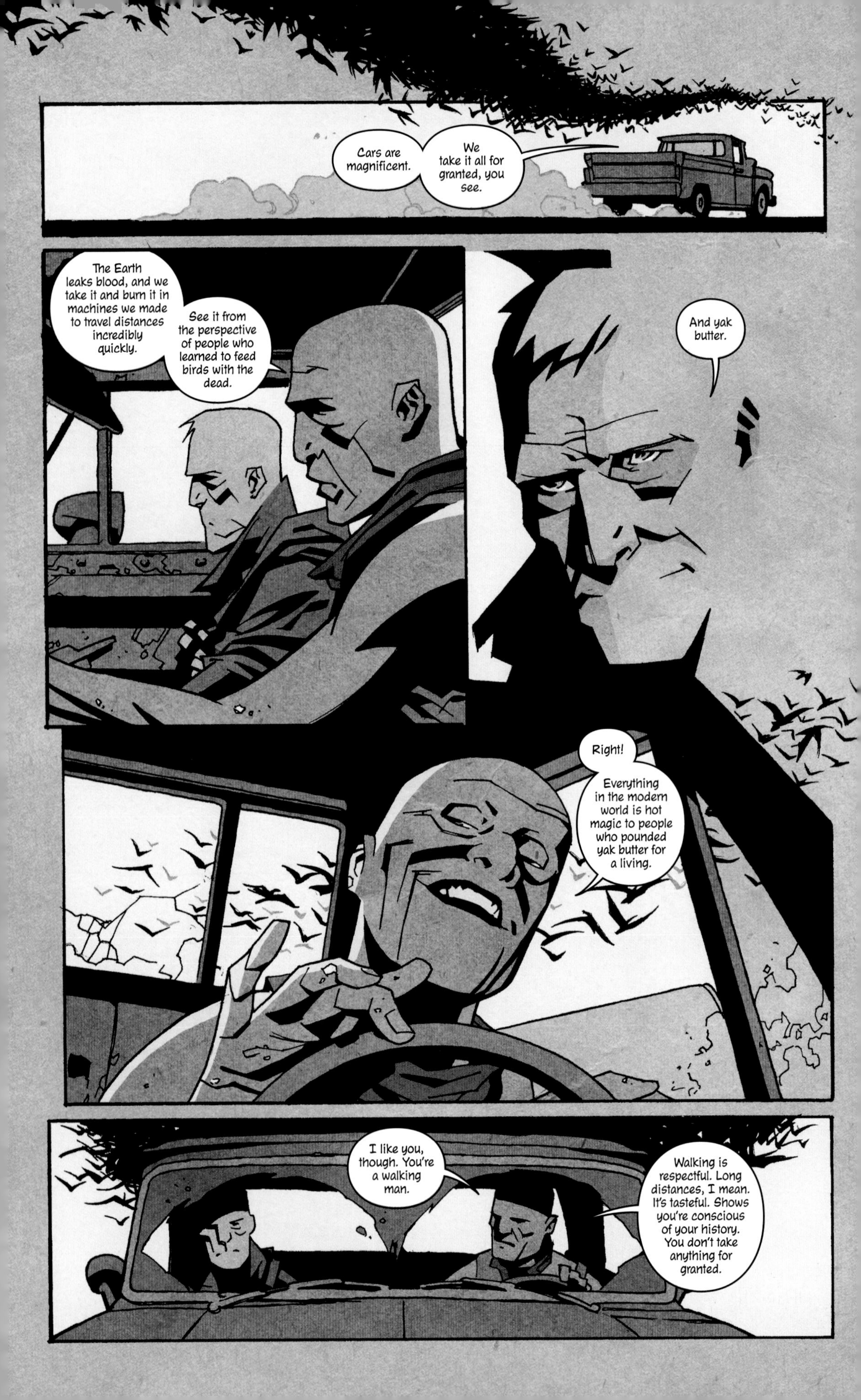
Cars are magnificent.
We take it all for granted, you see.
The Earth leaks blood, and we take it and burn it in machines we made to travel distances incredibly quickly.
See it from the perspective of people who learned to feed birds with the dead.
And yak butter.
Right!
Everything in the modern world is hot magic to people who pounded yak butter for a living.
I like you, though. You're a walking man.
Walking is respectful. Long distances, I mean. It's tasteful. Shows you're conscious of your history. You don't take anything for granted.

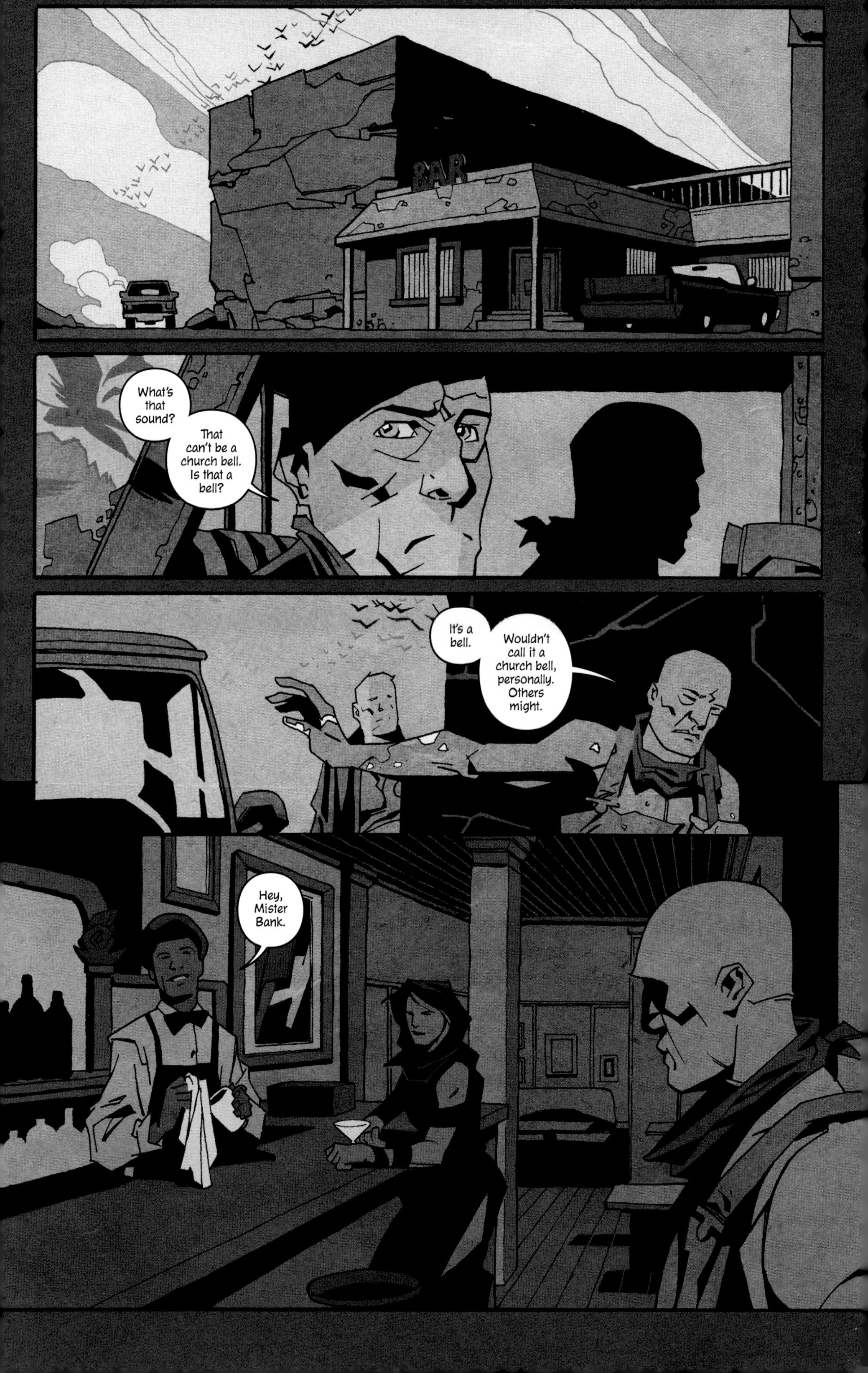
What's that sound?
That can't be a church bell. Is that a bell?
It's a bell.
Wouldn't call it a church bell, personally. Others might.
Hey, Mister Bank.

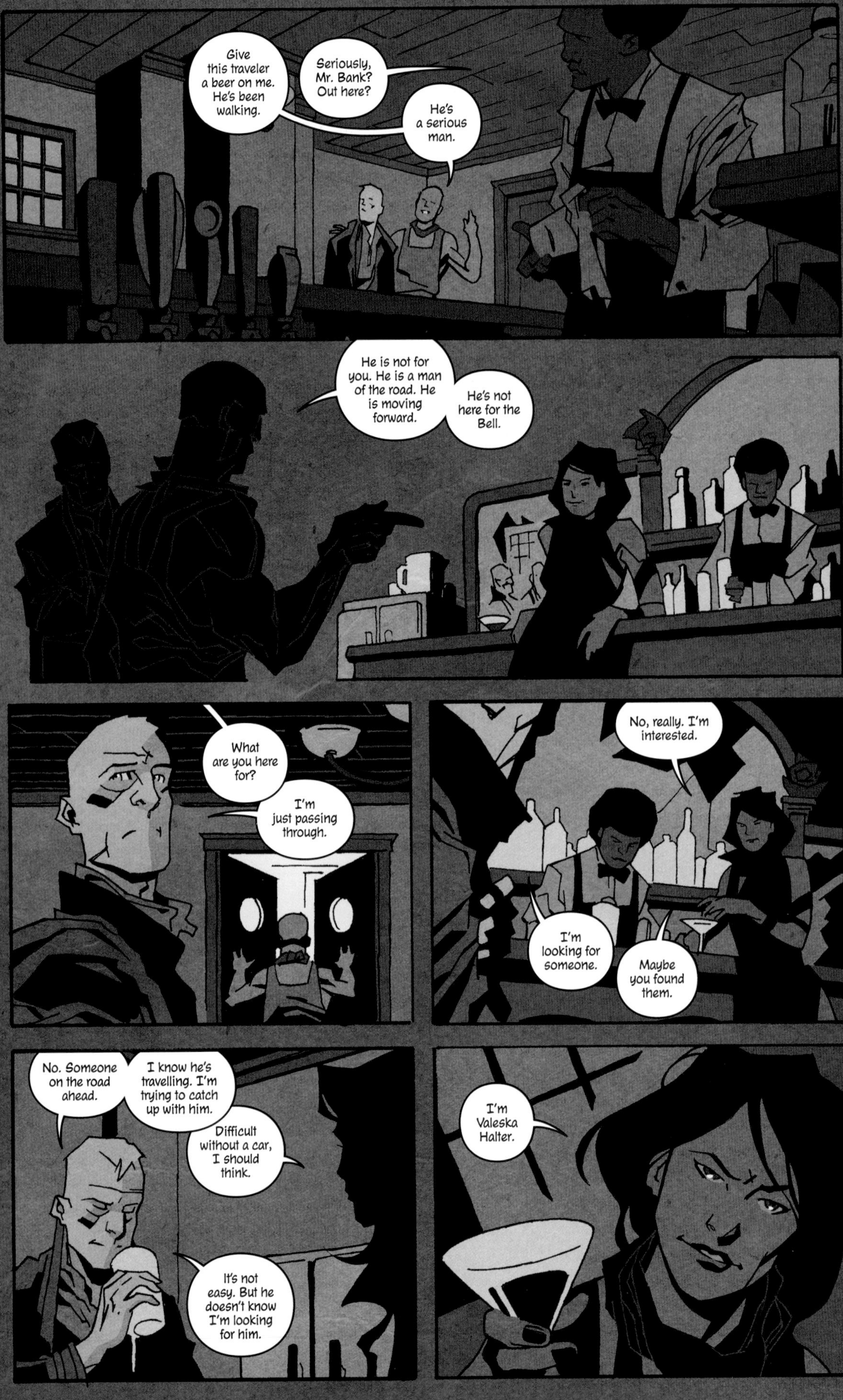

Give this traveler a beer on me. He's been walking.
Seriously, Mr. Bank? Out here?
He's a serious man.
He is not for you. He is a man of the road. He is moving forward.
He's not here for the Bell.
What are you here for?
I'm just passing through.
No, really. I'm interested.
I'm looking for someone.
Maybe you found them.
No. Someone on the road ahead.
I know he's travelling. I'm trying to catch up with him.
Difficult without a car, I should think.
It's not easy. But he doesn't know I'm looking for him.
I'm Valeska Halter.

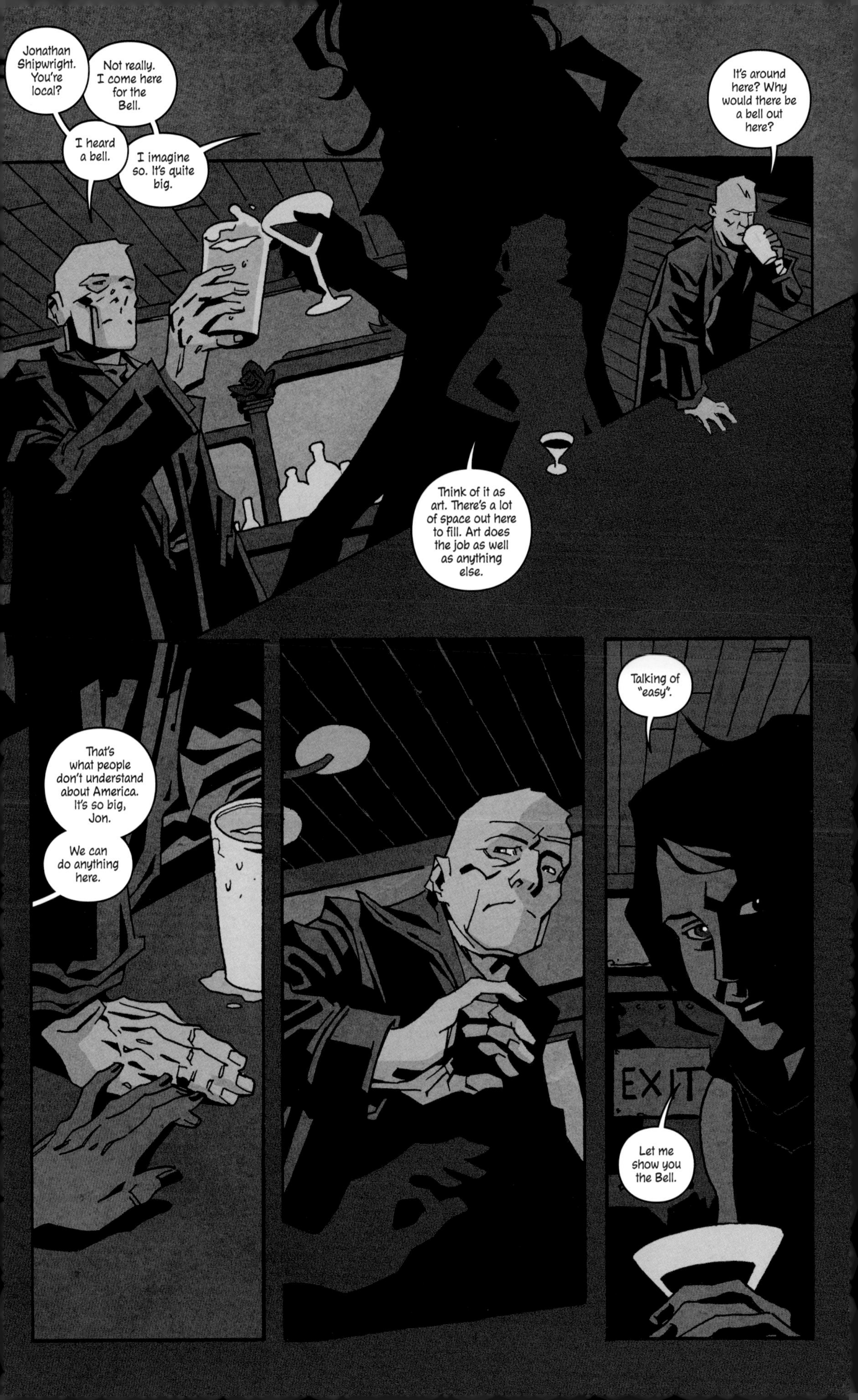
Jonathan Shipwright. You're local?
Not really. I come here for the Bell.
I heard a bell.
I imagine so. It's quite big.
It's around here? Why would there be a bell out here?
Think of it as art. There's a lot of space out here to fill. Art does the job as well as anything else.
That's what people don't understand about America. It's so big, Jon.
We can do anything here.
Talking of "easy".
EXIT
Let me show you the Bell.

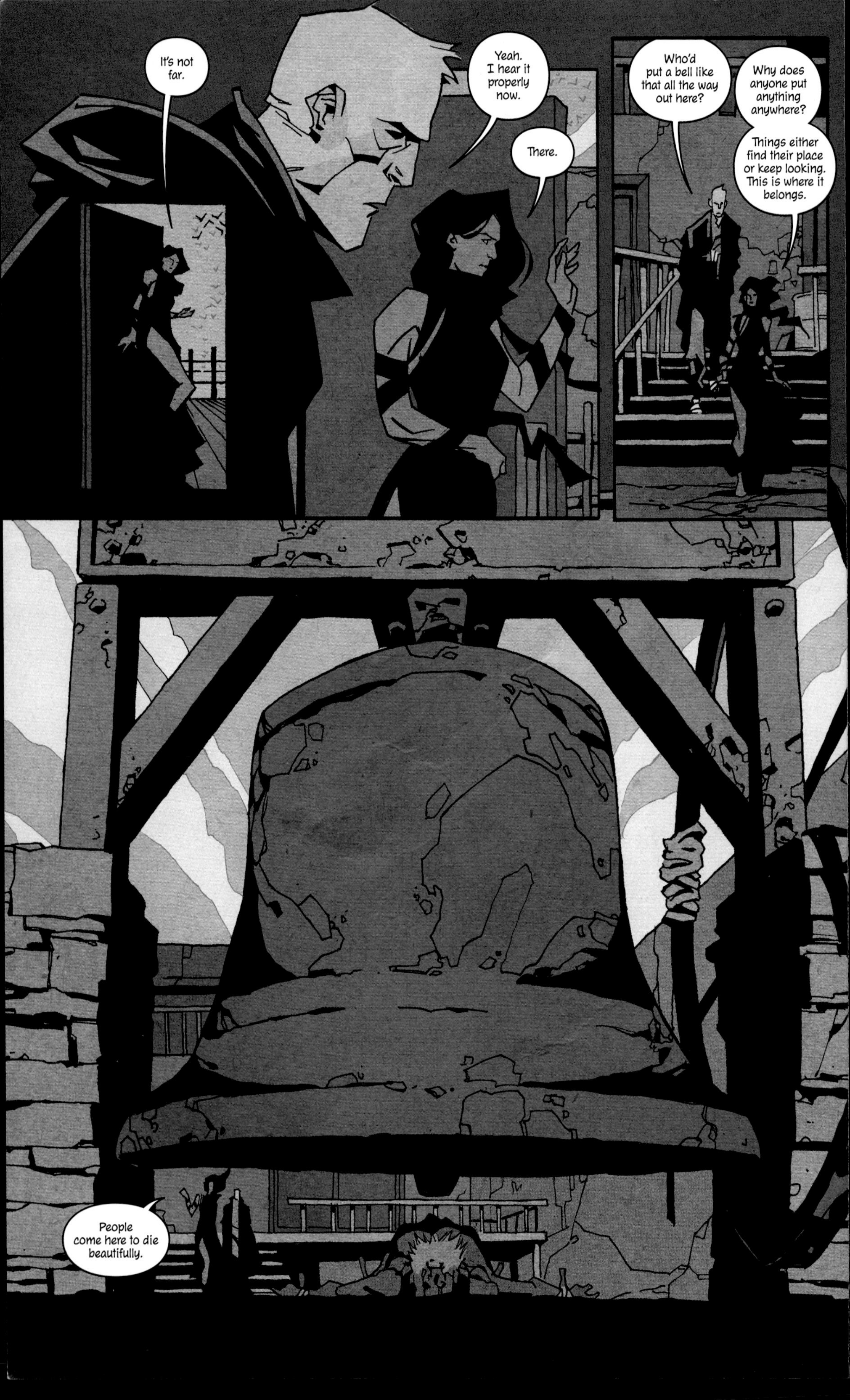
It's not far.
Yeah. I hear it properly now.
There.
Who'd put a bell like that all the way out here?
Why does anyone put anything anywhere?
Things either find their place or keep looking. This is where it belongs.
People come here to die beautifully.

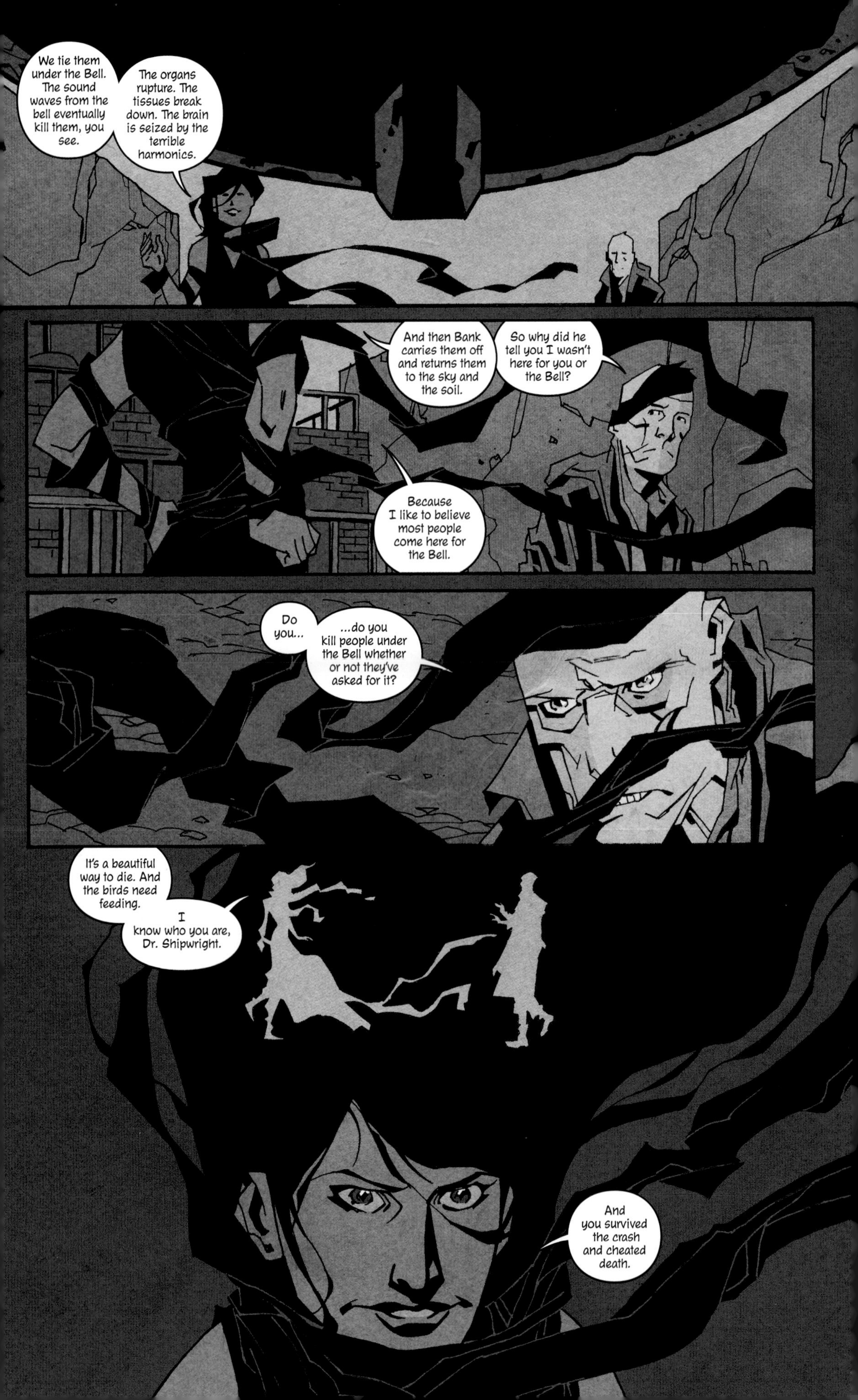
We tie them under the Bell. The sound waves from the bell eventually kill them, you see.
The organs rupture. The tissues break down. The brain is seized by the terrible harmonics.
And then Bank carries them off and returns them to the sky and the soil.
So why did he tell you I wasn't here for you or the Bell?
Because I like to believe most people come here for the Bell.
Do you...
...do you kill people under the Bell whether or not they've asked for it?
It's a beautiful way to die. And the birds need feeding.
I know who you are, Dr. Shipwright.
And you survived the crash and cheated death.

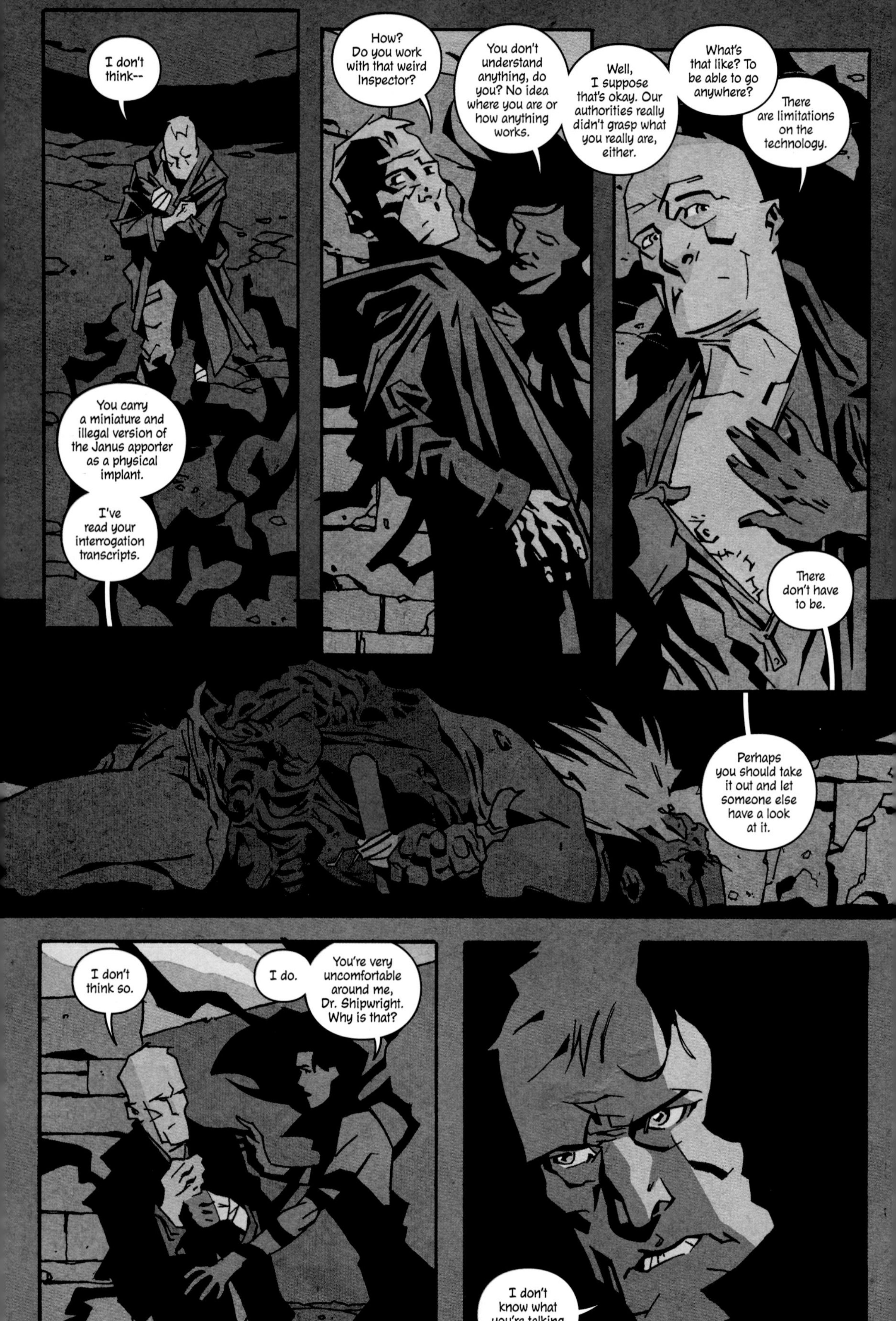
I don't think--
You carry a miniature and illegal version of the Janus apporter as a physical implant.
I've read your interrogation transcripts.
How? Do you work with that weird Inspector?
You don't understand anything, do you? No idea where you are or how anything works.
Well, I suppose that's okay. Our authorities really didn't grasp what you really are, either.
What's that like? To be able to go anywhere?
There are limitations on the technology.
There don't have to be.
Perhaps you should take it out and let someone else have a look at it.
I don't think so.
I do.
You're very uncomfortable around me, Dr. Shipwright. Why is that?
I don't know what you're talking about.

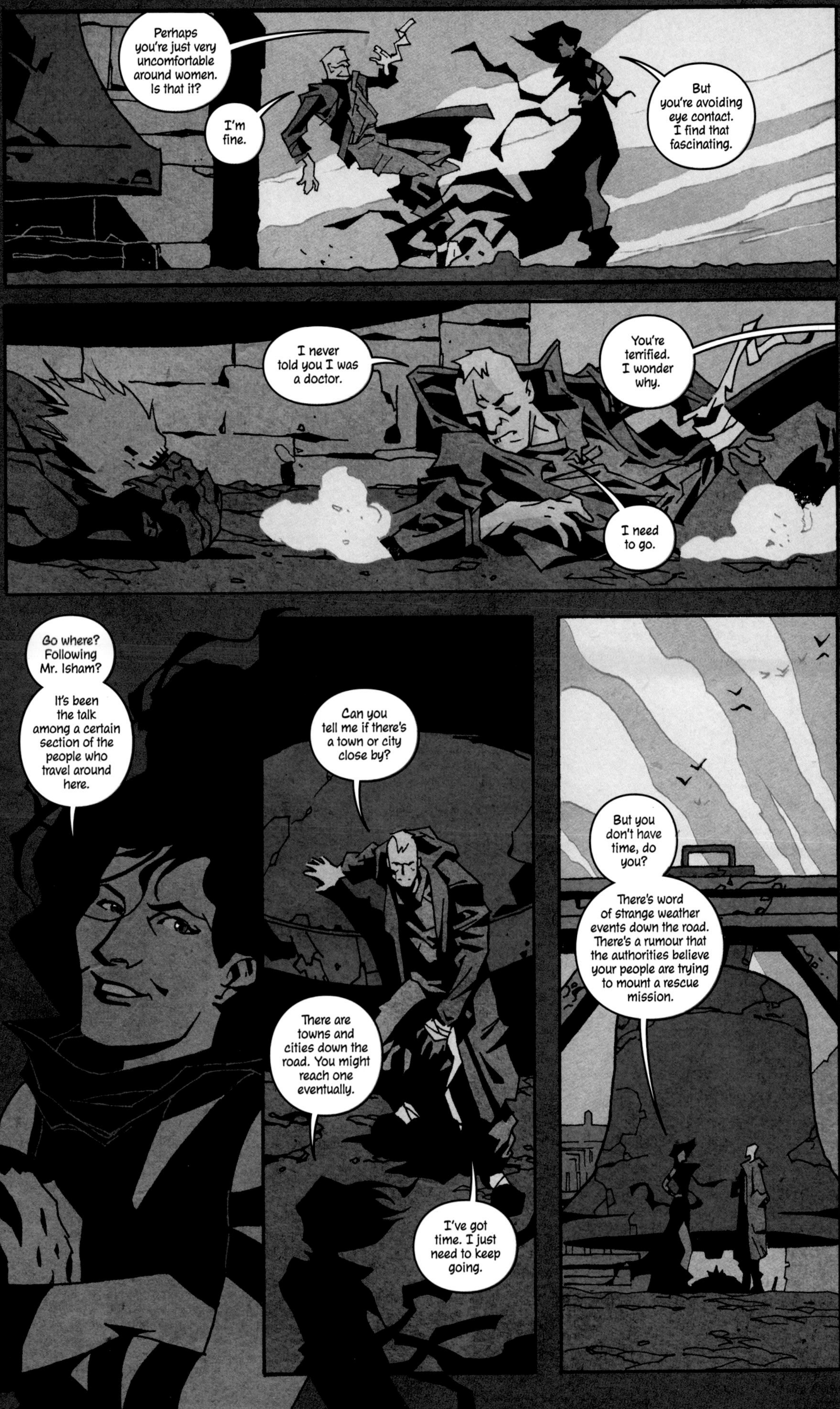
Perhaps you're just very uncomfortable around women. Is that it?
I'm fine.
But you're avoiding eye contact. I find that fascinating.
I never told you I was a doctor.
You're terrified. I wonder why.
I need to go.
Go where? Following Mr. Isham?
It's been the talk among a certain section of the people who travel around here.
Can you tell me if there's a town or city close by?
There are towns and cities down the road. You might reach one eventually.
I've got time. I just need to keep going.
But you don't have time, do you?
There's word of strange weather events down the road. There's a rumour that the authorities believe your people are trying to mount a rescue mission.

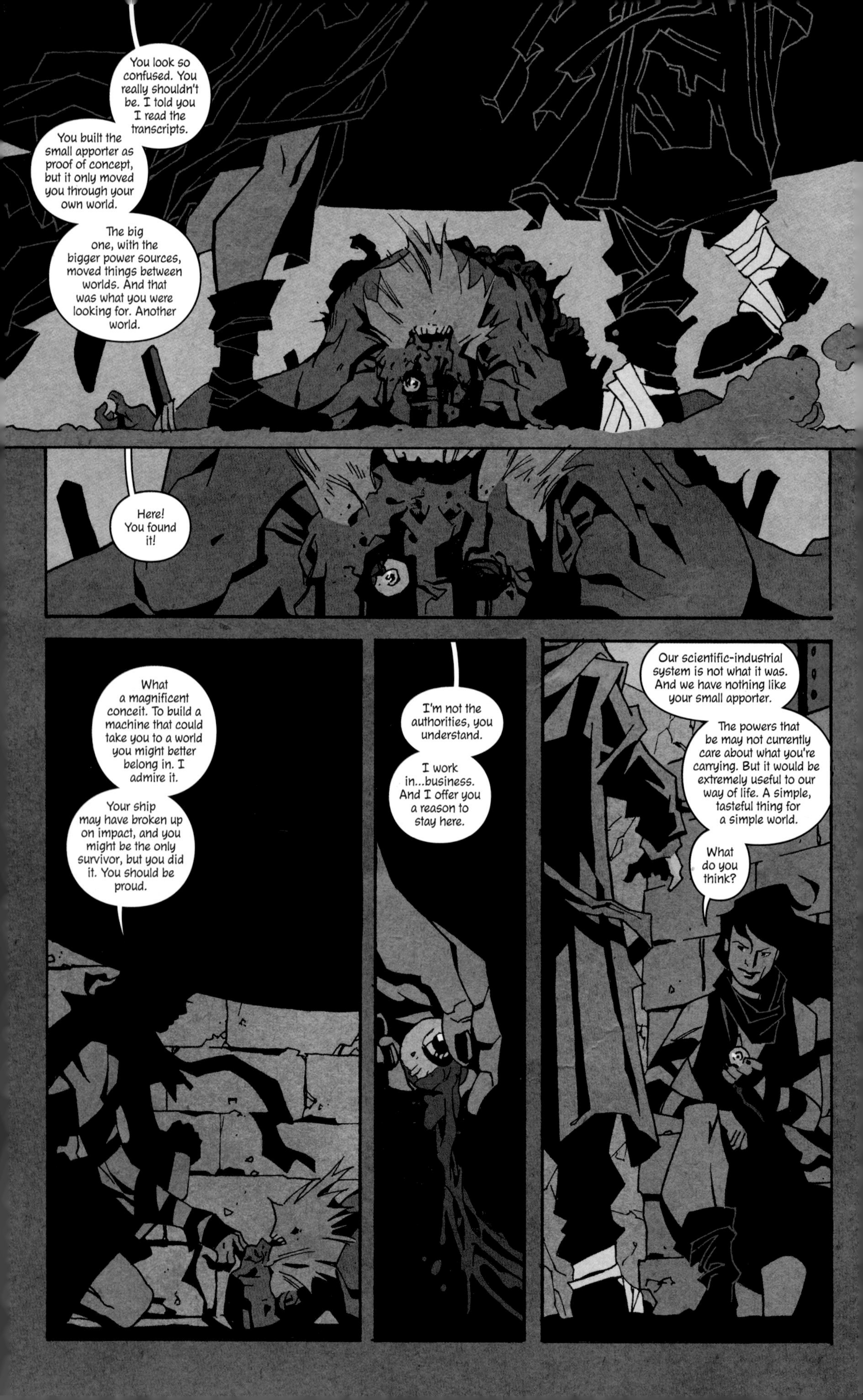
You look so confused. You really shouldn't be. I told you I read the transcripts.
You built the small apporter as proof of concept, but it only moved you through your own world.
The big one, with the bigger power sources, moved things between worlds. And that was what you were looking for. Another world.
Here! You found it!
What a magnificent conceit. To build a machine that could take you to a world you might better belong in. I admire it.
Your ship may have broken up on impact, and you might be the only survivor, but you did it. You should be proud.
I'm not the authorities, you understand.
I work in...business. And I offer you a reason to stay here.
Our scientific-industrial system is not what it was. And we have nothing like your small apporter.
The powers that be may not currently care about what you're carrying. But it would be extremely useful to our way of life. A simple, tasteful thing for a simple world.
What do you think?

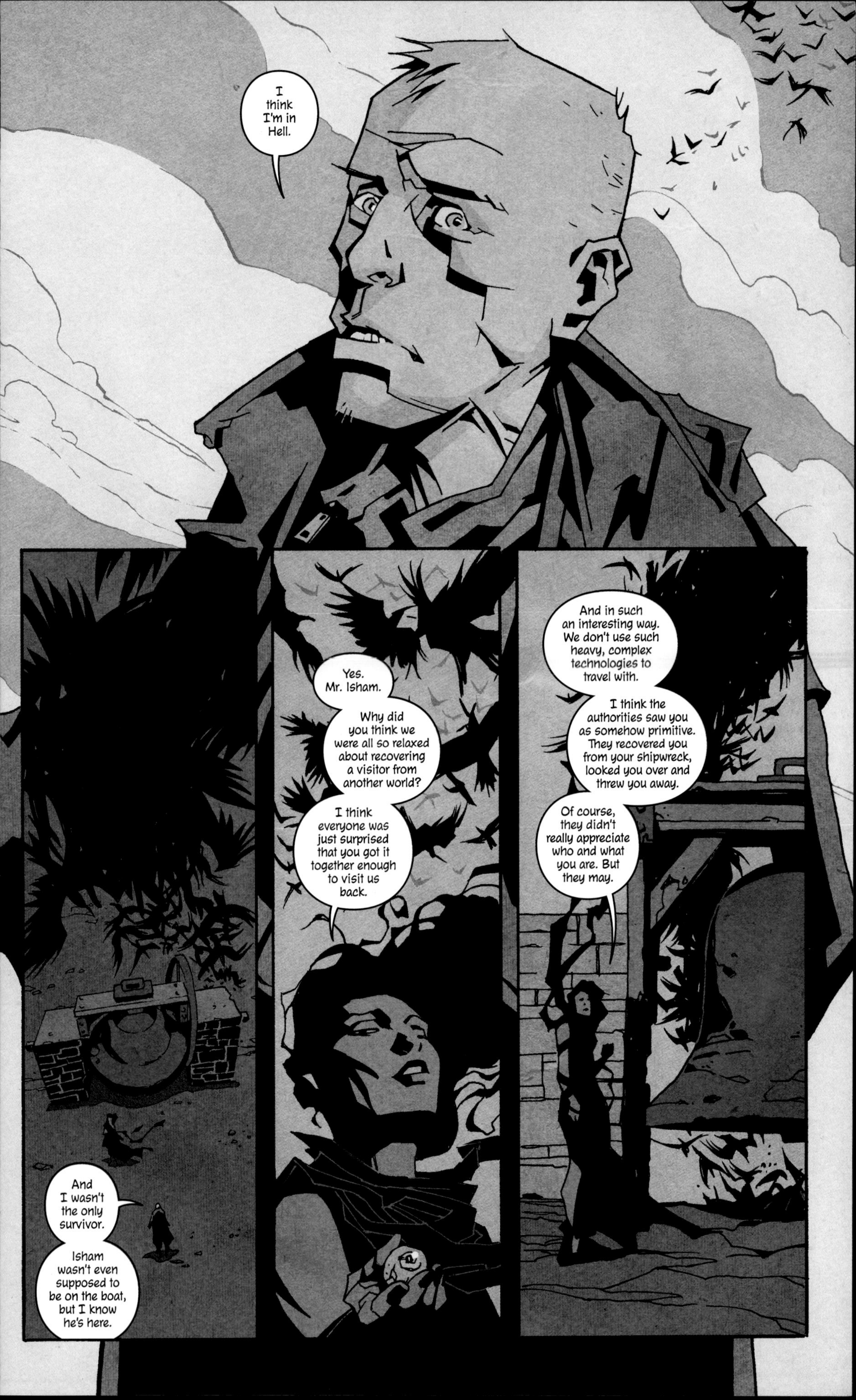

I think I'm in Hell.
And I wasn't the only survivor.
Isham wasn't even supposed to be on the boat, but I know he's here.
Yes. Mr. Isham.
Why did you think we were all so relaxed about recovering a visitor from another world?
I think everyone was just surprised that you got it together enough to visit us back.
And in such an interesting way. We don't use such heavy, complex technologies to travel with.
I think the authorities saw you as somehow primitive. They recovered you from your shipwreck, looked you over and threw you away.
Of course, they didn't really appreciate who and what you are. But they may.

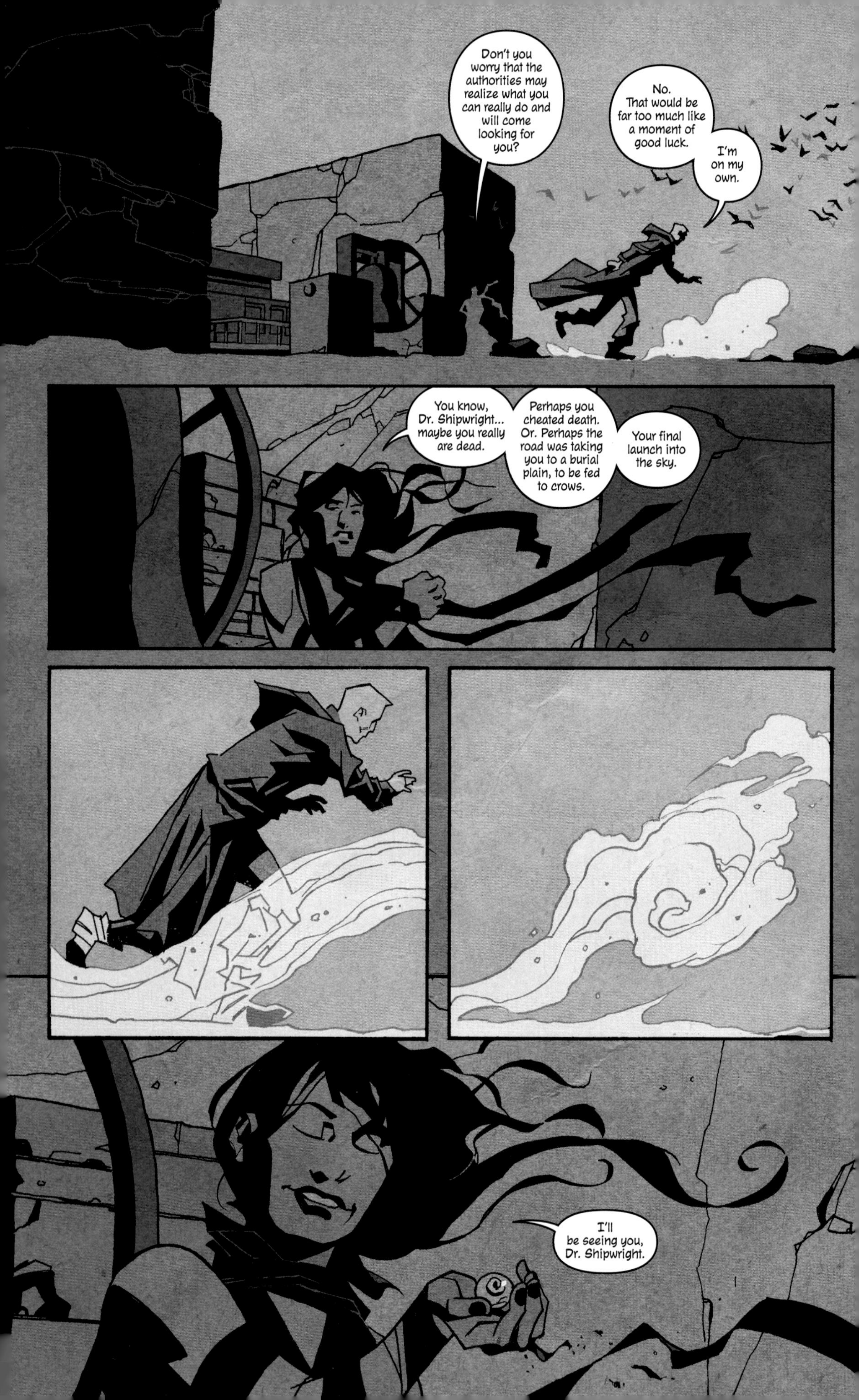
Don't you worry that the authorities may realize what you can really do and will come looking for you?
No. That would be far too much like a moment of good luck.
I'm on my own.
You know, Dr. Shipwright... maybe you really are dead.
Perhaps you cheated death. Or. Perhaps the road was taking you to a burial plain, to be fed to crows.
Your final launch into the sky.
I'll be seeing you, Dr. Shipwright.

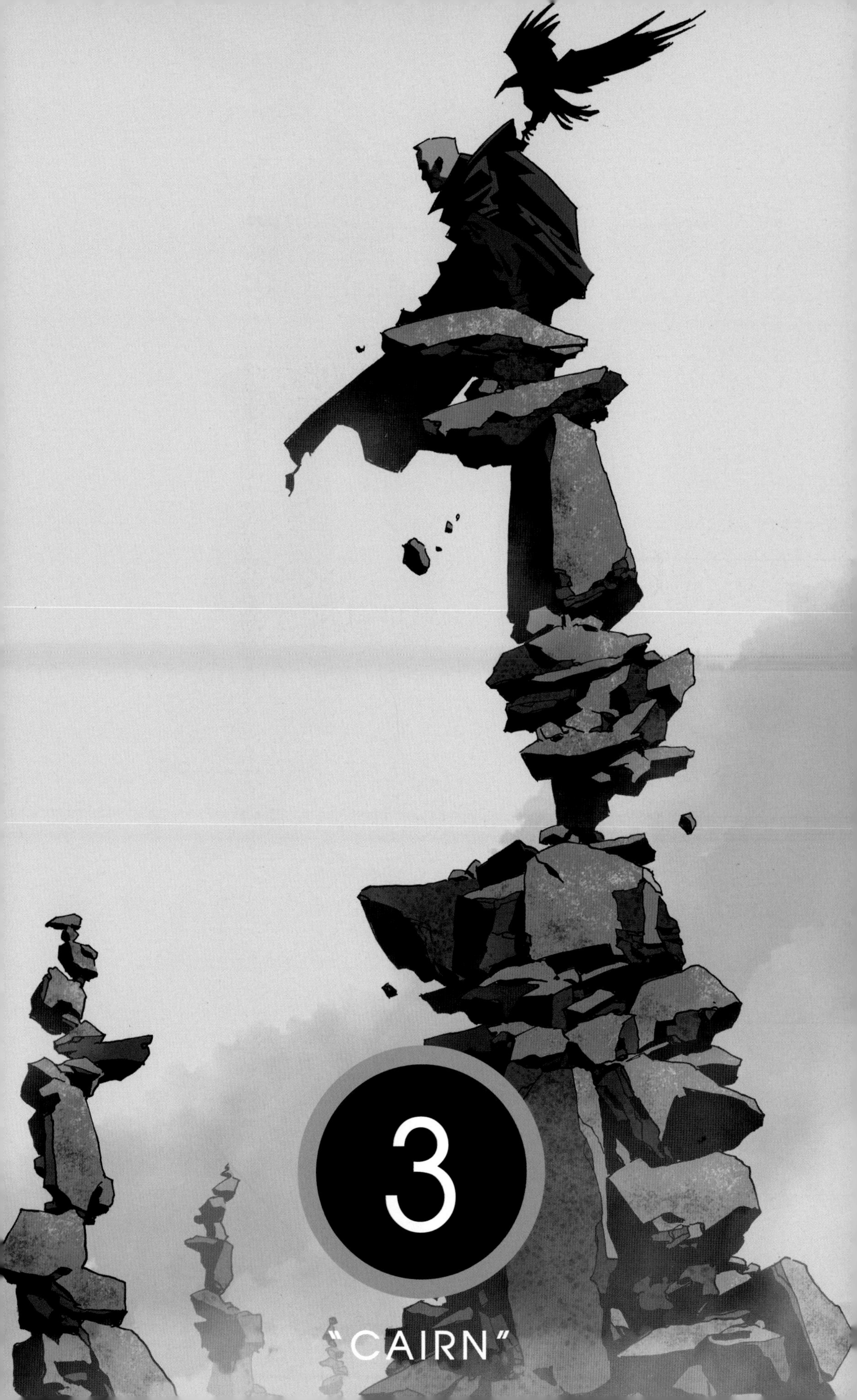
3
"CAIRN"

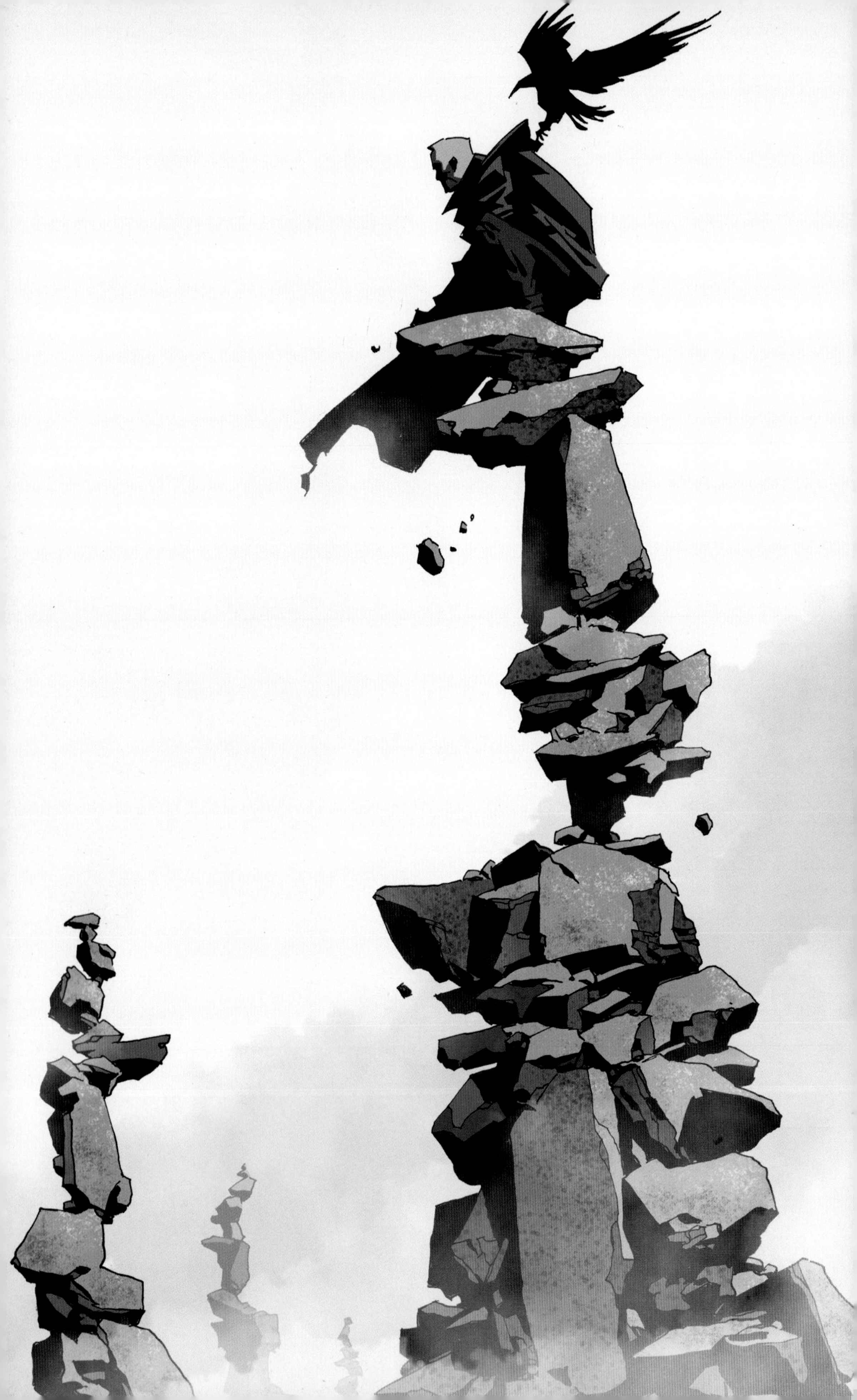

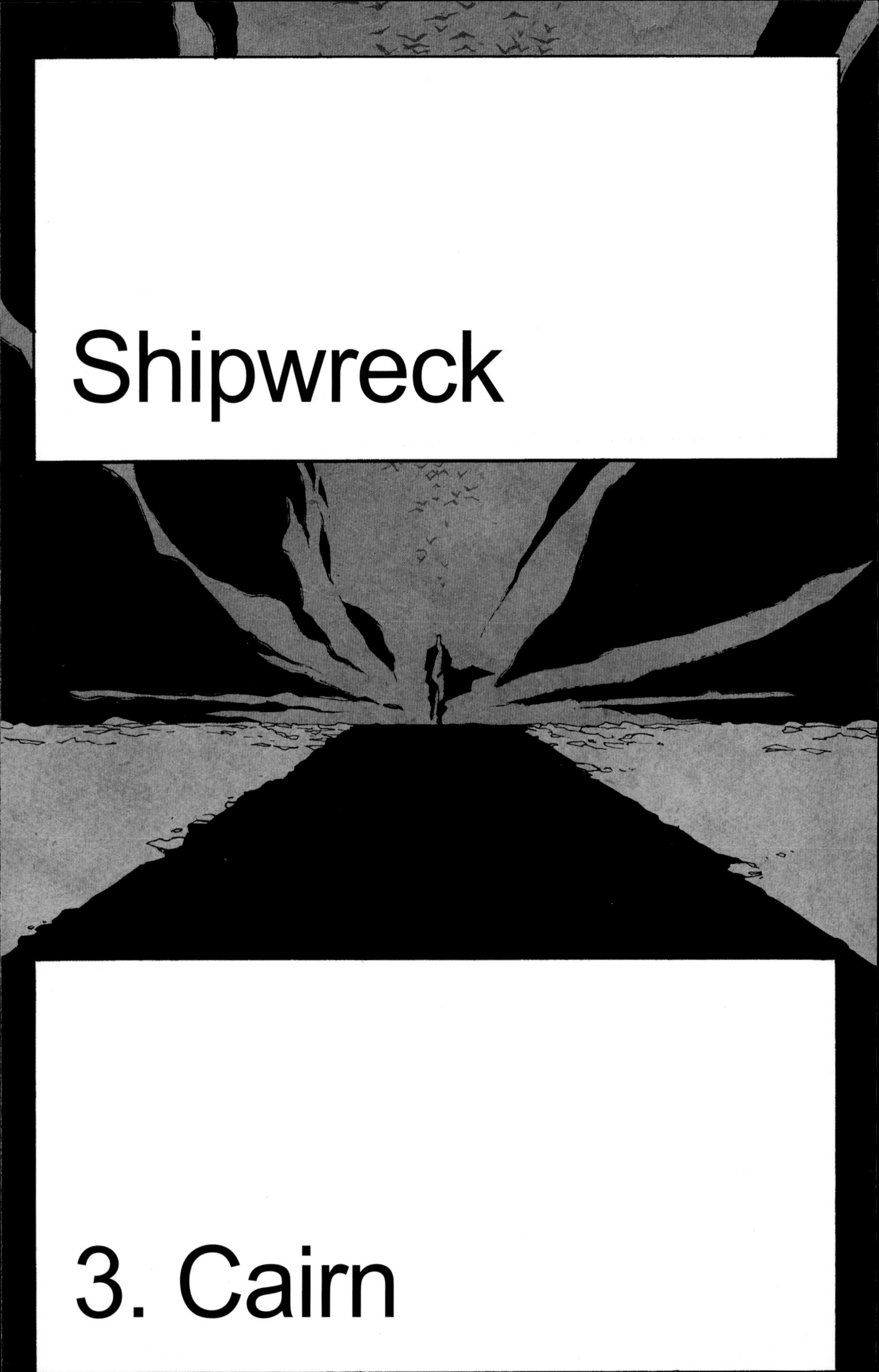
Shipwreck
3. Cairn

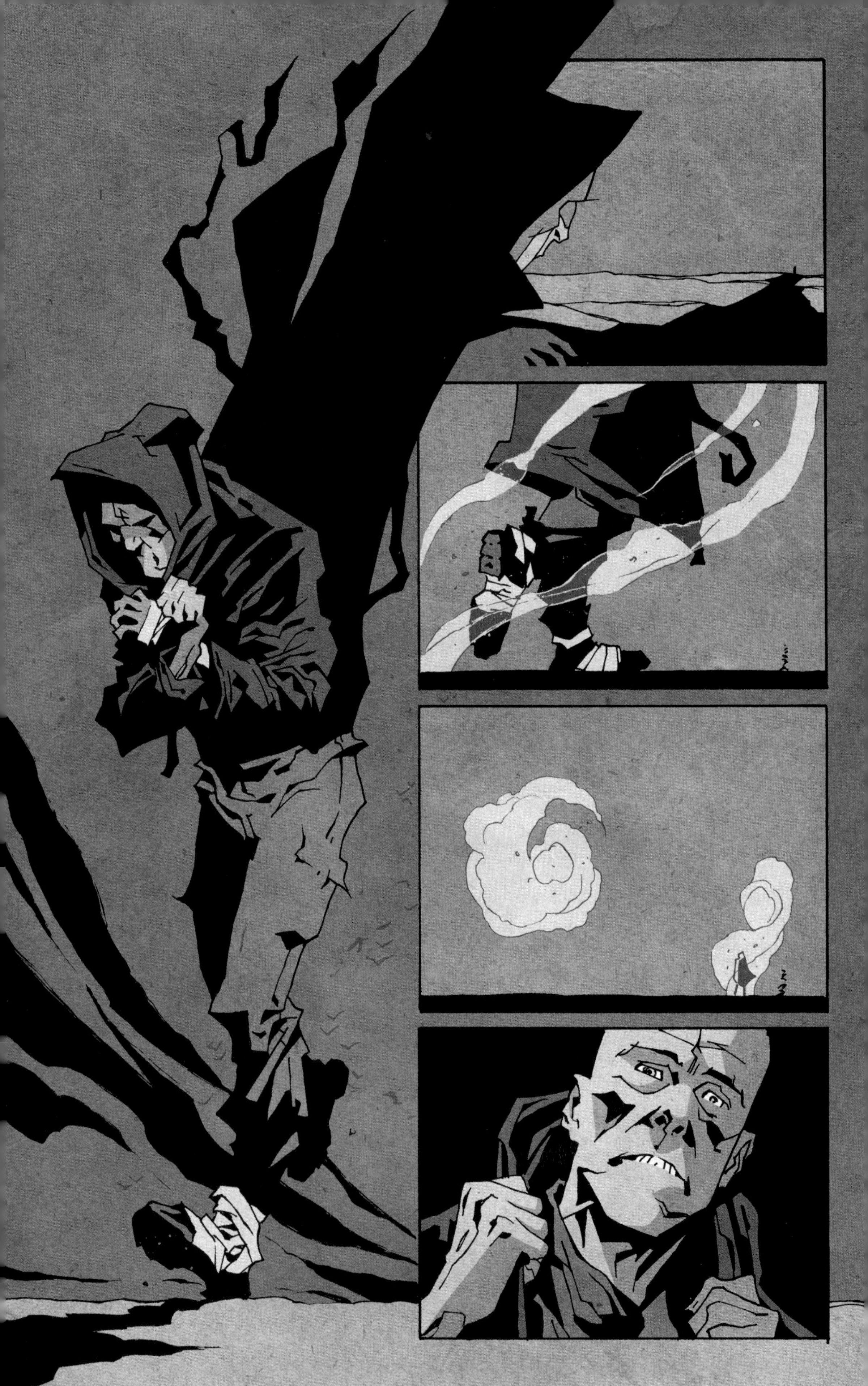

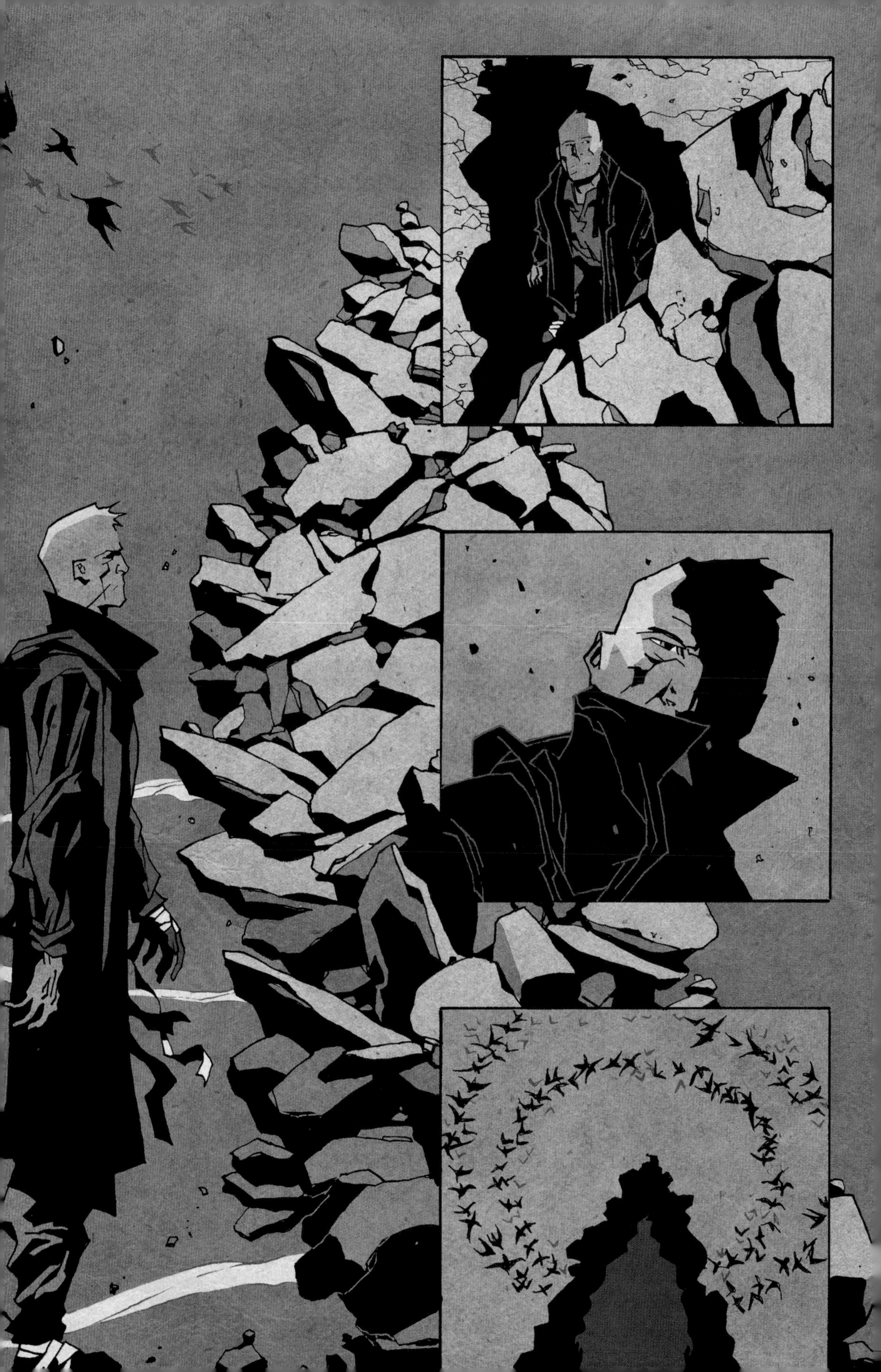

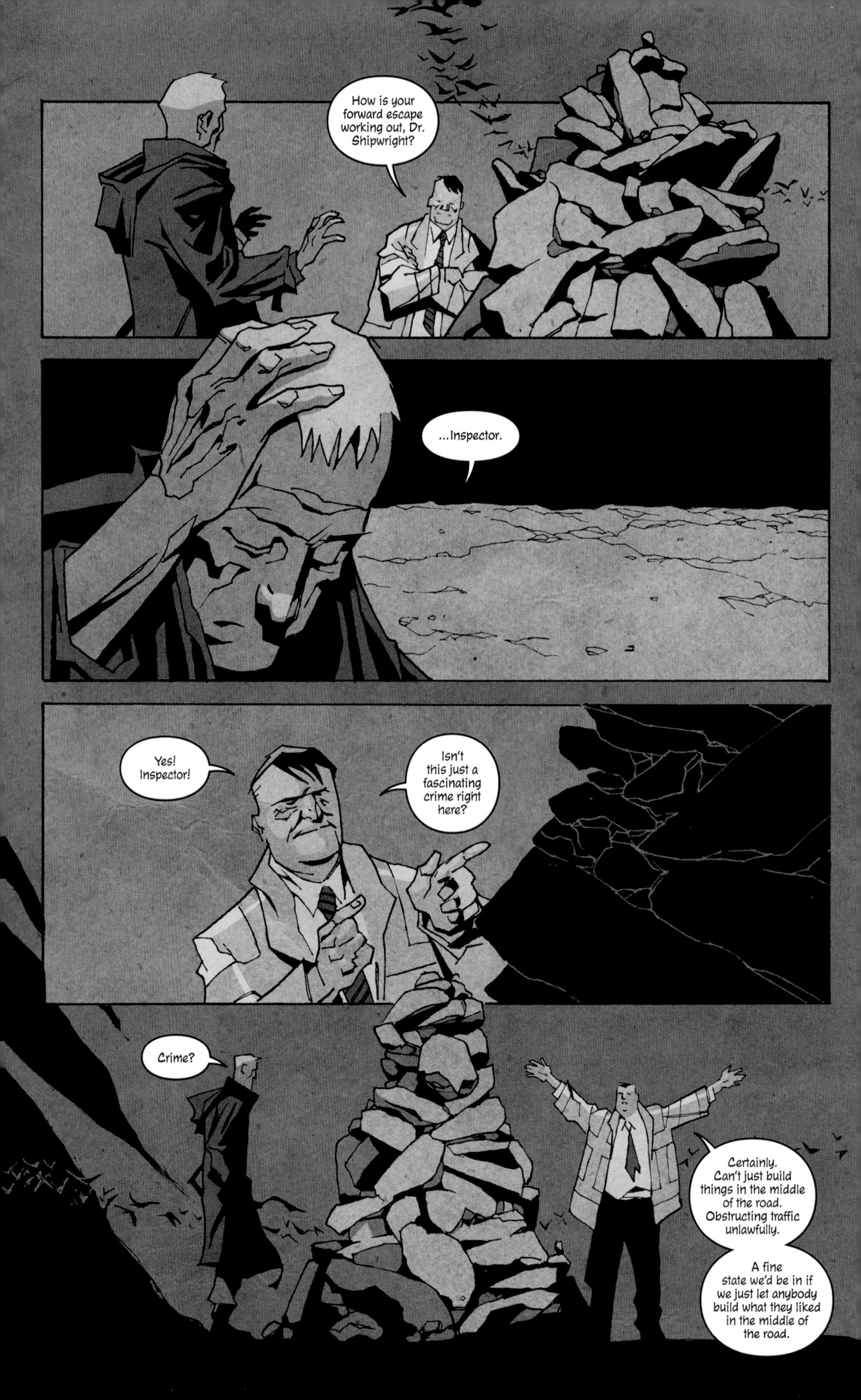
How is your forward escape working out, Dr. Shipwright?
...Inspector.
Yes! Inspector!
Isn't this just a fascinating crime right here?
Crime?
Certainly. Can't just build things in the middle of the road. Obstructing traffic unlawfully.
A fine state we'd be in if we just let anybody build what they liked in the middle of the road.

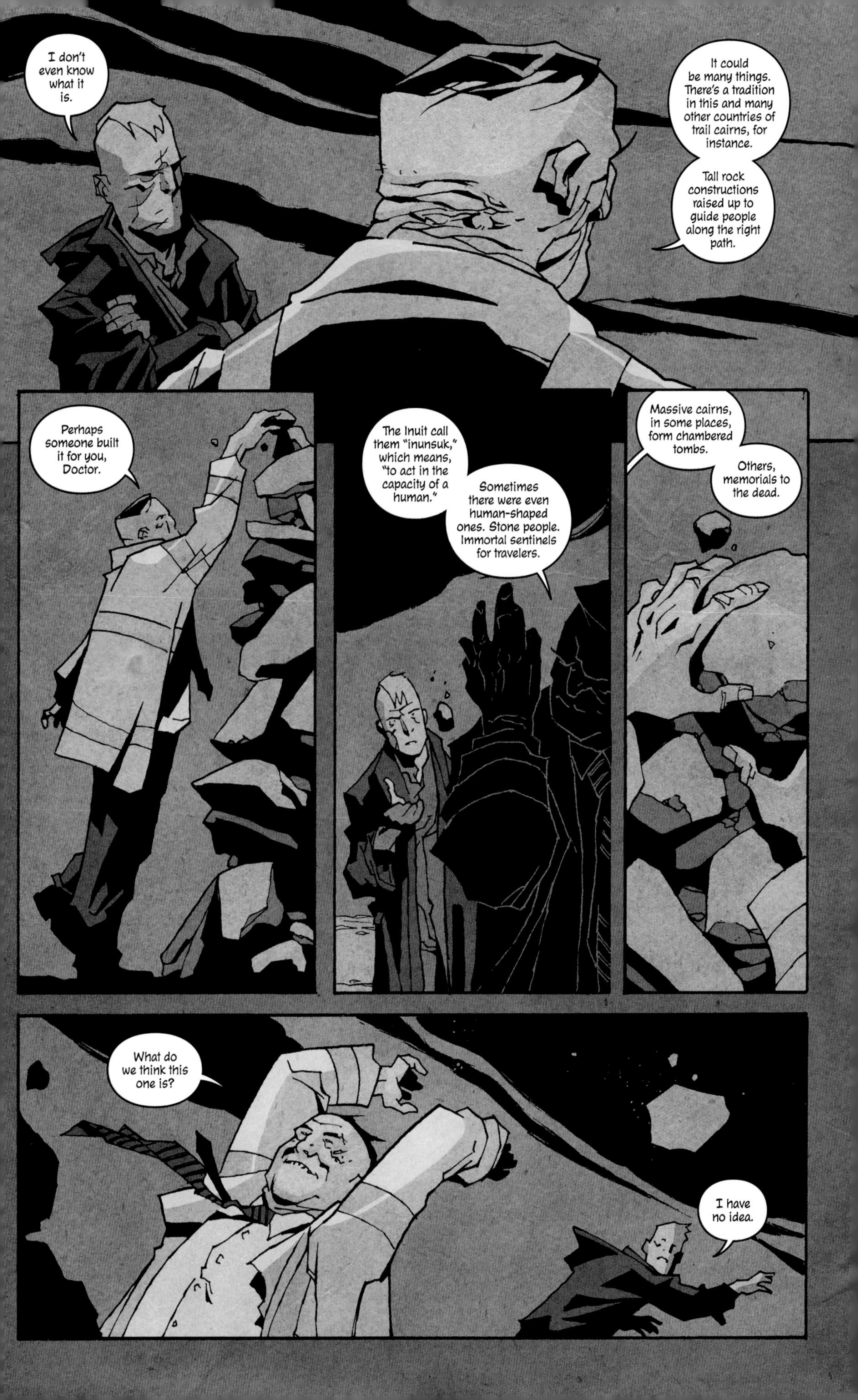
I don't even know what it is.
It could be many things. There's a tradition in this and many other countries of trail cairns, for instance.
Tall rock constructions raised up to guide people along the right path.
Perhaps someone built it for you, Doctor.
The Inuit call them "inunsuk," which means, "to act in the capacity of a human."
Sometimes there were even human-shaped ones. Stone people. Immortal sentinels for travelers.
Massive cairns, in some places, form chambered tombs.
Others, memorials to the dead.
What do we think this one is?
I have no idea.

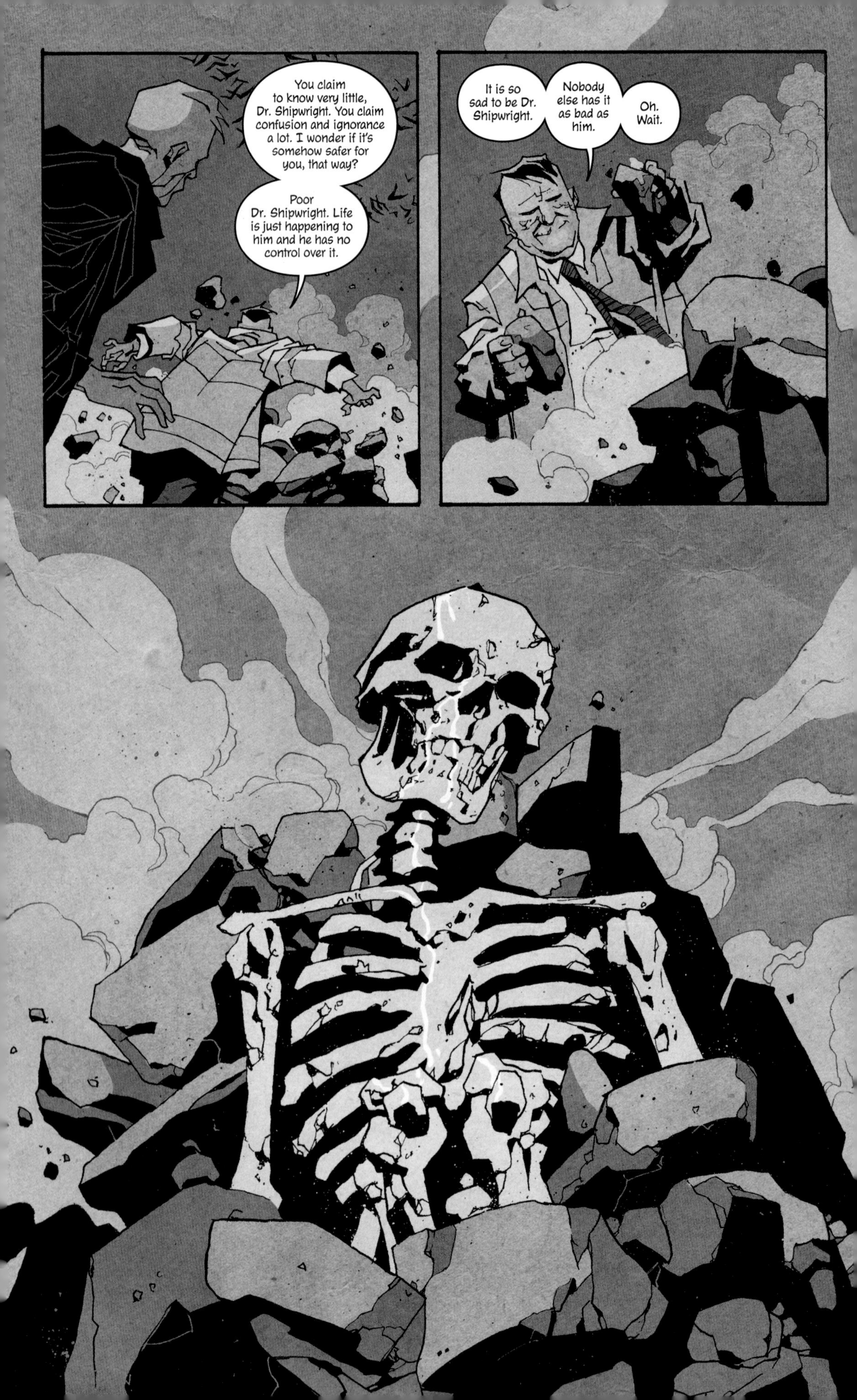
You claim to know very little, Dr. Shipwright. You claim confusion and ignorance a lot. I wonder if it's somehow safer for you, that way?
Poor Dr. Shipwright. Life is just happening to him and he has no control over it.
It is so sad to be Dr. Shipwright.
Nobody else has it as bad as him.
Oh. Wait.

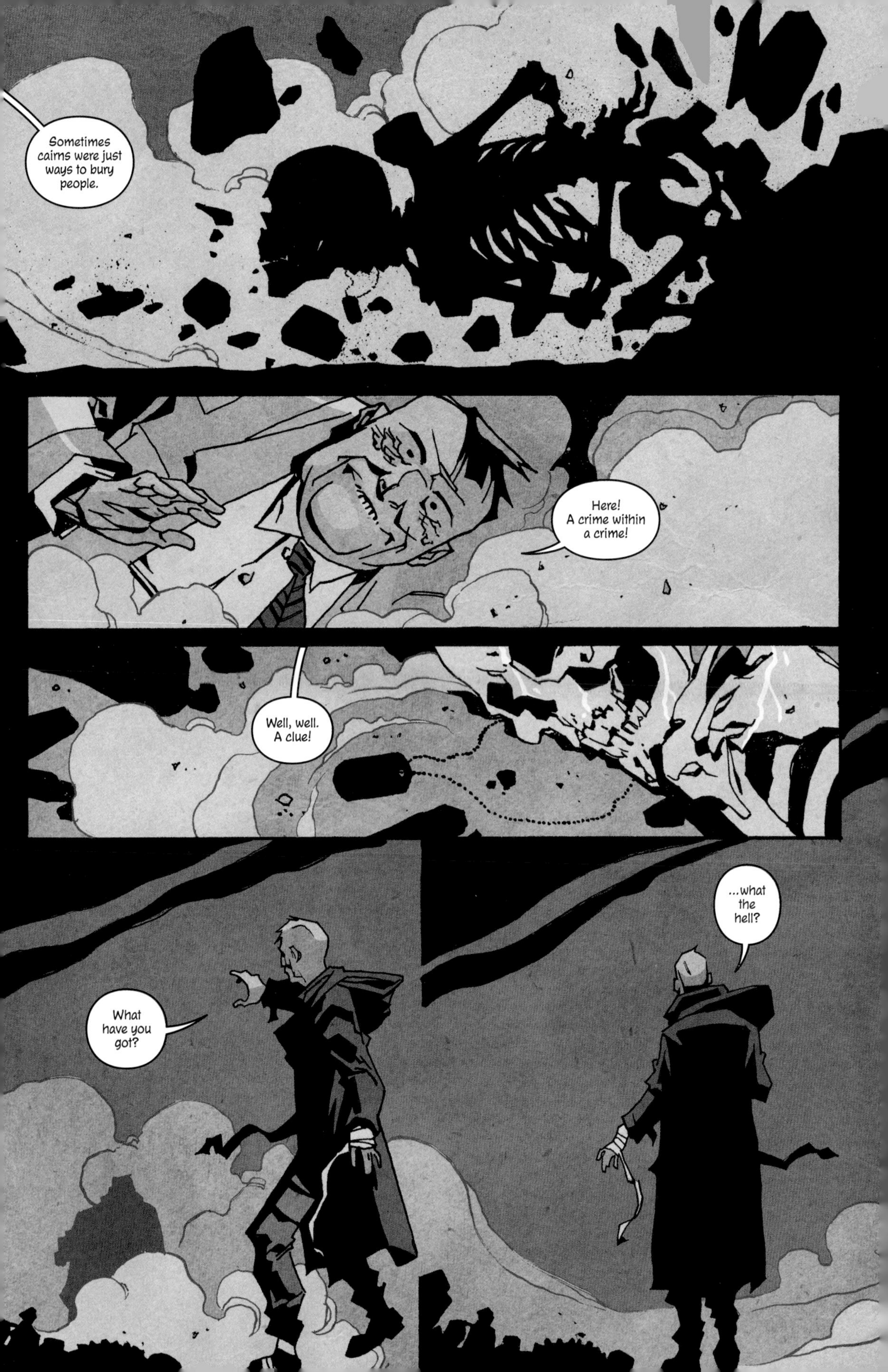

Sometimes cairns were just ways to bury people.
Here! A crime within a crime!
Well, well. A clue!
What have you got?
...what the hell?

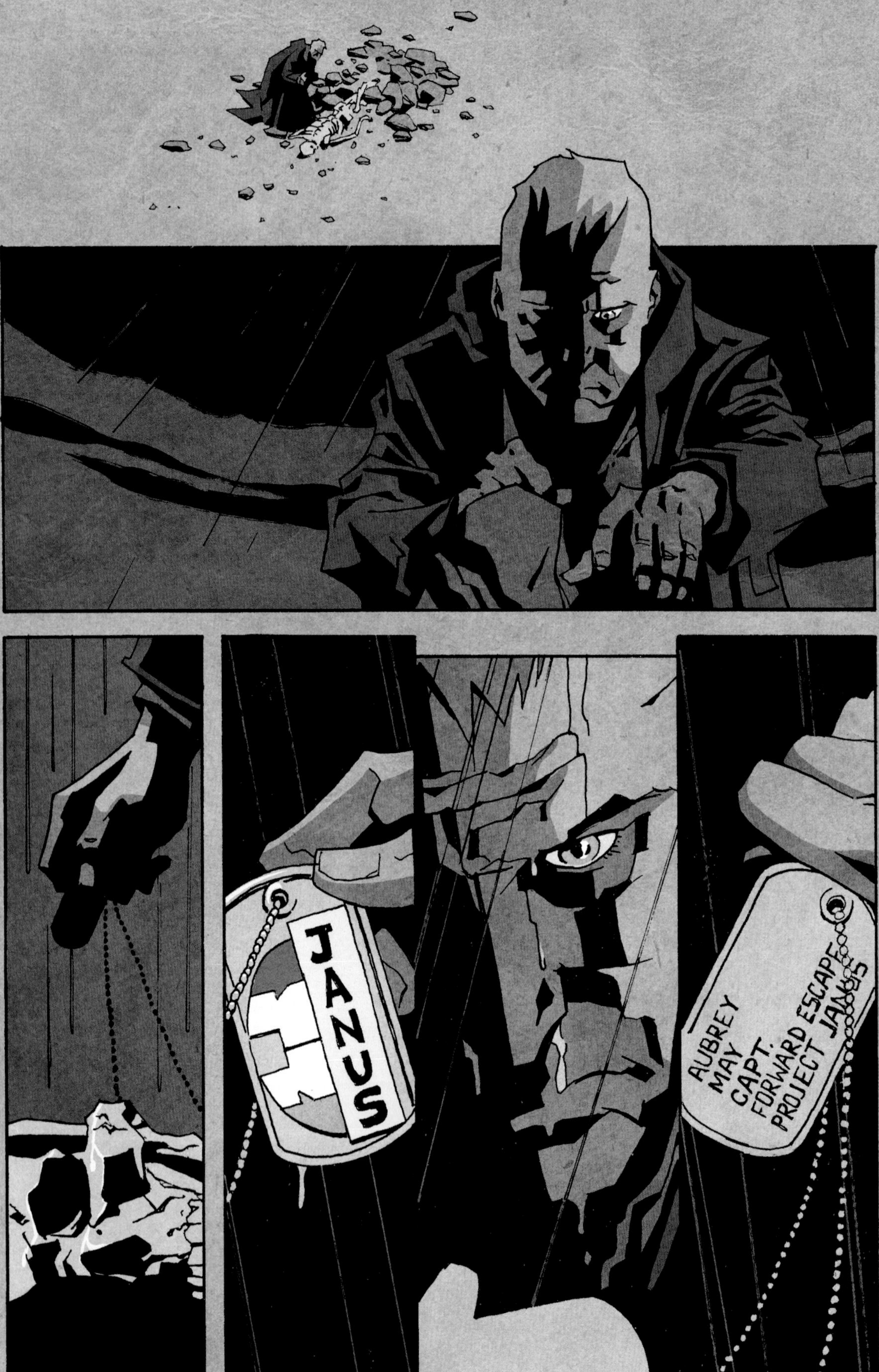
JANUS
AUBREY
MAY
CAPT.
FORWARD ESCAPE
PROJECT JANUS

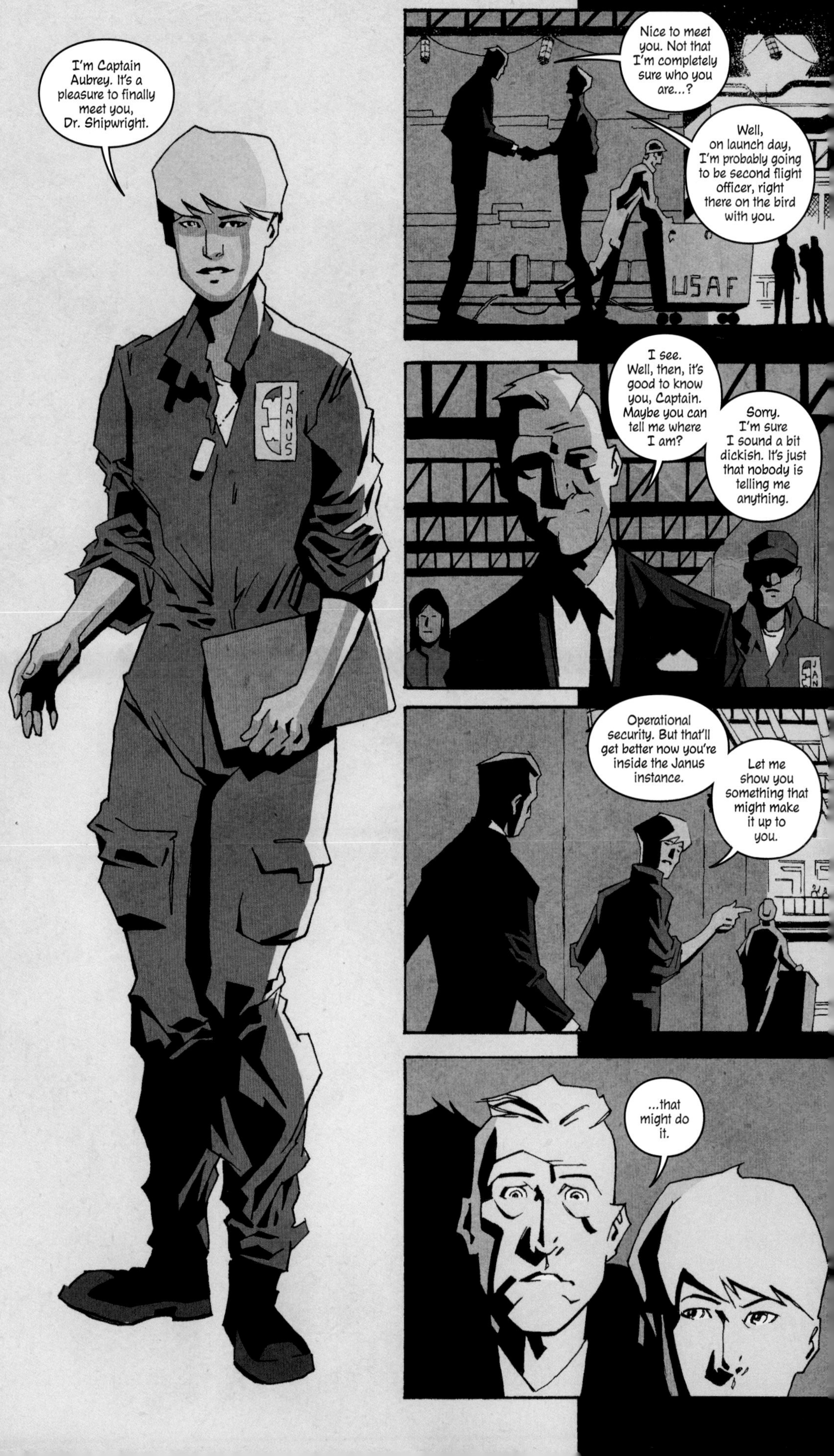
I'm Captain Aubrey. It's a pleasure to finally meet you, Dr. Shipwright.
JANUS
Nice to meet you. Not that I'm completely sure who you are...?
Well, on launch day, I'm probably going to be second flight officer, right there on the bird with you.
USAF
I see. Well, then, it's good to know you, Captain. Maybe you can tell me where I am?
Sorry. I'm sure I sound a bit dickish. It's just that nobody is telling me anything.
Operational security. But that'll get better now you're inside the Janus instance.
Let me show you something that might make it up to you.
...that might do it.

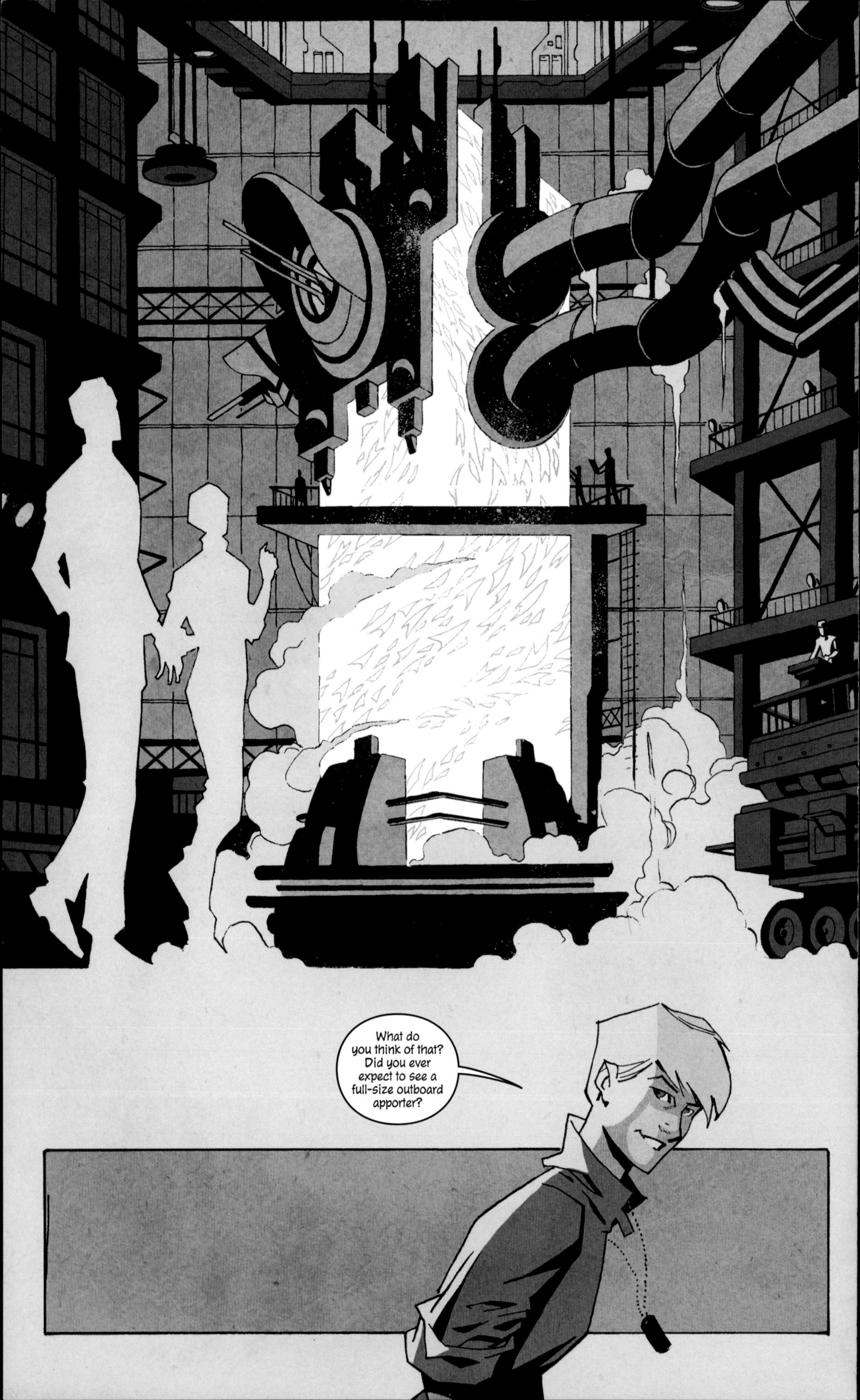
What do you think of that? Did you ever expect to see a full-size outboard apporter?

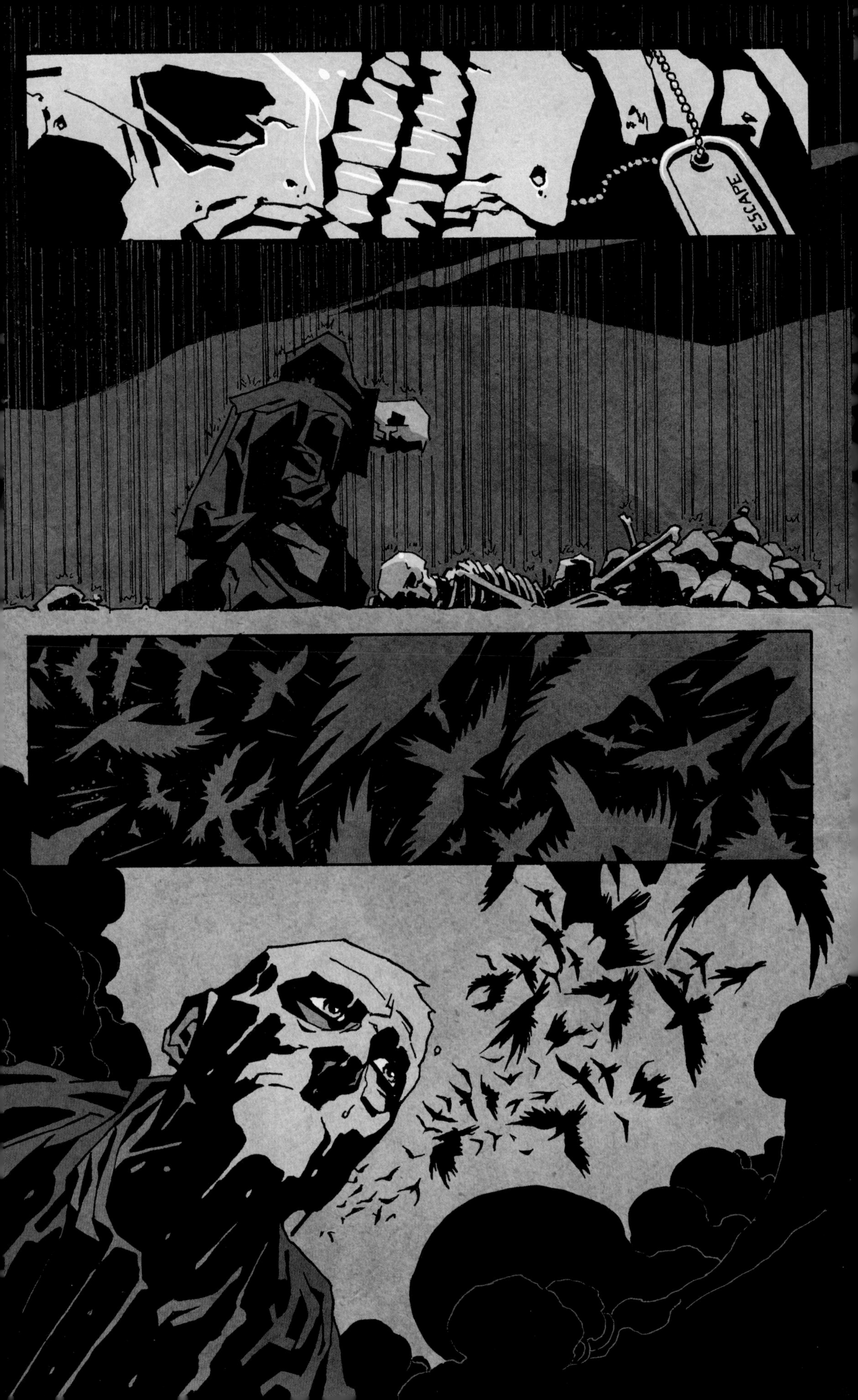
ESCAPE

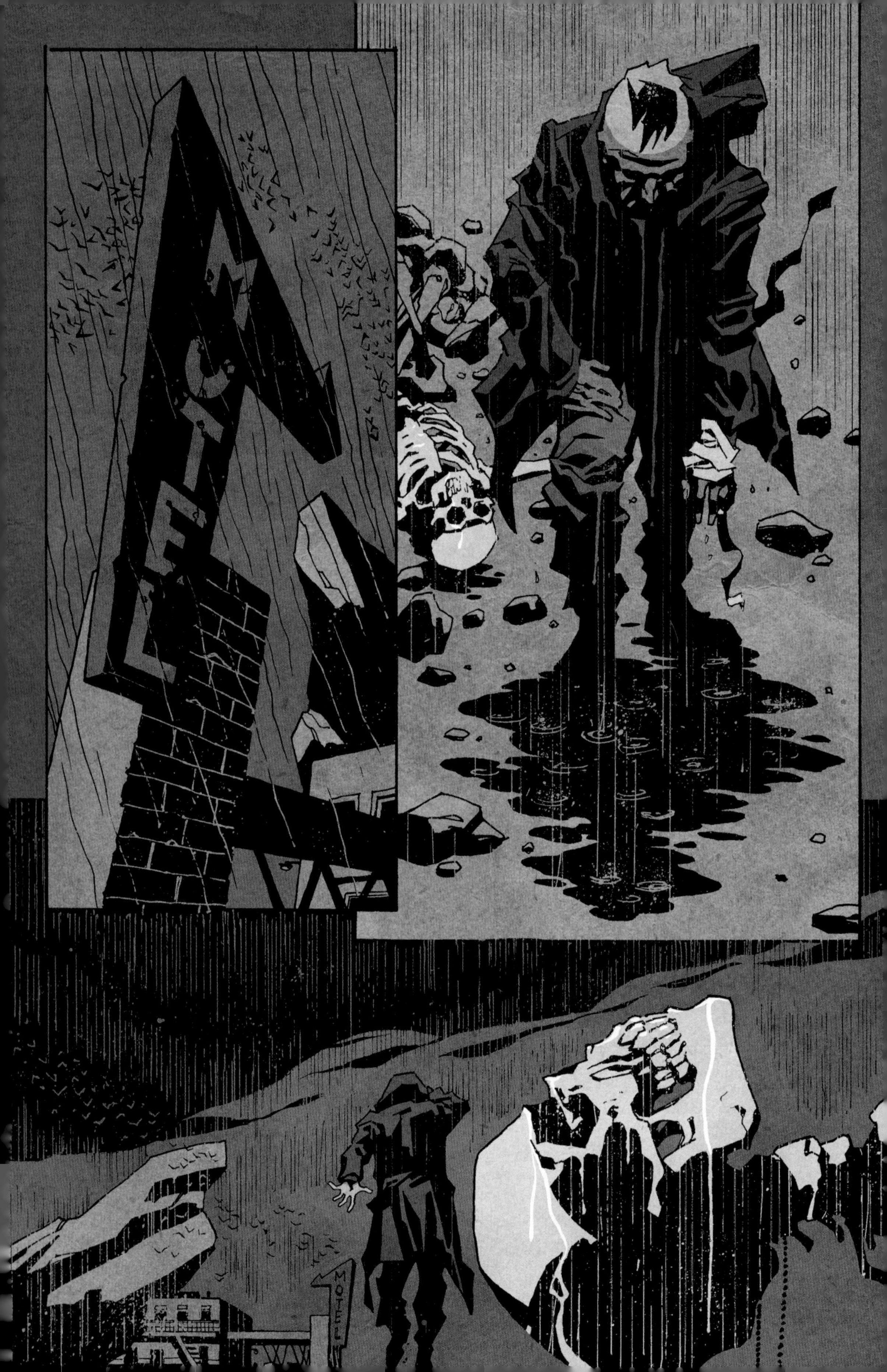
MOTEL

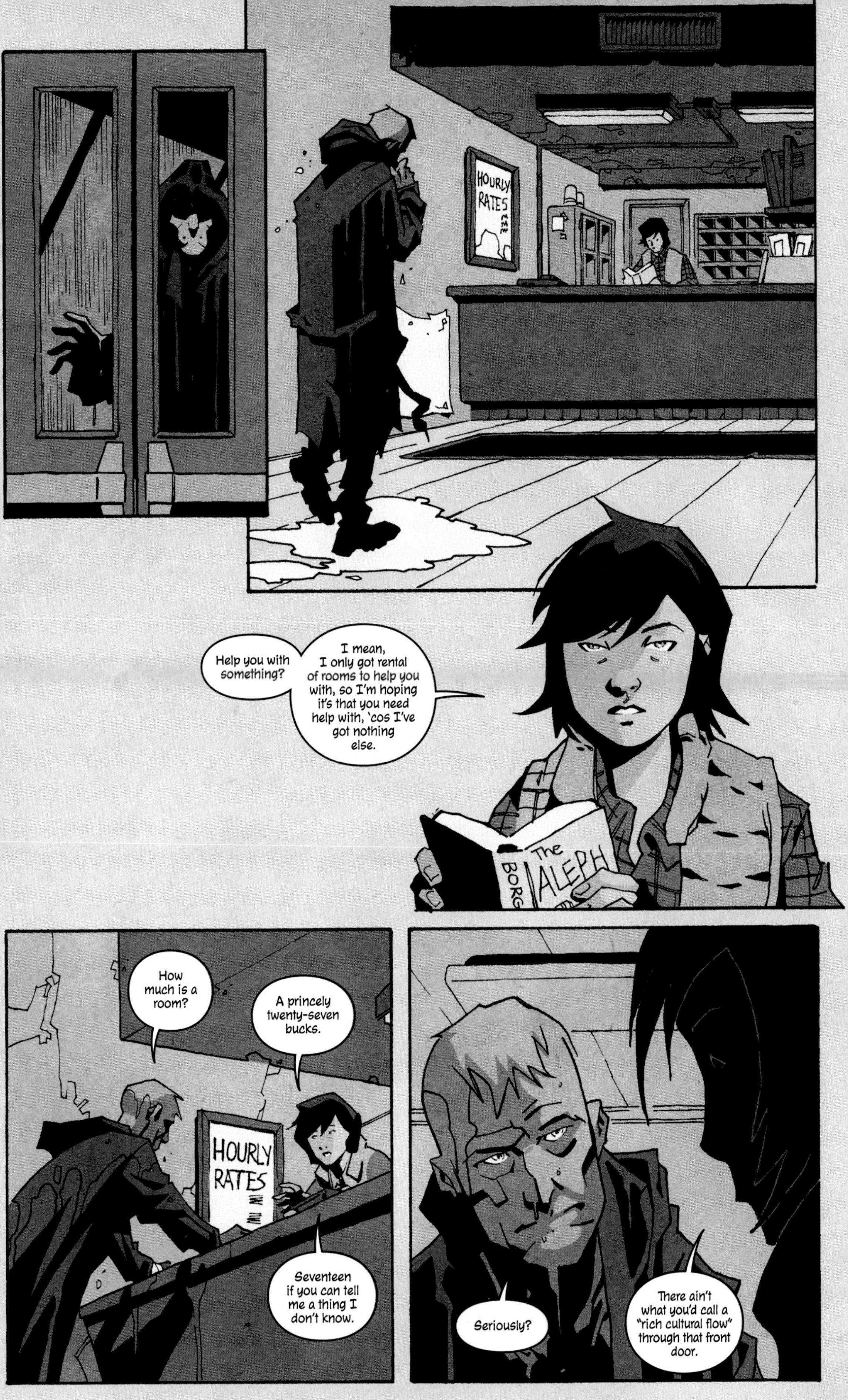
HOURLY RATES
Help you with something?
I mean, I only got rental of rooms to help you with, so I'm hoping it's that you need help with, 'cos I've got nothing else.
The ALEPH
How much is a room?
A princely twenty-seven bucks.
HOURLY RATES
Seventeen if you can tell me a thing I don't know.
Seriously?
There ain't what you'd call a "rich cultural flow" through that front door.

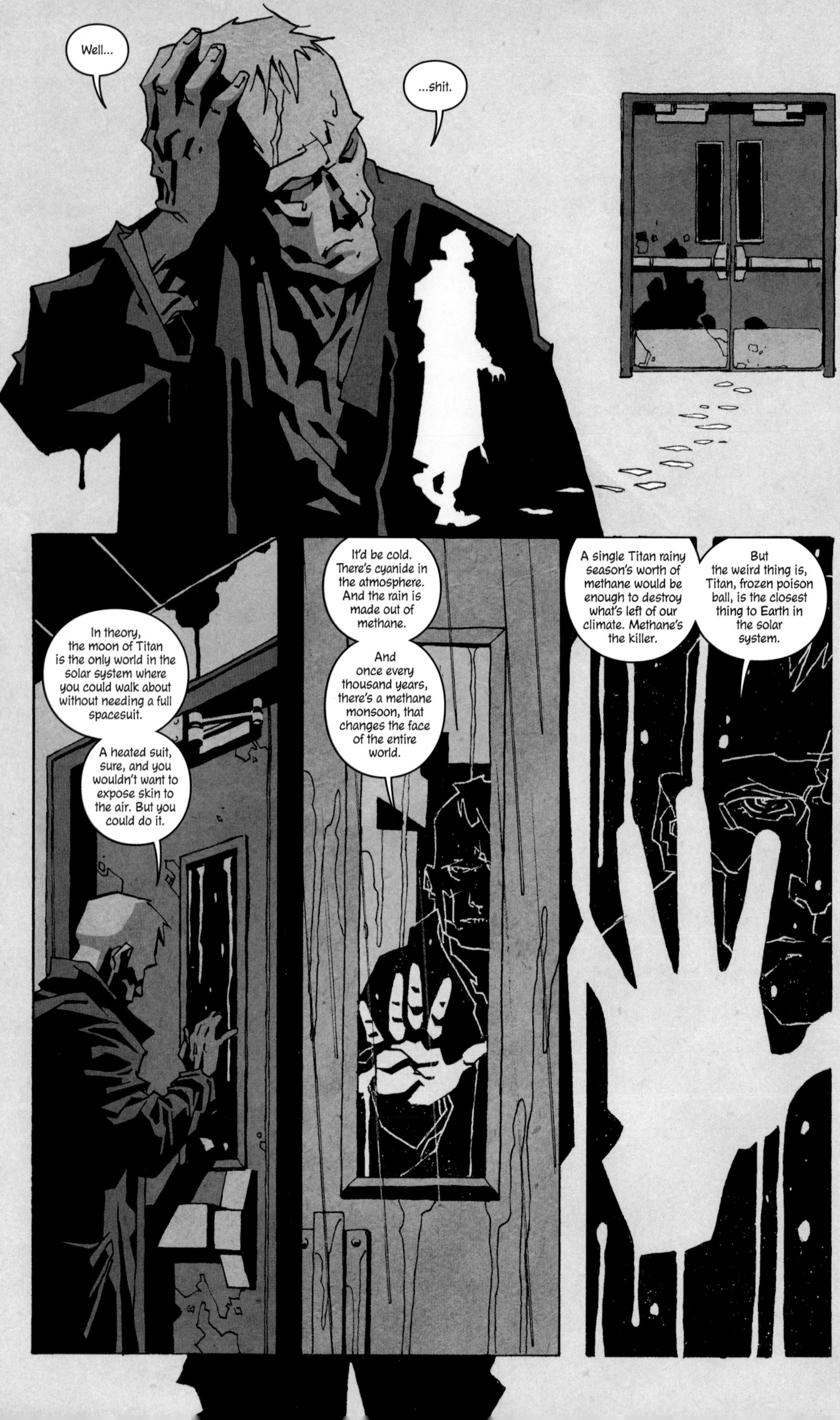
Well...
...shit.
In theory, the moon of Titan is the only world in the solar system where you could walk about without needing a full spacesuit.
A heated suit, sure, and you wouldn't want to expose skin to the air. But you could do it.
It'd be cold. There's cyanide in the atmosphere. And the rain is made out of methane.
And once every thousand years, there's a methane monsoon, that changes the face of the entire world.
A single Titan rainy season's worth of methane would be enough to destroy what's left of our climate. Methane's the killer.
But the weird thing is, Titan, frozen poison ball, is the closest thing to Earth in the solar system.

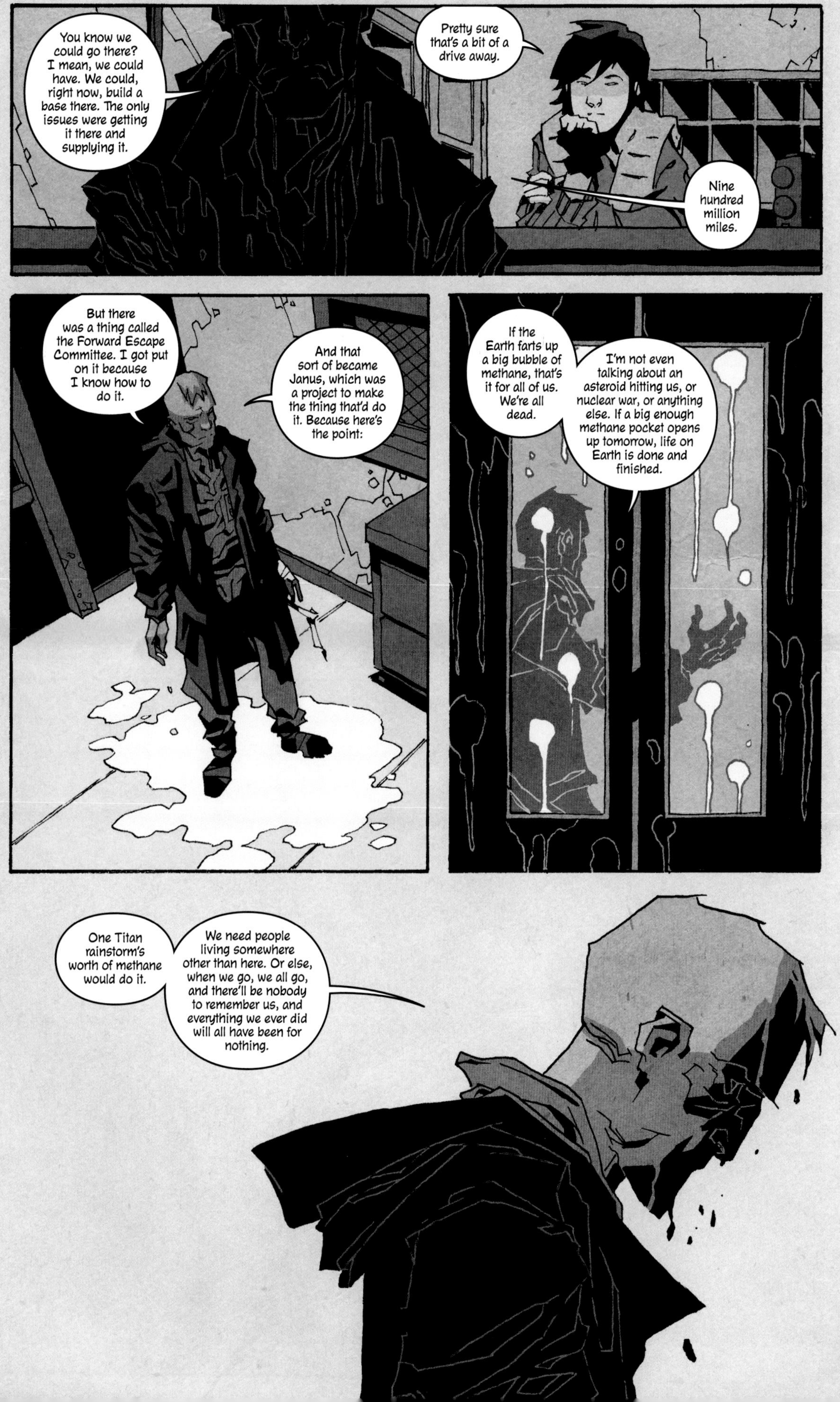
You know we could go there? I mean, we could have. We could, right now, build a base there. The only issues were getting it there and supplying it.
Pretty sure that's a bit of a drive away.
Nine hundred million miles.
But there was a thing called the Forward Escape Committee. I got put on it because I know how to do it.
And that sort of became Janus, which was a project to make the thing that'd do it. Because here's the point:
If the Earth farts up a big bubble of methane, that's it for all of us. We're all dead.
I'm not even talking about an asteroid hitting us, or nuclear war, or anything else. If a big enough methane pocket opens up tomorrow, life on Earth is done and finished.
One Titan rainstorm's worth of methane would do it.
We need people living somewhere other than here. Or else, when we go, we all go, and there'll be nobody to remember us, and everything we ever did will all have been for nothing.

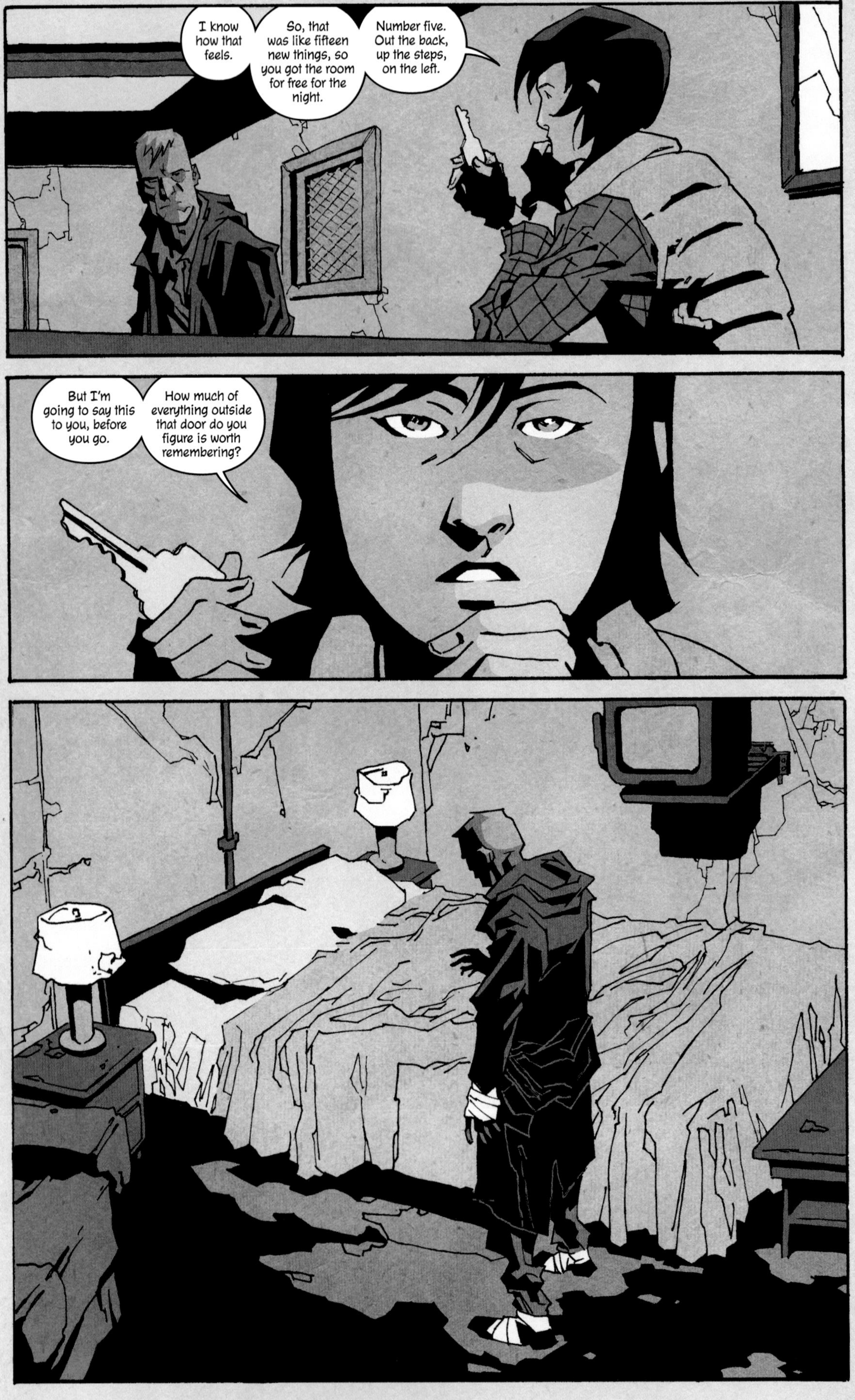
I know how that feels.
So, that was like fifteen new things, so you got the room for free for the night.
Number five. Out the back, up the steps, on the left.
But I'm going to say this to you, before you go.
How much of everything outside that door do you figure is worth remembering?

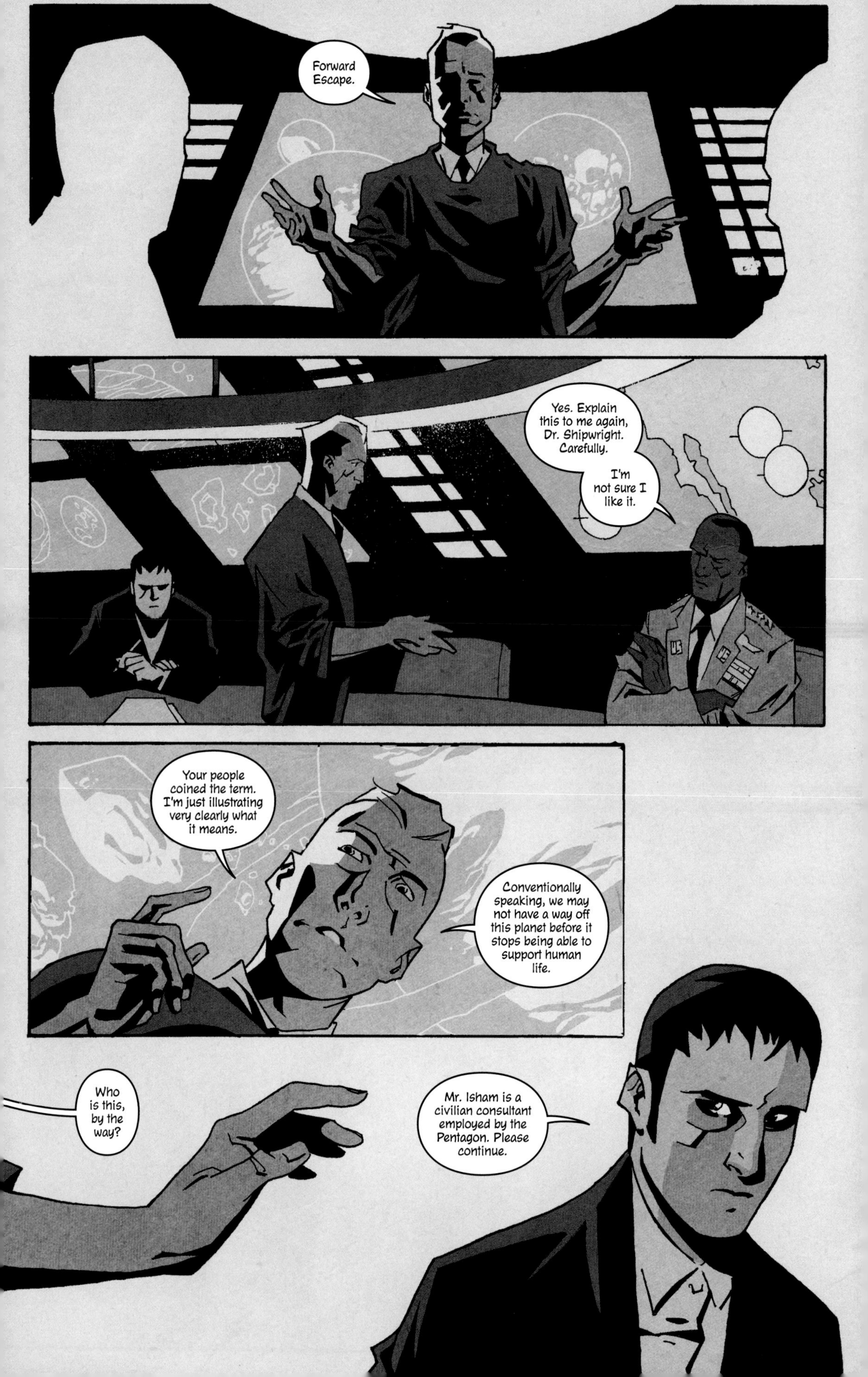
Forward Escape.
Yes. Explain this to me again, Dr. Shipwright. Carefully.
I'm not sure I like it.
Your people coined the term. I'm just illustrating very clearly what it means.
Conventionally speaking, we may not have a way off this planet before it stops being able to support human life.
Who is this, by the way?
Mr. Isham is a civilian consultant employed by the Pentagon. Please continue.

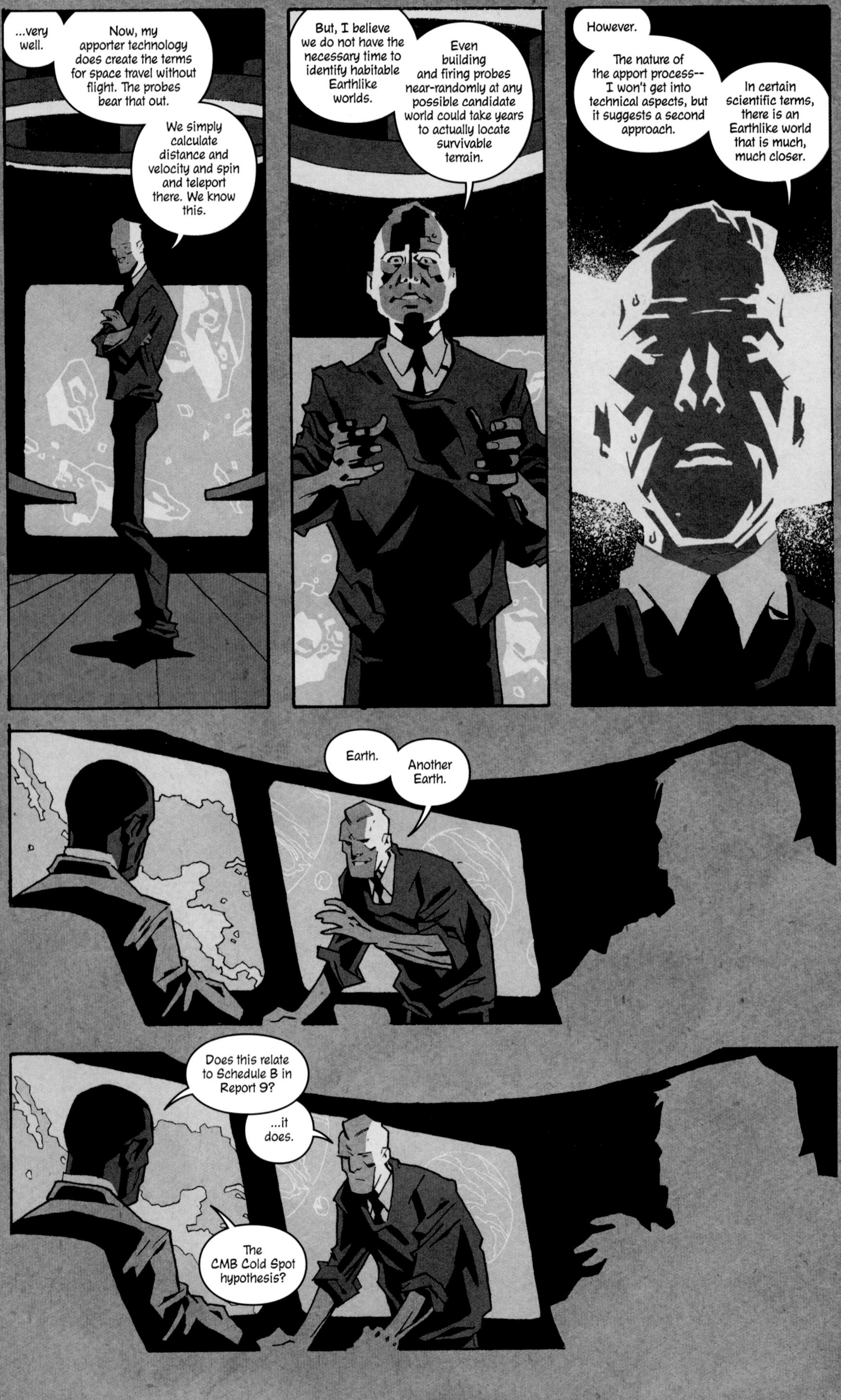
...very well.
Now, my apporter technology does create the terms for space travel without flight. The probes bear that out.
We simply calculate distance and velocity and spin and teleport there. We know this.
But, I believe we do not have the necessary time to identify habitable Earthlike worlds.
Even building and firing probes near-randomly at any possible candidate world could take years to actually locate survivable terrain.
However.
The nature of the apport process-- I won't get into technical aspects, but it suggests a second approach.
In certain scientific terms, there is an Earthlike world that is much, much closer.
Earth.
Another Earth.
Does this relate to Schedule B in Report 9?
...it does.
The CMB Cold Spot hypothesis?

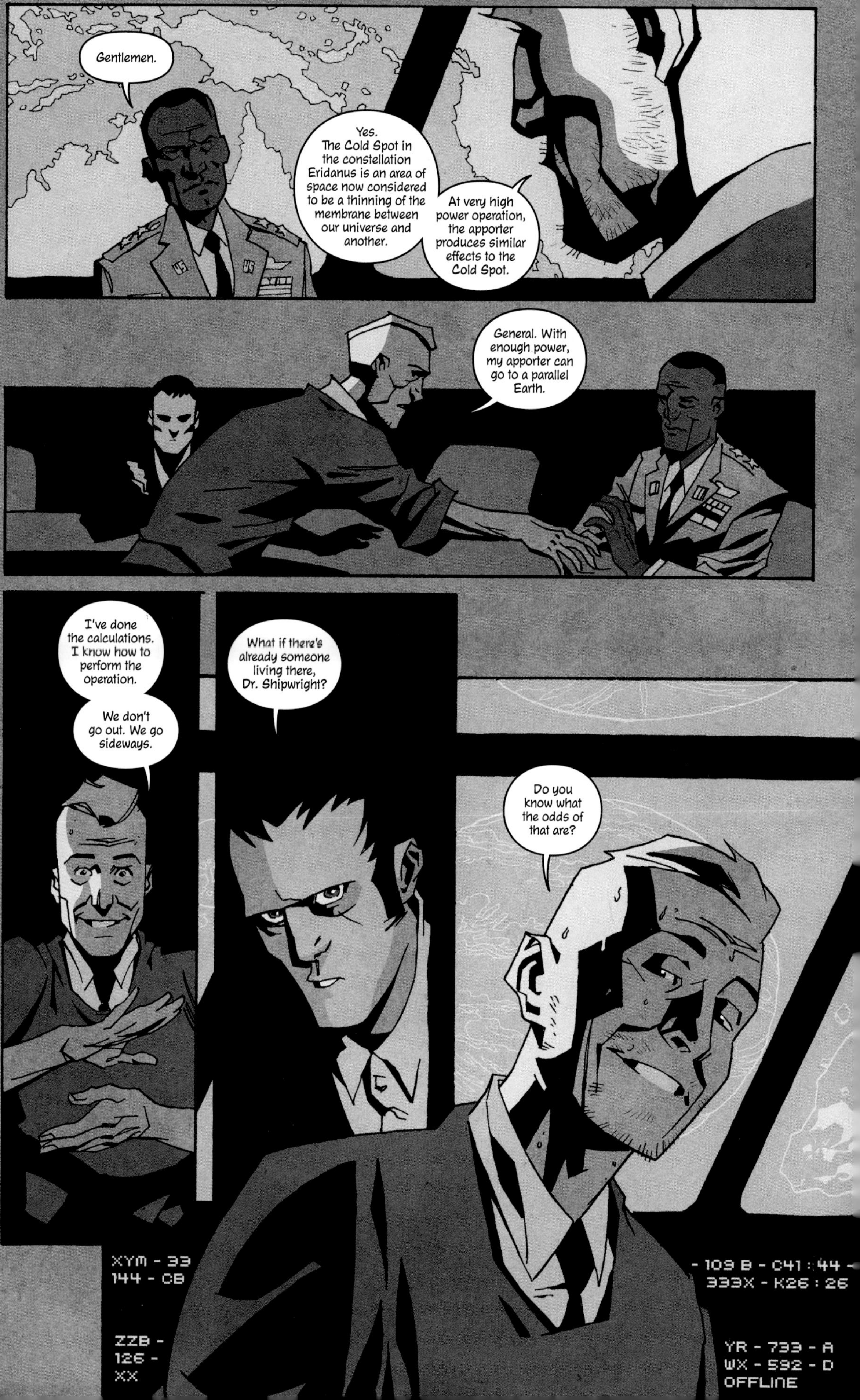
Gentlemen.
Yes. The Cold Spot in the constellation Eridanus is an area of space now considered to be a thinning of the membrane between our universe and another.
At very high power operation, the apporter produces similar effects to the Cold Spot.
General. With enough power, my apporter can go to a parallel Earth.
I've done the calculations. I know how to perform the operation.
We don't go out. We go sideways.
What if there's already someone living there, Dr. Shipwright?
Do you know what the odds of that are?
XYM - 33
144 - CB
ZZB -
126 -
XX
- 109 B - C41 : 44 -
333X - K26 : 26
YR - 733 - A
WX - 592 - D
OFFLINE

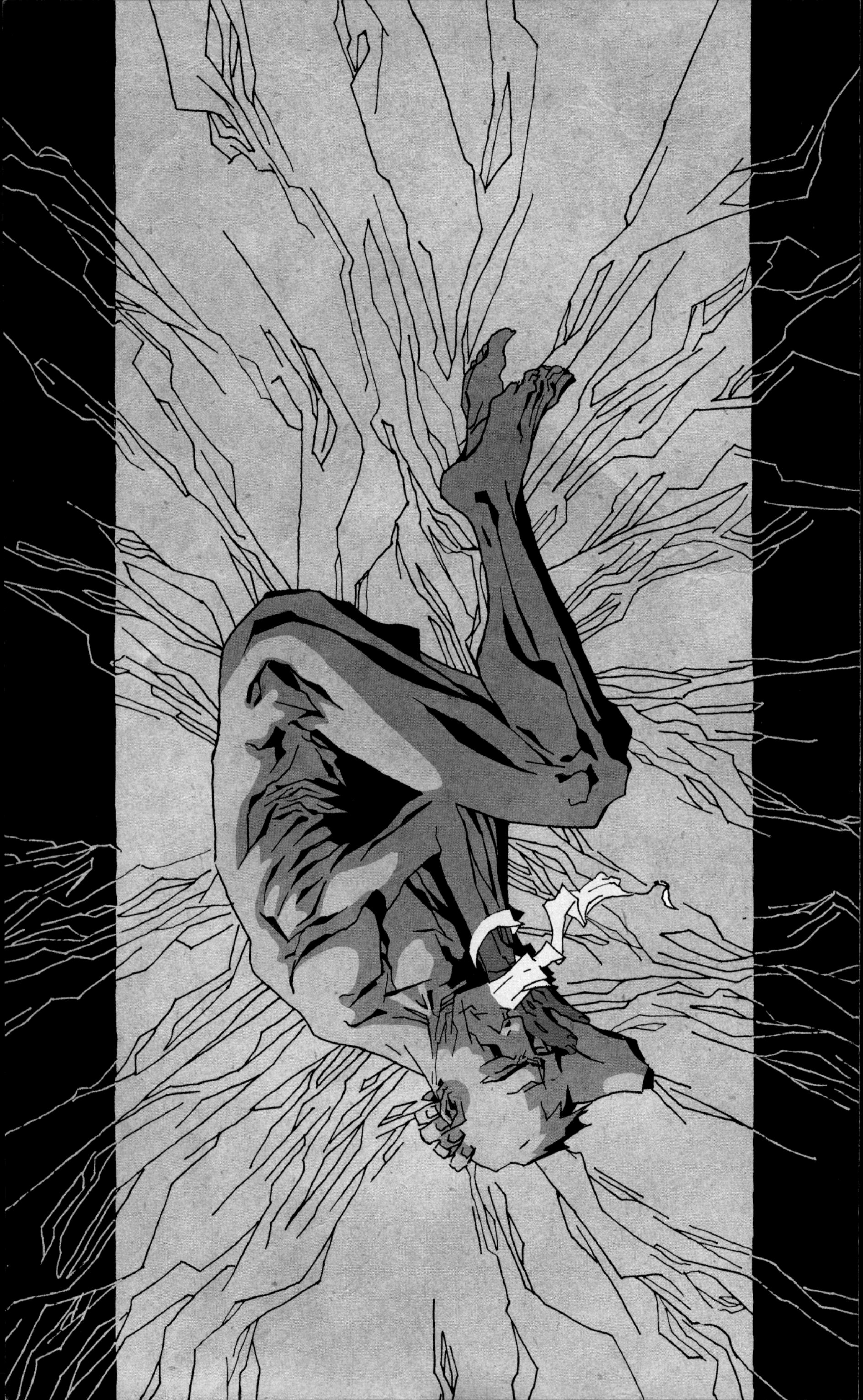

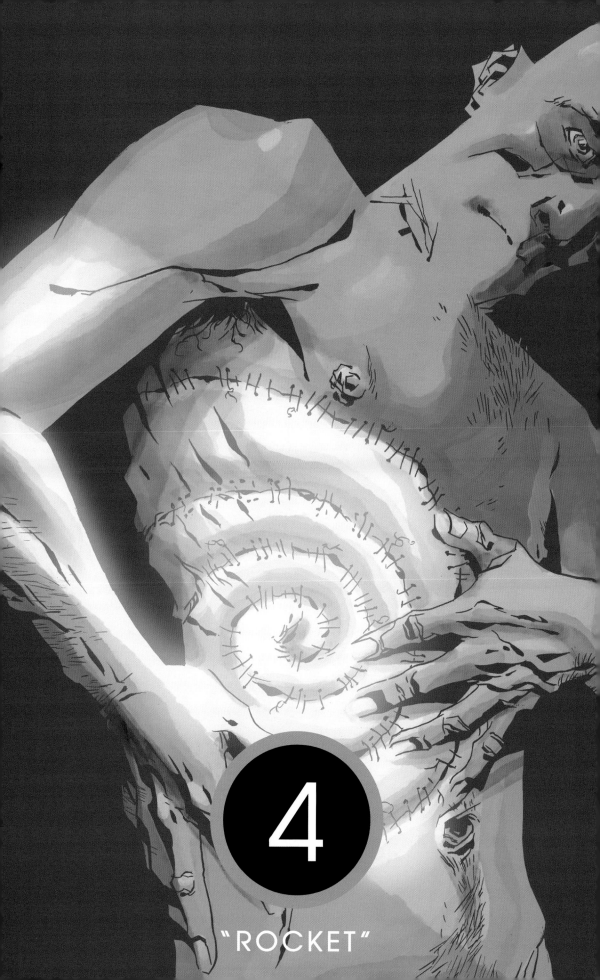

4

"ROCKET"

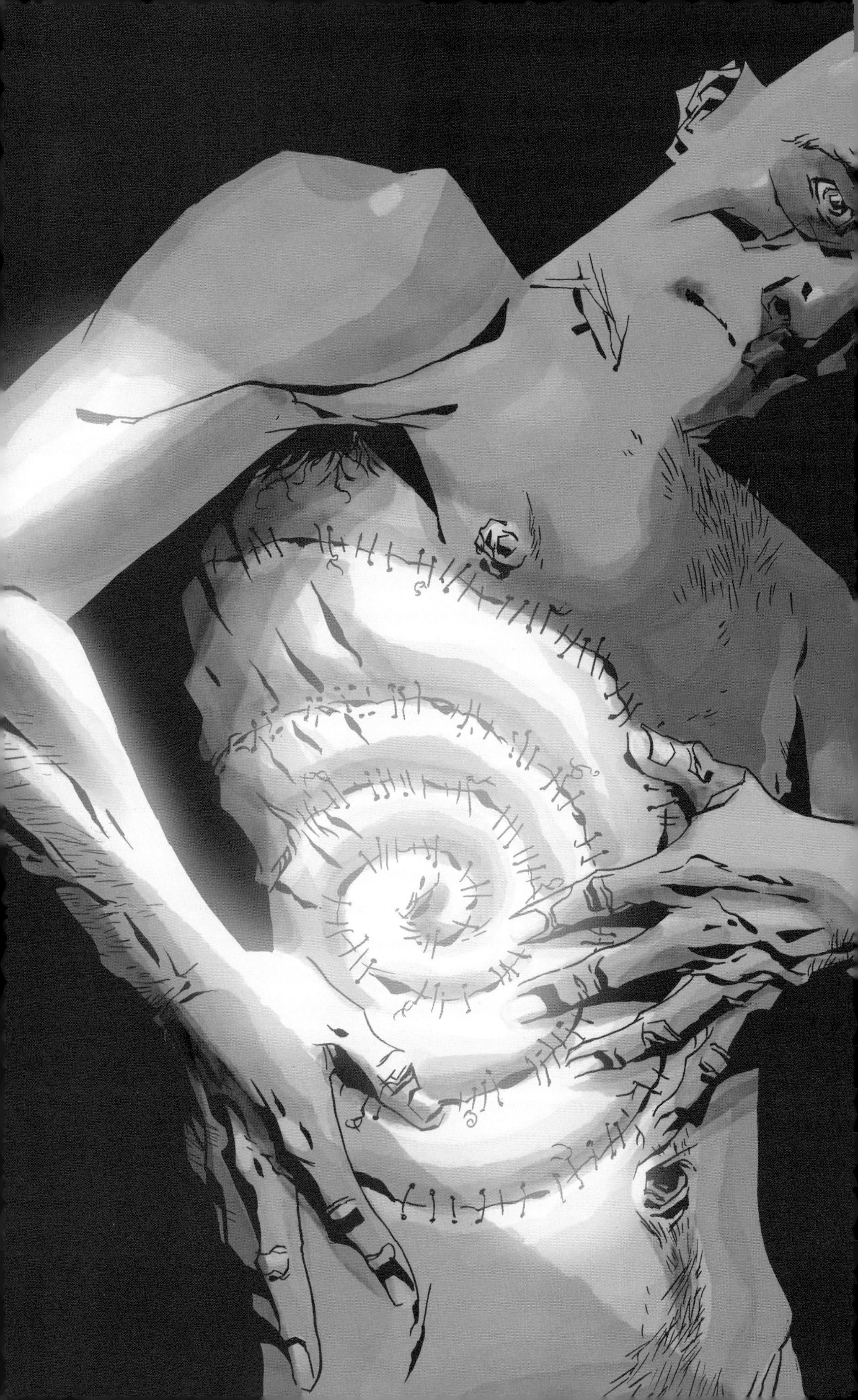

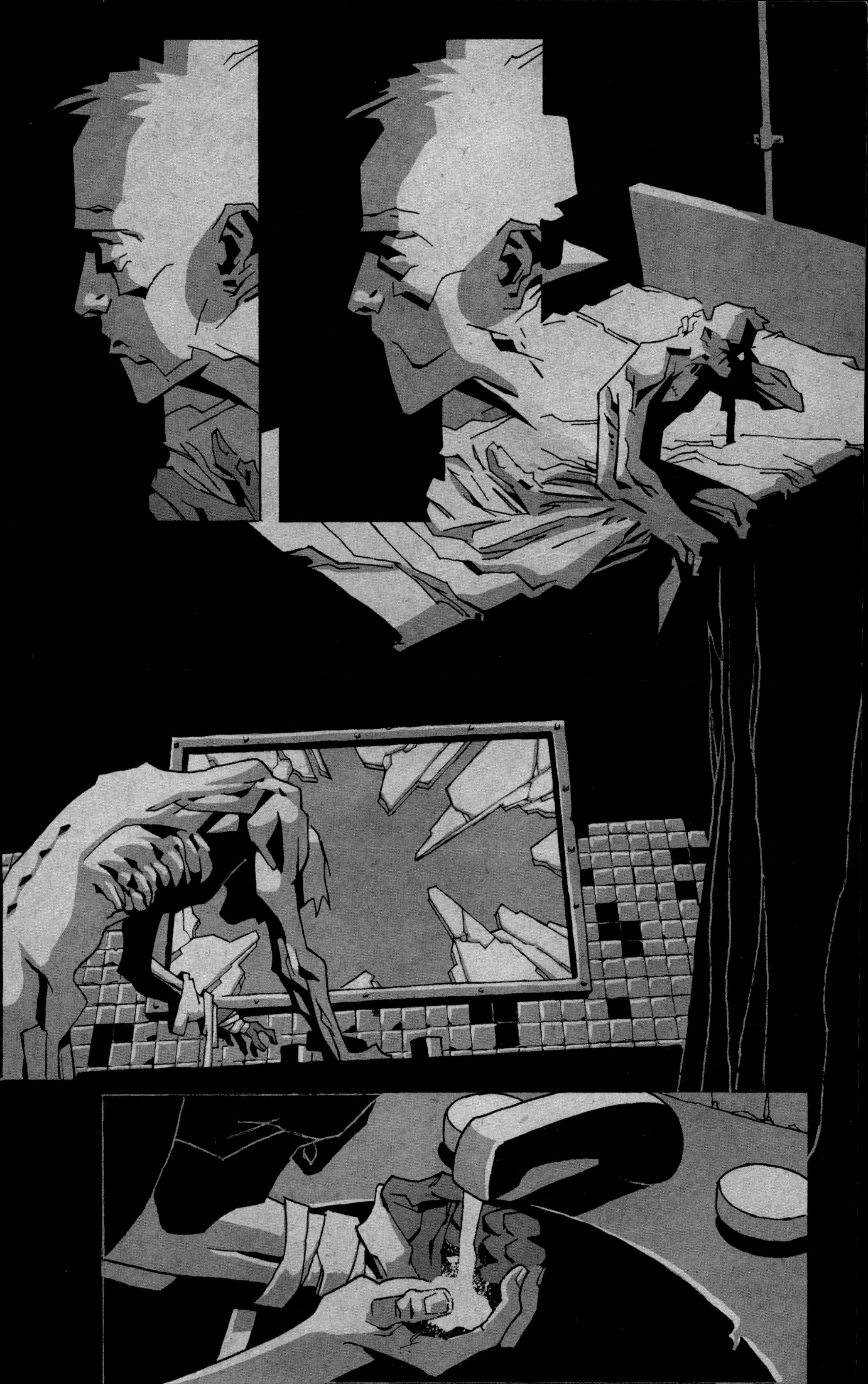

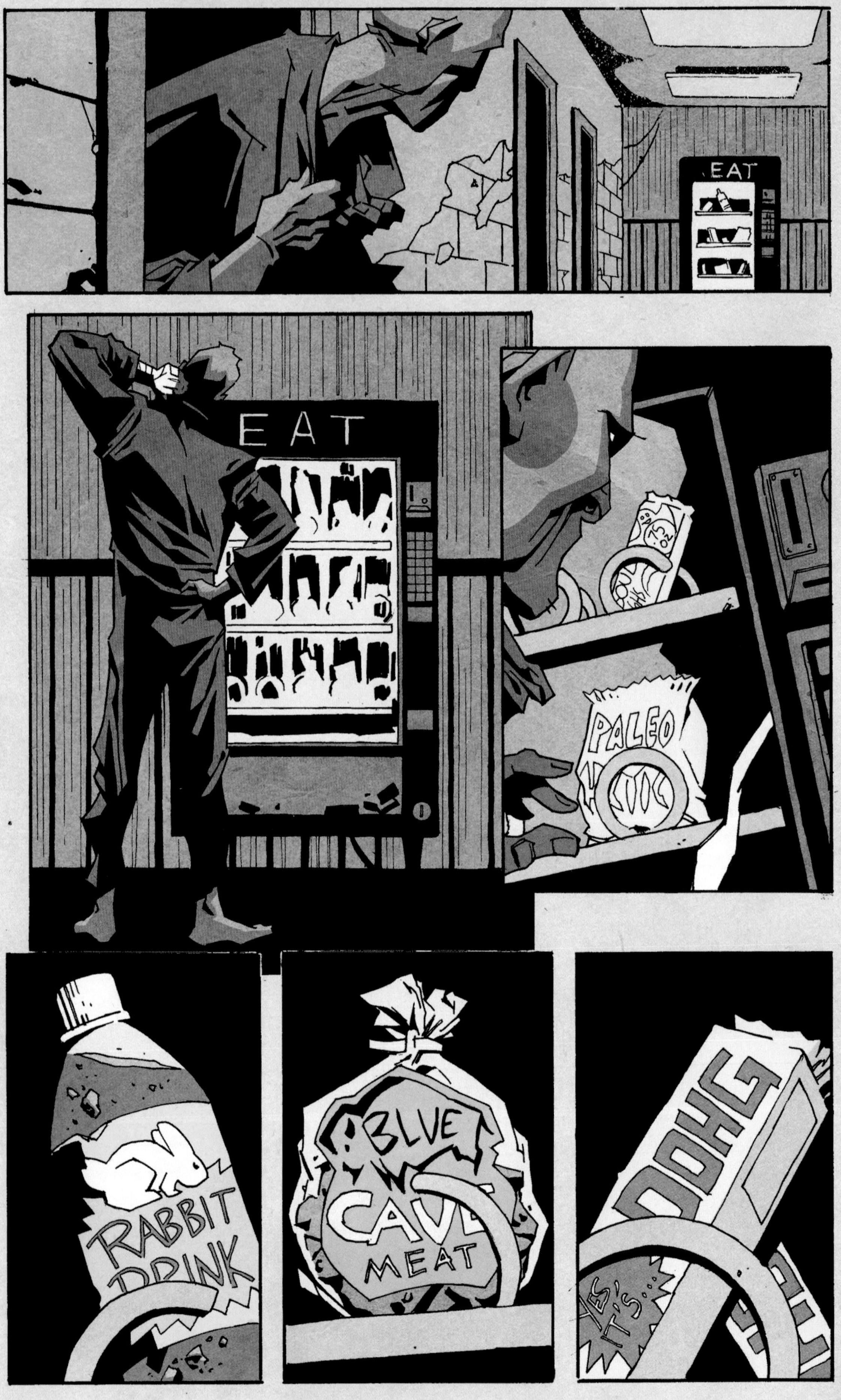
EAT
EAT
PALEO
RABBIT DRINK
BLUE
CAVE
MEAT
YES, IT'S...

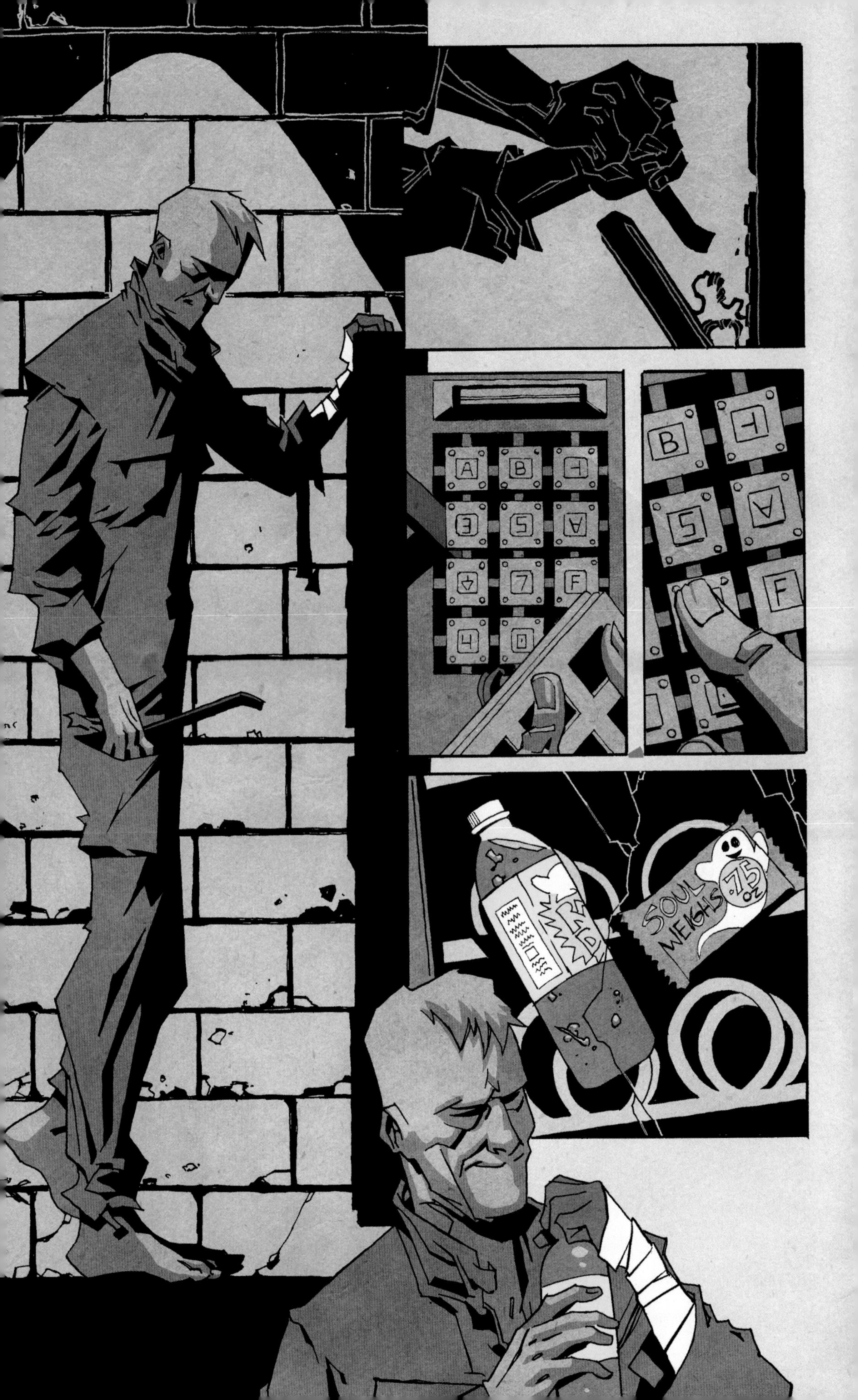
SOUL WEIGHS
.75 OZ

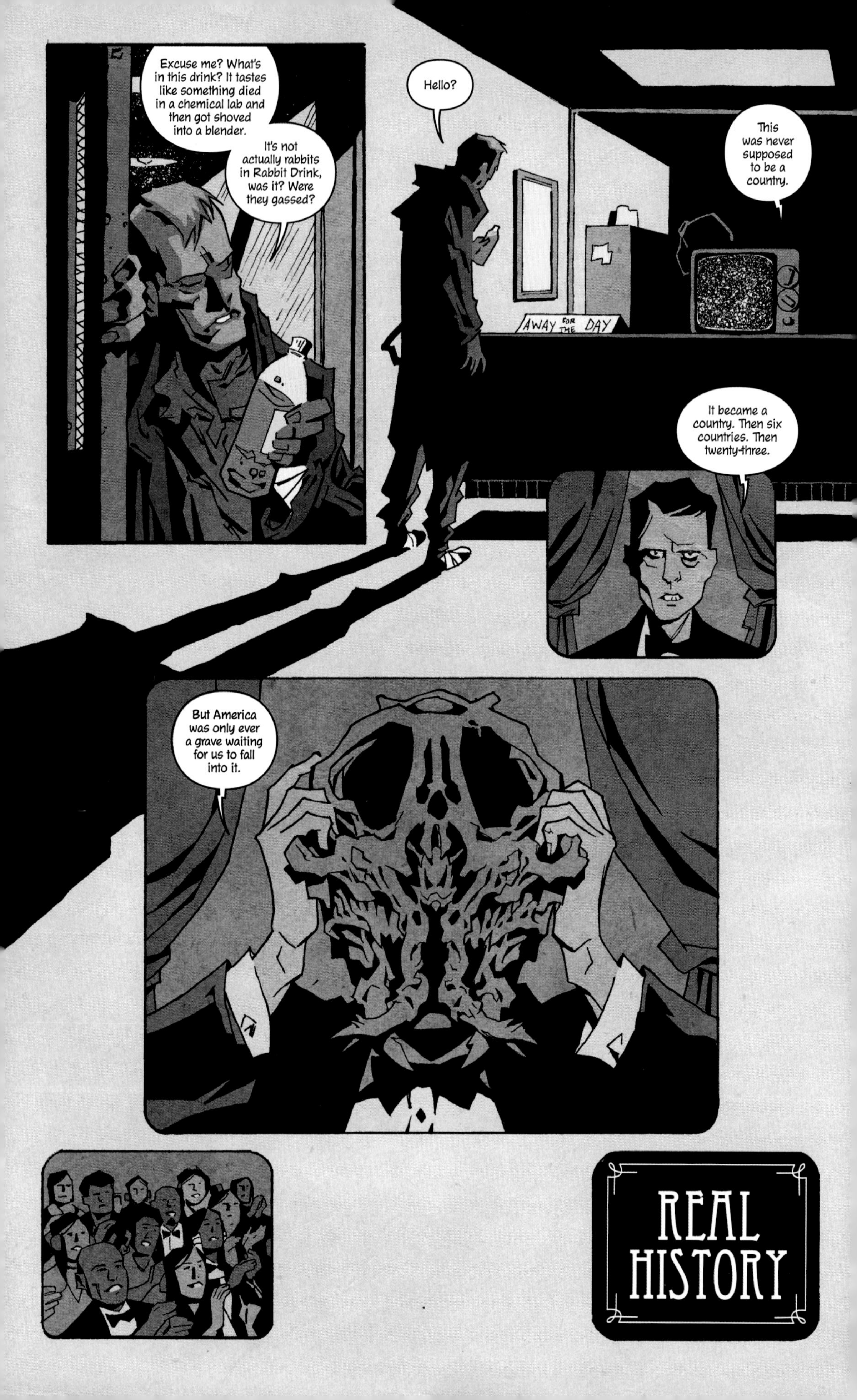
Excuse me? What's in this drink? It tastes like something died in a chemical lab and then got shoved into a blender.
It's not actually rabbits in Rabbit Drink, was it? Were they gassed?
Hello?
AWAY FOR THE DAY
This was never supposed to be a country.
It became a country. Then six countries. Then twenty-three.
But America was only ever a grave waiting for us to fall into it.
REAL HISTORY

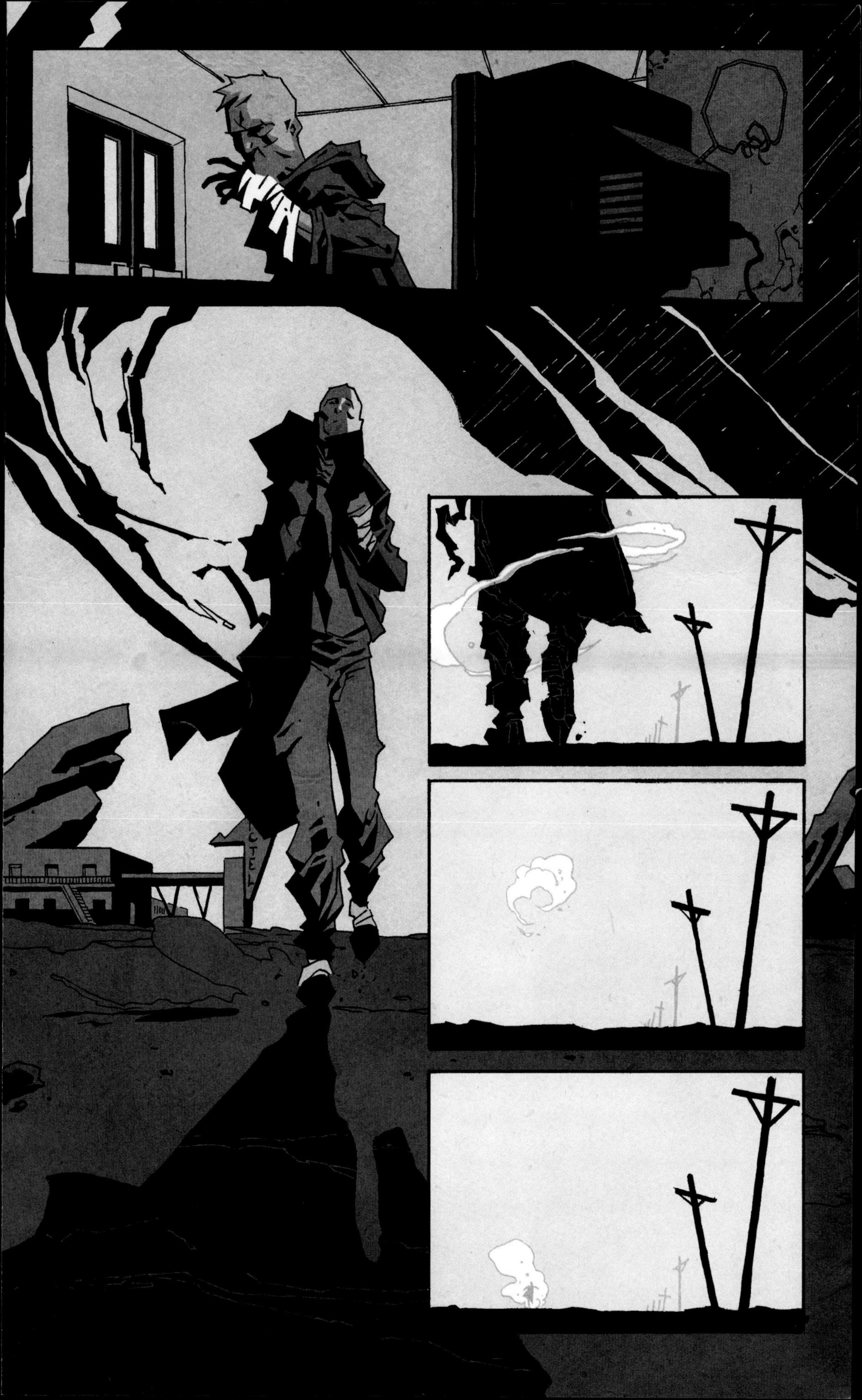

Shipwreck

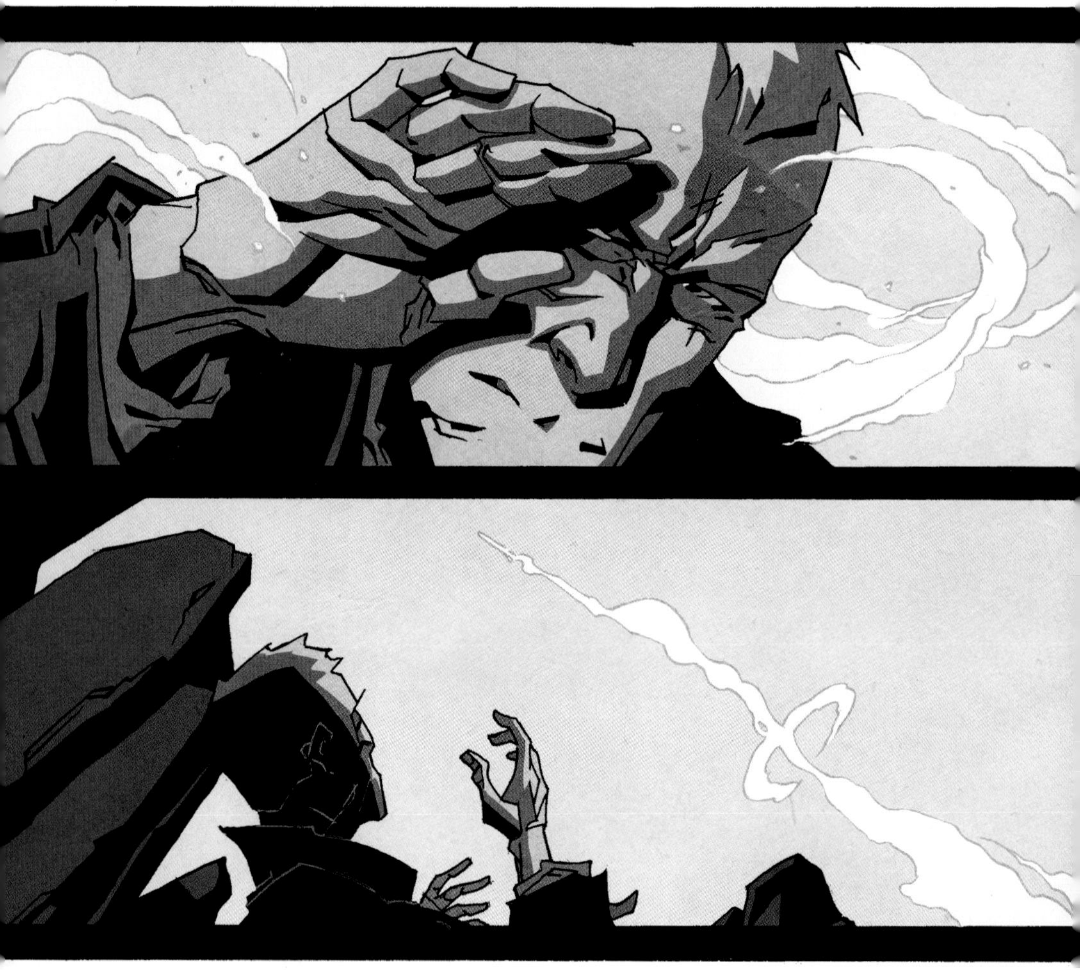

4. Rocket

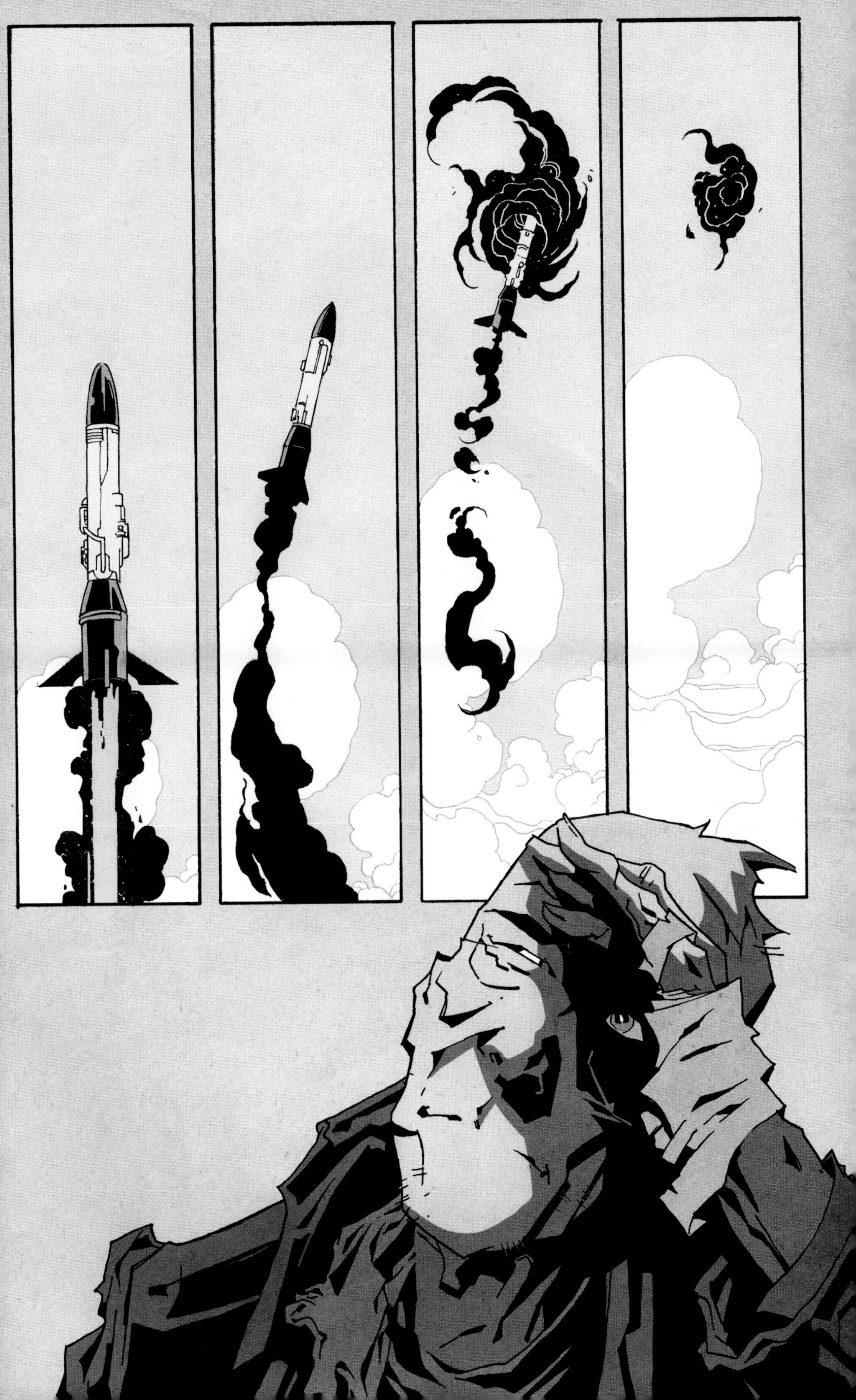

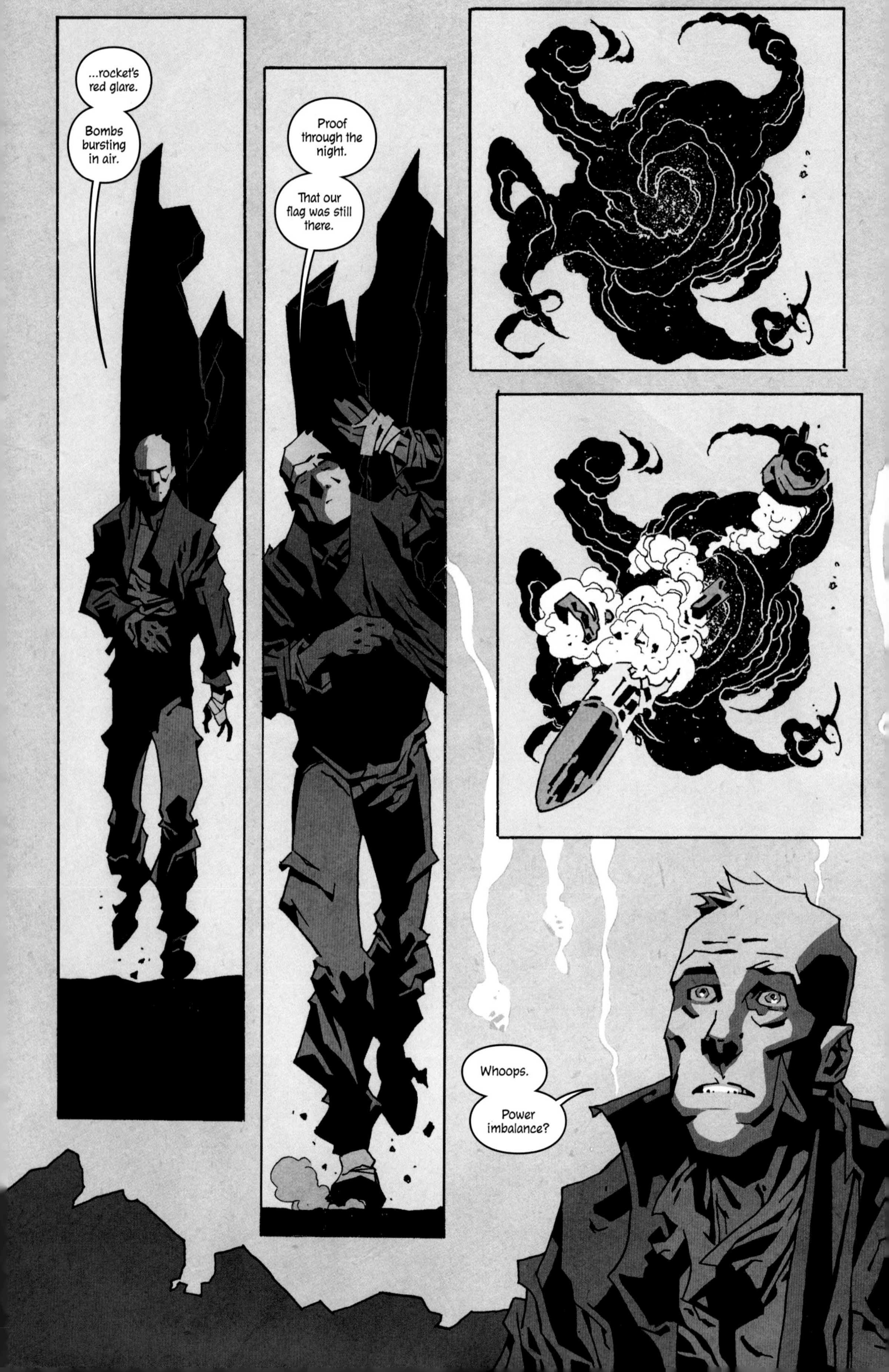

...rocket's red glare.
Bombs bursting in air.
Proof through the night.
That our flag was still there.
Whoops.
Power imbalance?

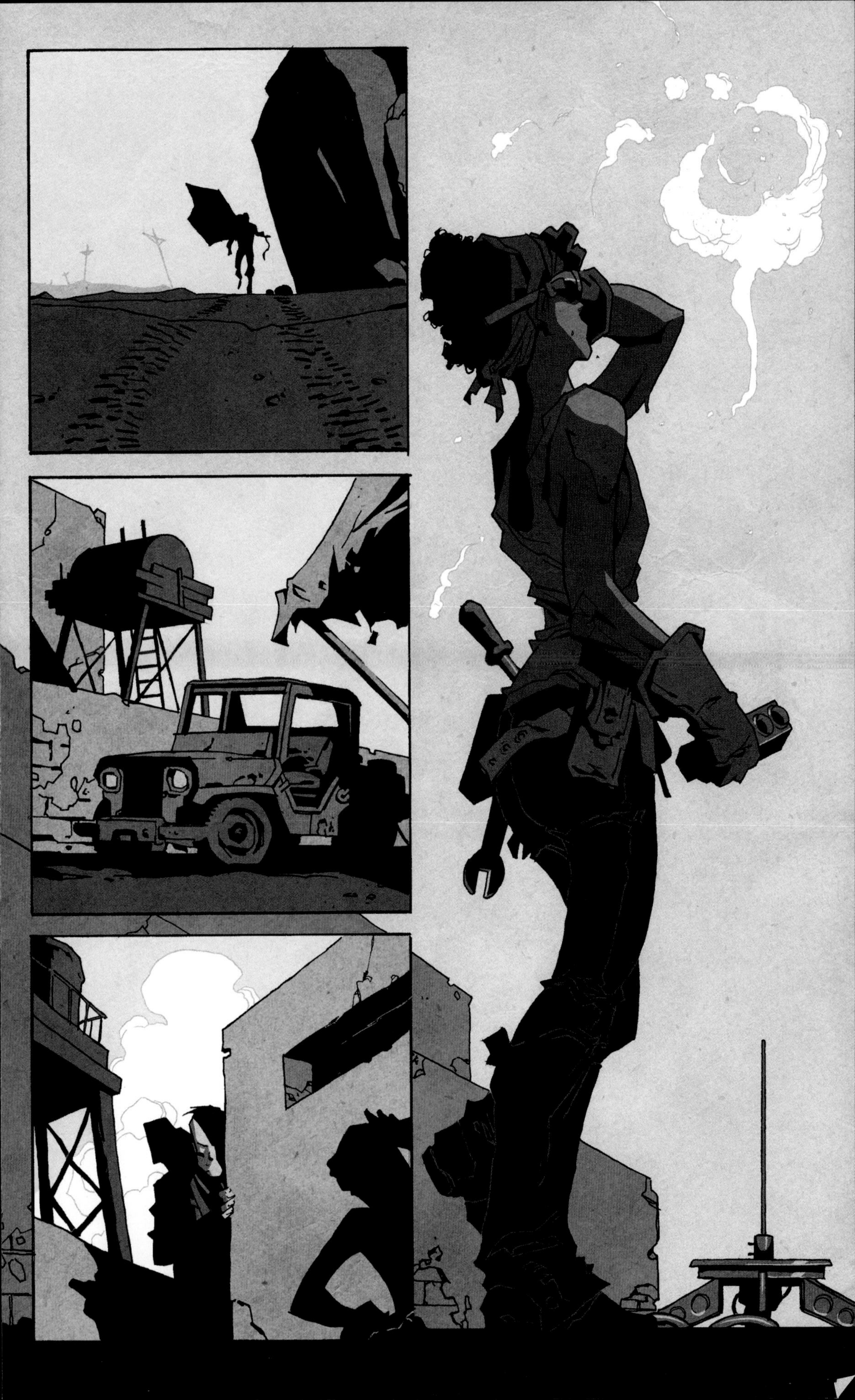

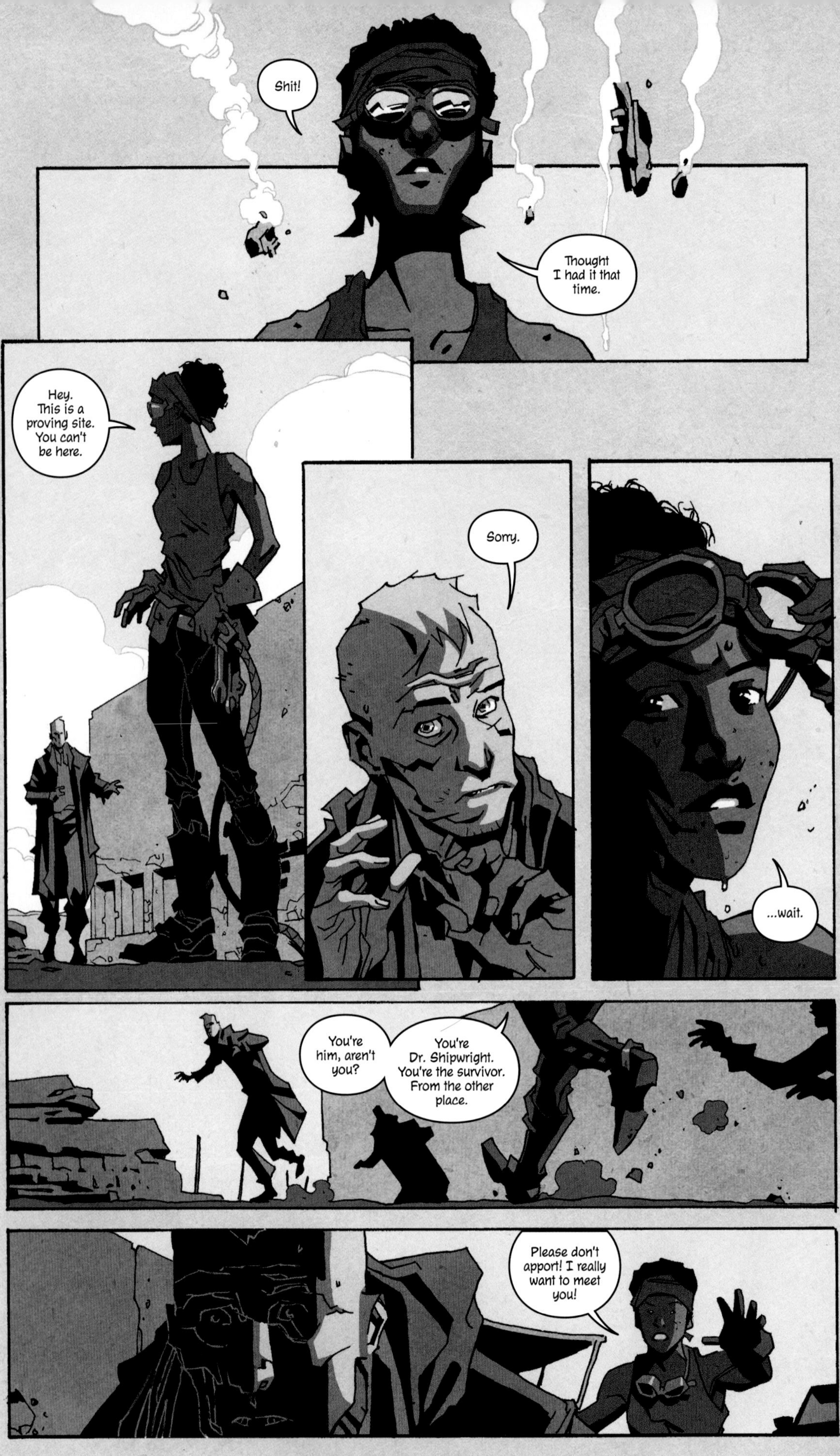
Shit!
Thought I had it that time.
Hey. This is a proving site. You can't be here.
Sorry.
...wait.
You're him, aren't you?
You're Dr. Shipwright. You're the survivor. From the other place.
Please don't apport! I really want to meet you!

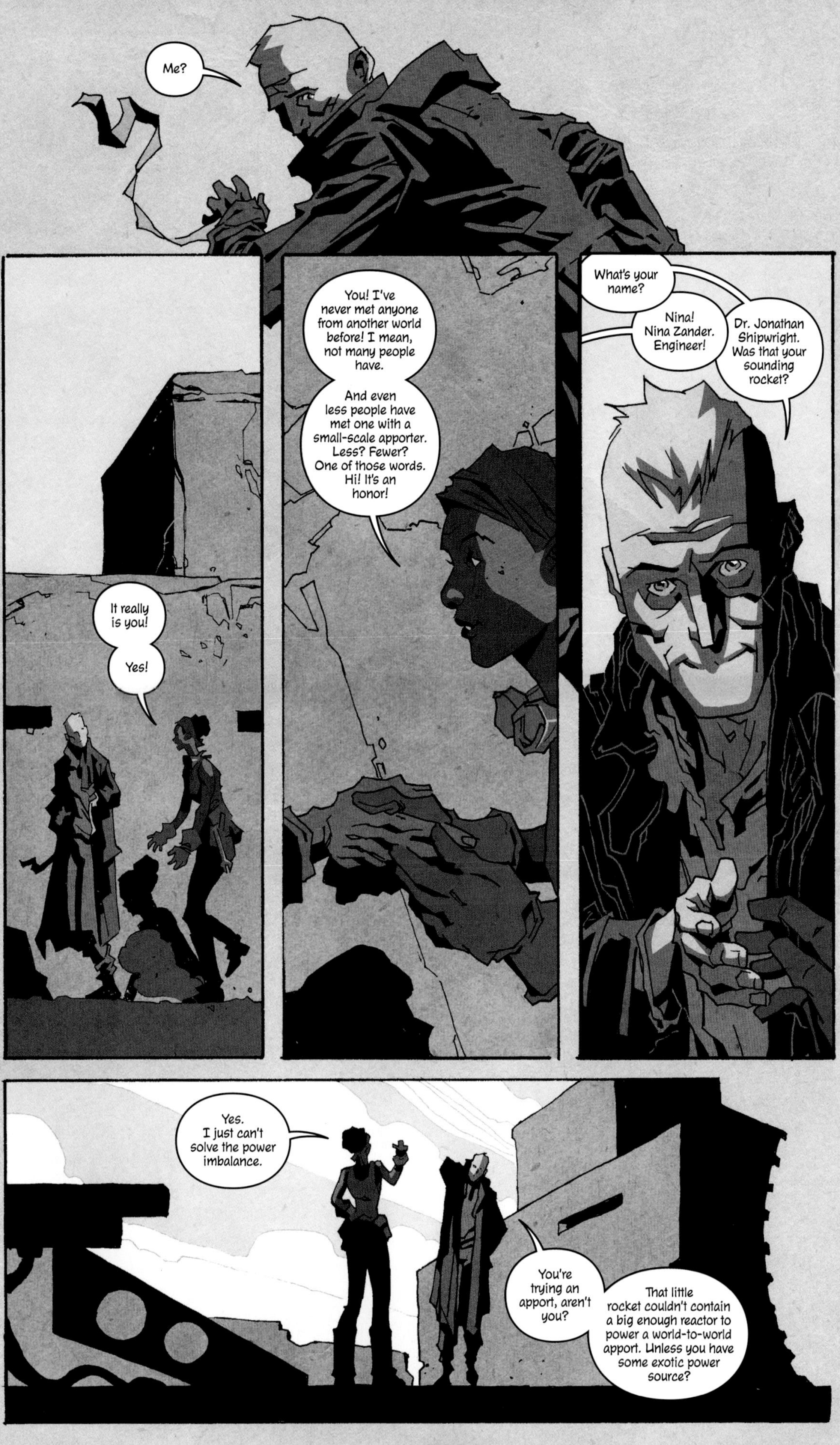
Me?
It really is you!
Yes!
You! I've never met anyone from another world before! I mean, not many people have.
And even less people have met one with a small-scale apporter. Less? Fewer? One of those words. Hi! It's an honor!
What's your name?
Nina! Nina Zander. Engineer!
Dr. Jonathan Shipwright. Was that your sounding rocket?
Yes. I just can't solve the power imbalance.
You're trying an apport, aren't you?
That little rocket couldn't contain a big enough reactor to power a world-to-world apport. Unless you have some exotic power source?

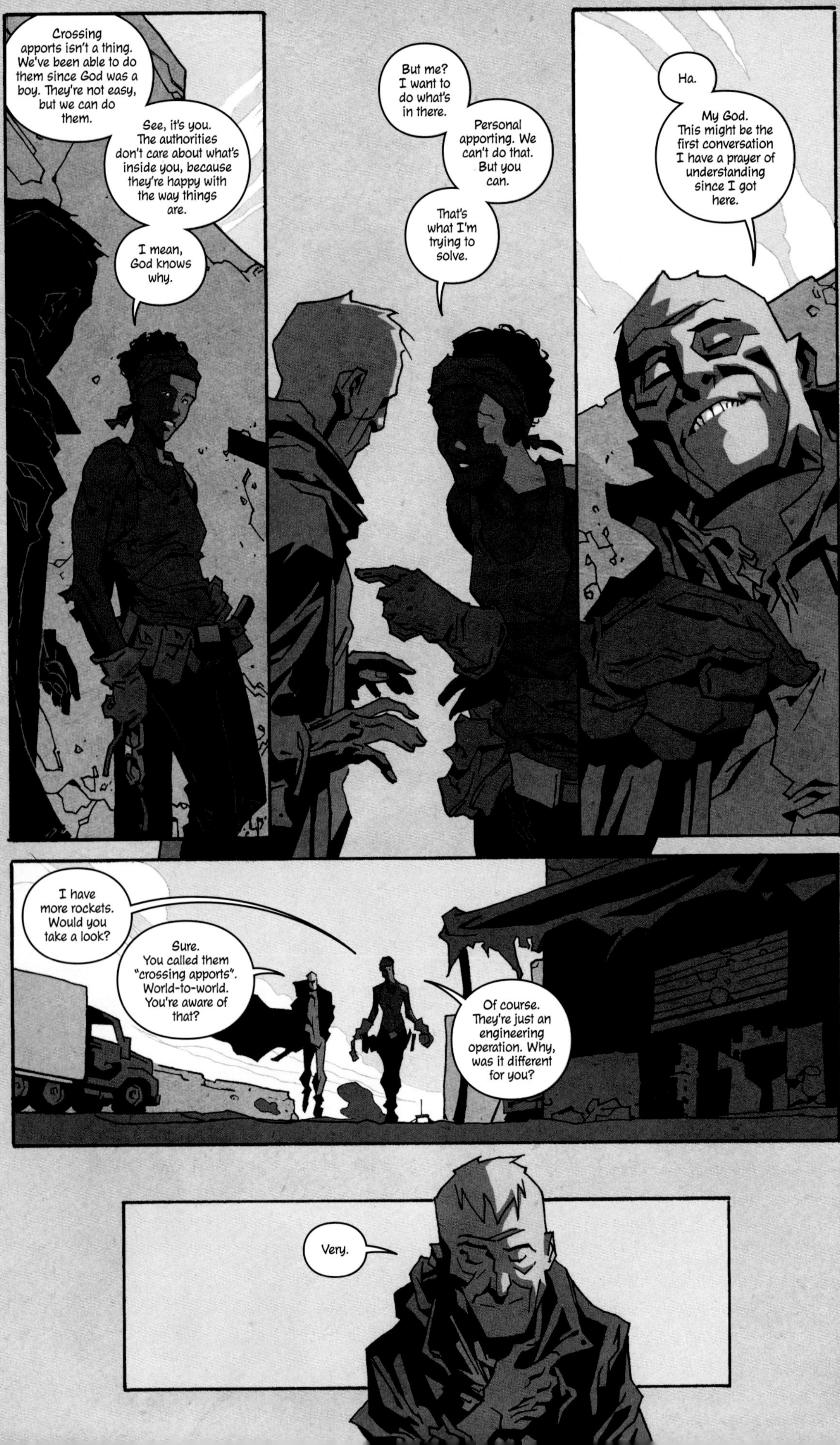
Crossing apports isn't a thing. We've been able to do them since God was a boy. They're not easy, but we can do them.
See, it's you. The authorities don't care about what's inside you, because they're happy with the way things are.
I mean, God knows why.
But me? I want to do what's in there.
Personal apporting. We can't do that. But you can.
That's what I'm trying to solve.
Ha.
My God. This might be the first conversation I have a prayer of understanding since I got here.
I have more rockets. Would you take a look?
Sure. You called them "crossing apports". World-to-world. You're aware of that?
Of course. They're just an engineering operation. Why, was it different for you?
Very.

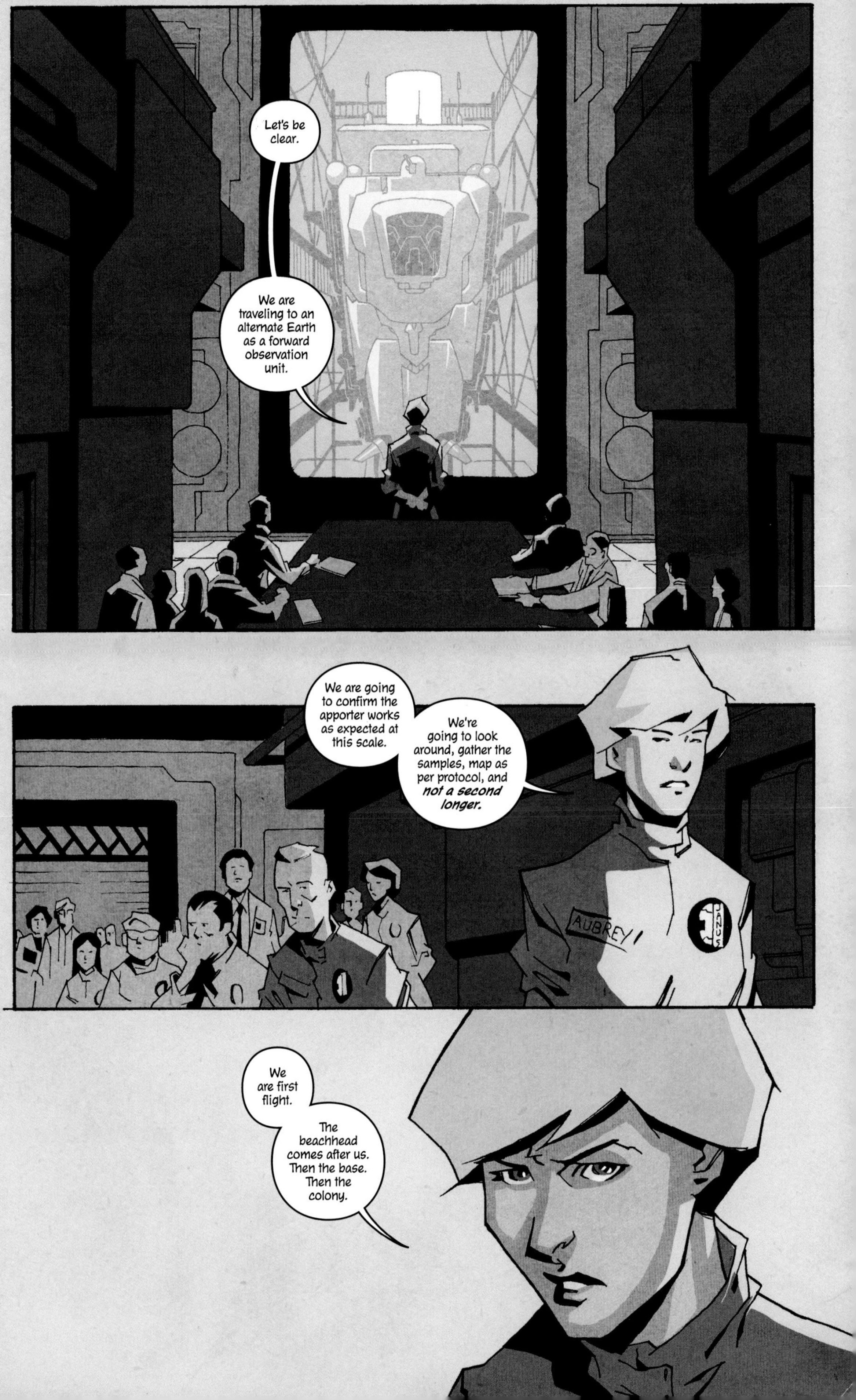
Let's be clear.
We are traveling to an alternate Earth as a forward observation unit.
We are going to confirm the apporter works as expected at this scale.
We're going to look around, gather the samples, map as per protocol, and ***not a second longer.***
AUBREY
JANUS
We are first flight.
The beachhead comes after us. Then the base. Then the colony.

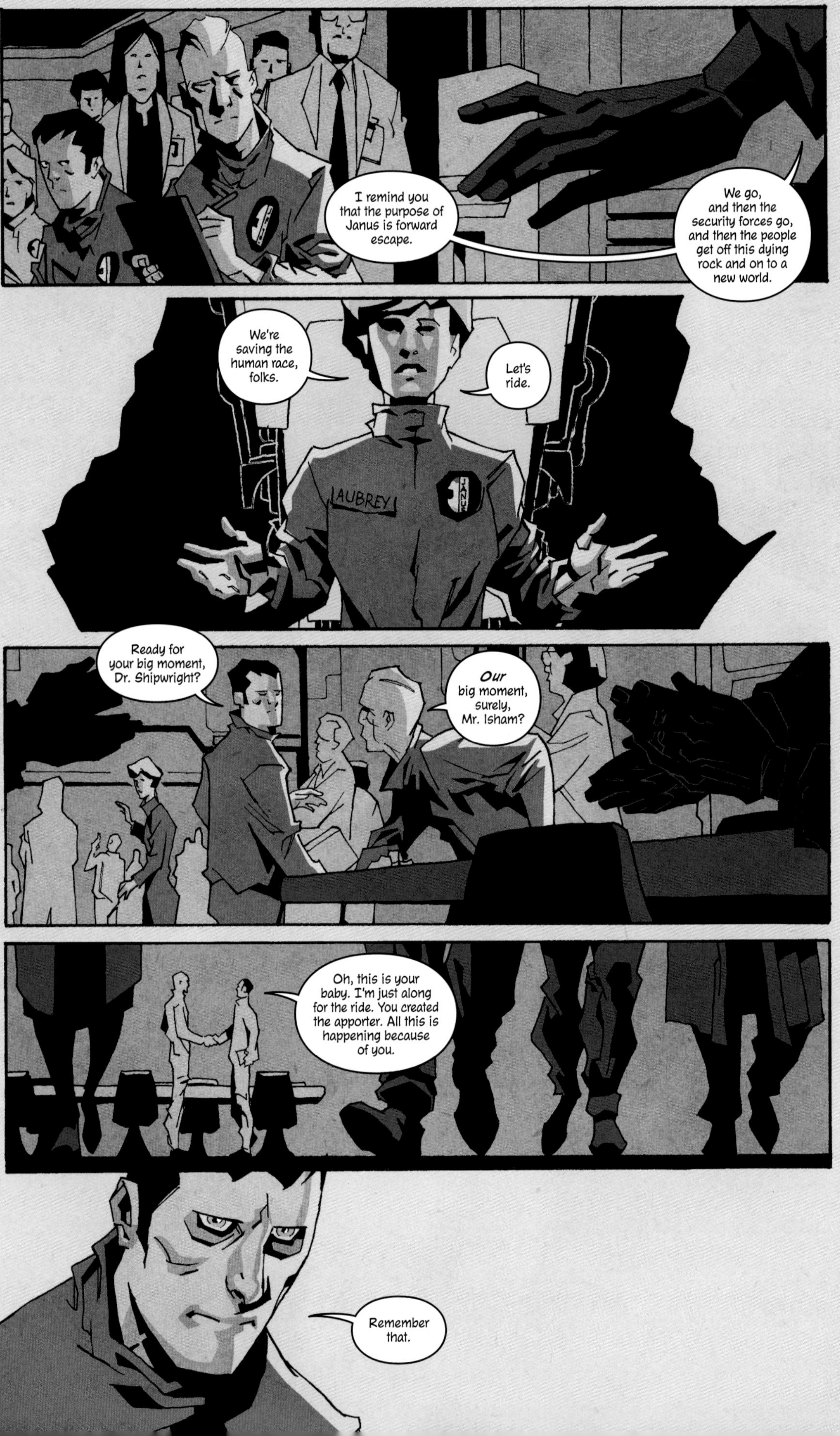
I remind you that the purpose of Janus is forward escape.
We go, and then the security forces go, and then the people get off this dying rock and on to a new world.
We're saving the human race, folks.
Let's ride.
AUBREY
Ready for your big moment, Dr. Shipwright?
Our big moment, surely, Mr. Isham?
Oh, this is your baby. I'm just along for the ride. You created the apporter. All this is happening because of you.
Remember that.

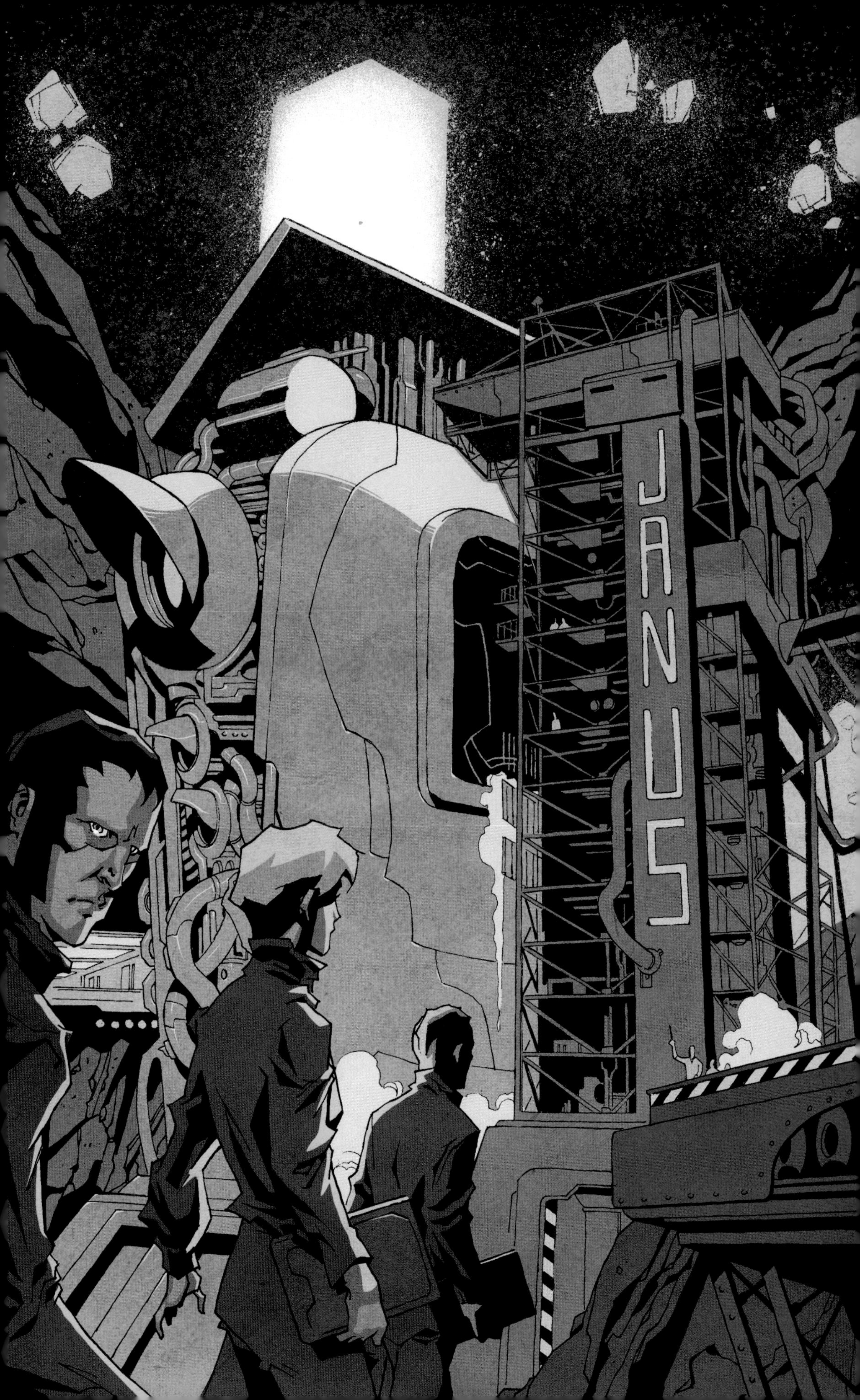
JANUS

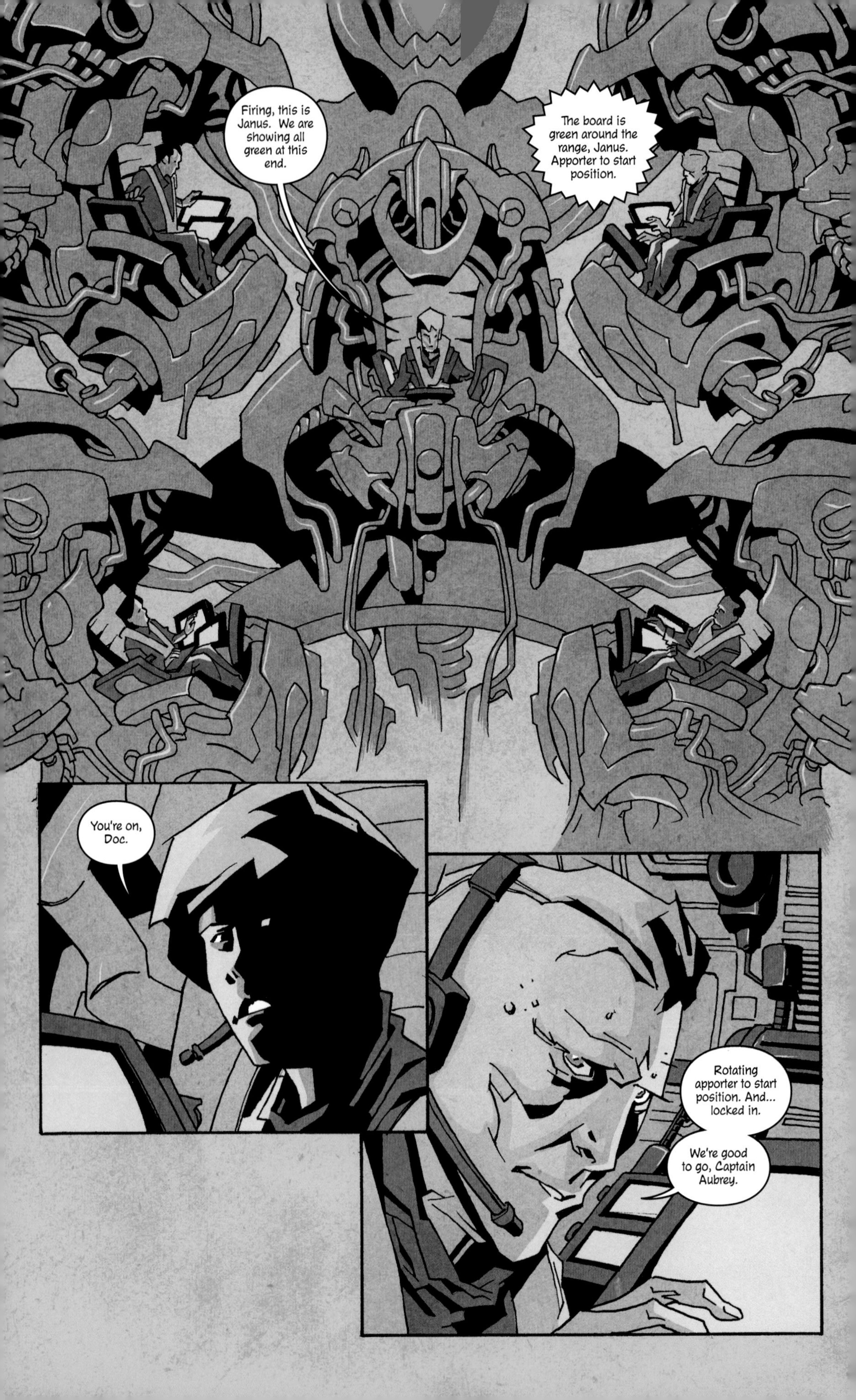
Firing, this is Janus. We are showing all green at this end.
The board is green around the range, Janus. Apporter to start position.
You're on, Doc.
Rotating apporter to start position. And... locked in.
We're good to go, Captain Aubrey.

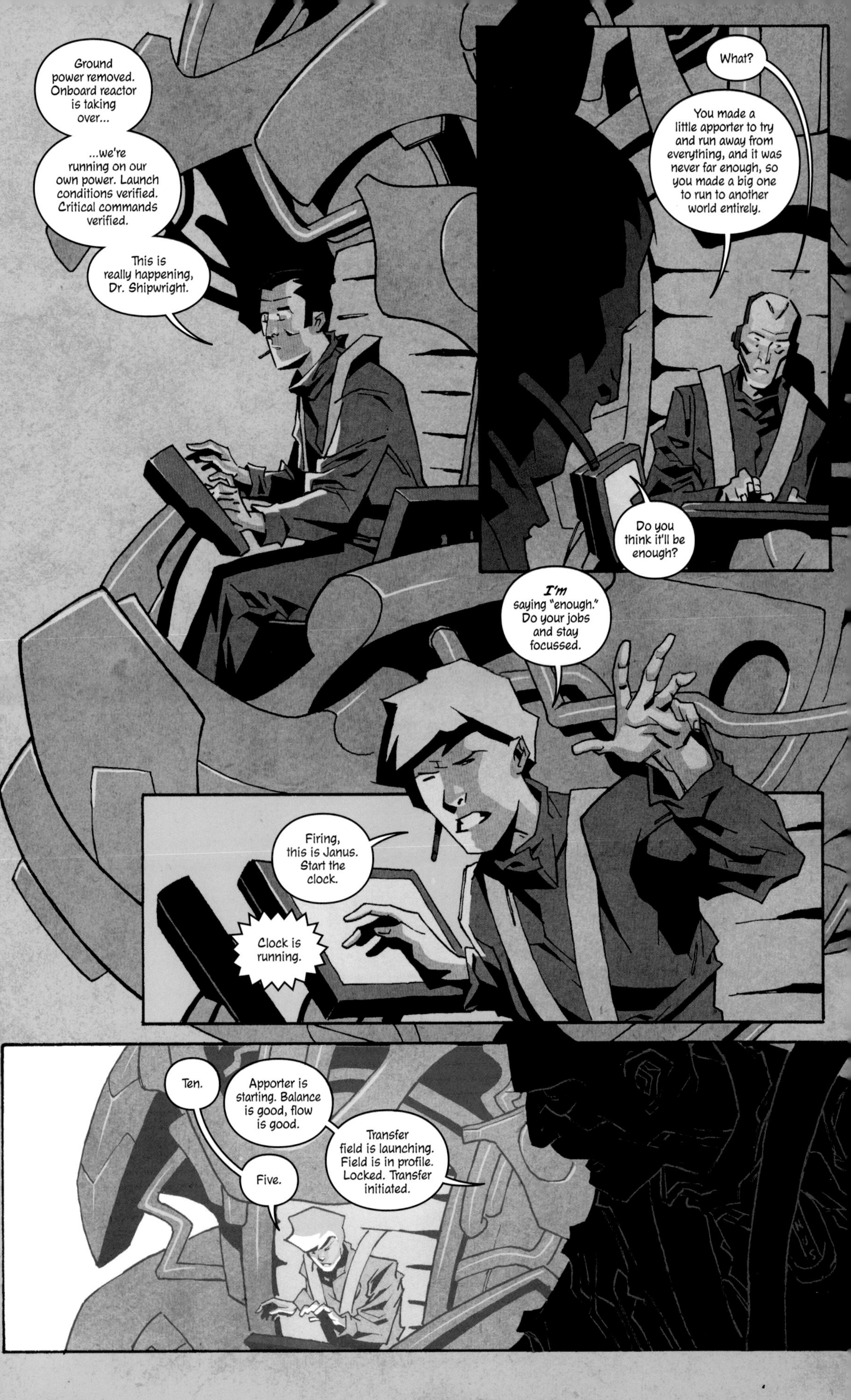
Ground power removed. Onboard reactor is taking over...
...we're running on our own power. Launch conditions verified. Critical commands verified.
This is really happening, Dr. Shipwright.
What?
You made a little apporter to try and run away from everything, and it was never far enough, so you made a big one to run to another world entirely.
Do you think it'll be enough?
I'm saying "enough." Do your jobs and stay focussed.
Firing, this is Janus. Start the clock.
Clock is running.
Ten.
Apporter is starting. Balance is good, flow is good.
Transfer field is launching. Field is in profile. Locked. Transfer initiated.
Five.

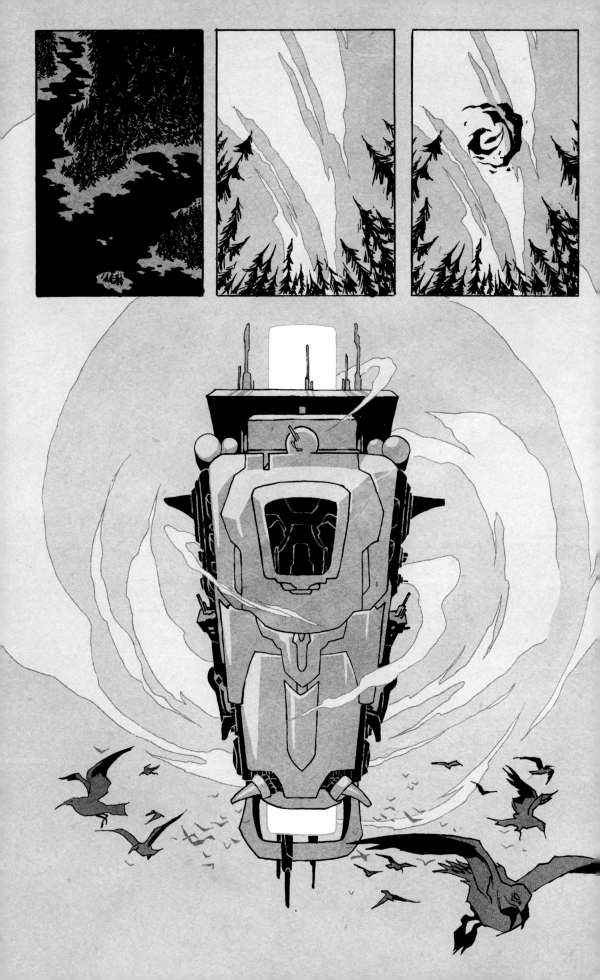

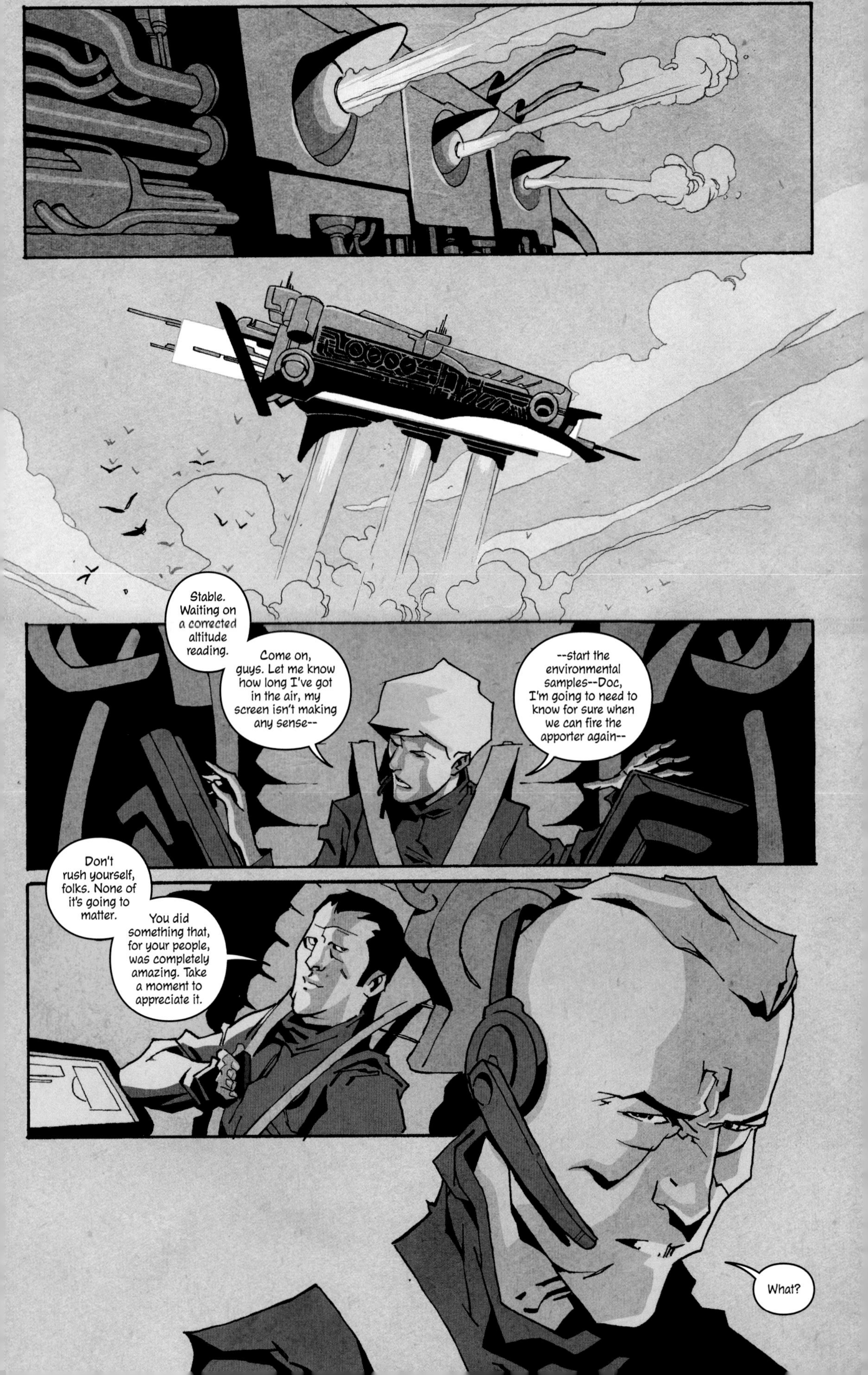
Stable. Waiting on a corrected altitude reading.
Come on, guys. Let me know how long I've got in the air, my screen isn't making any sense--
--start the environmental samples--Doc, I'm going to need to know for sure when we can fire the apporter again--
Don't rush yourself, folks. None of it's going to matter.
You did something that, for your people, was completely amazing. Take a moment to appreciate it.
What?

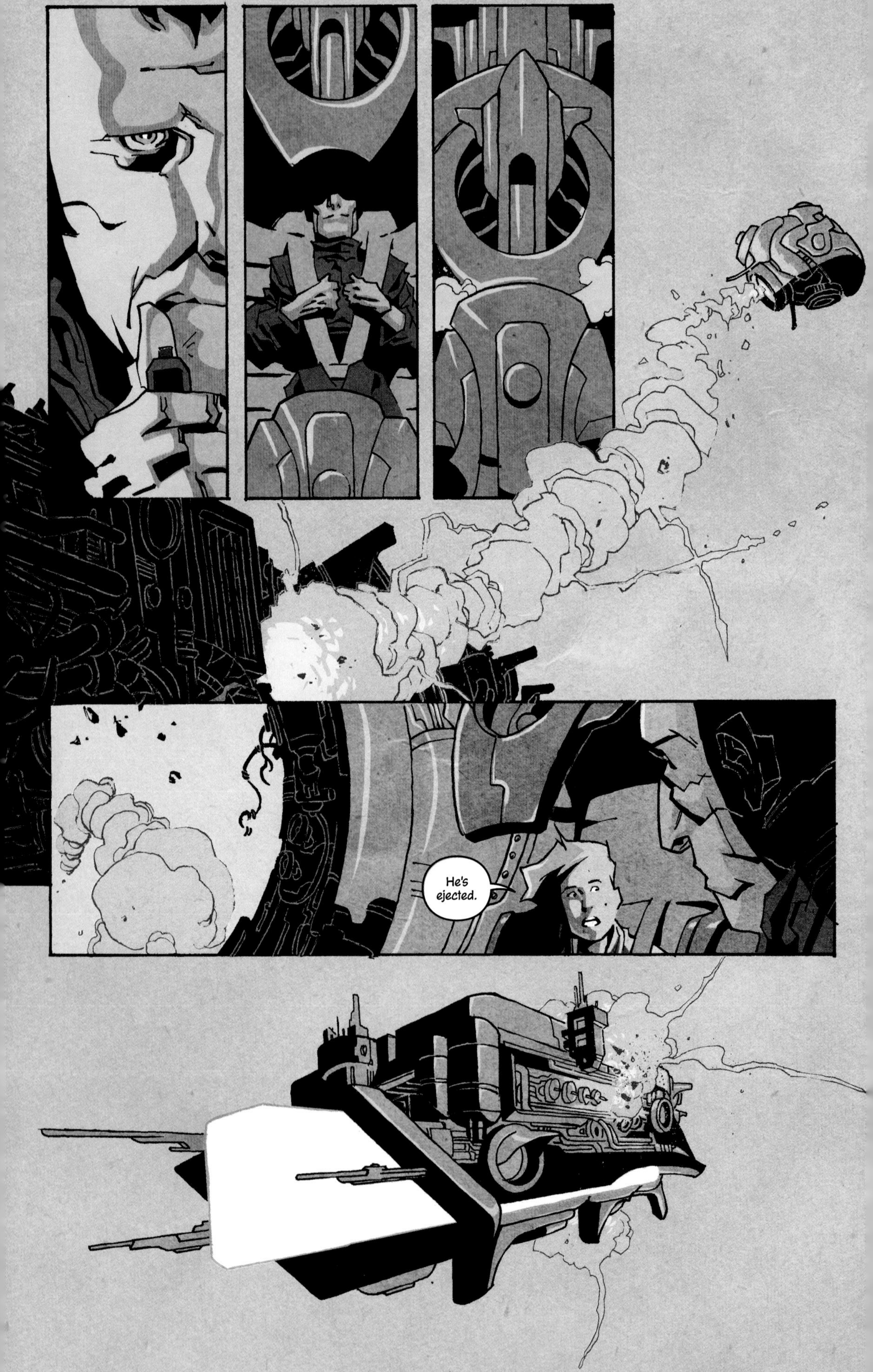
He's ejected.

5

"BEACON"

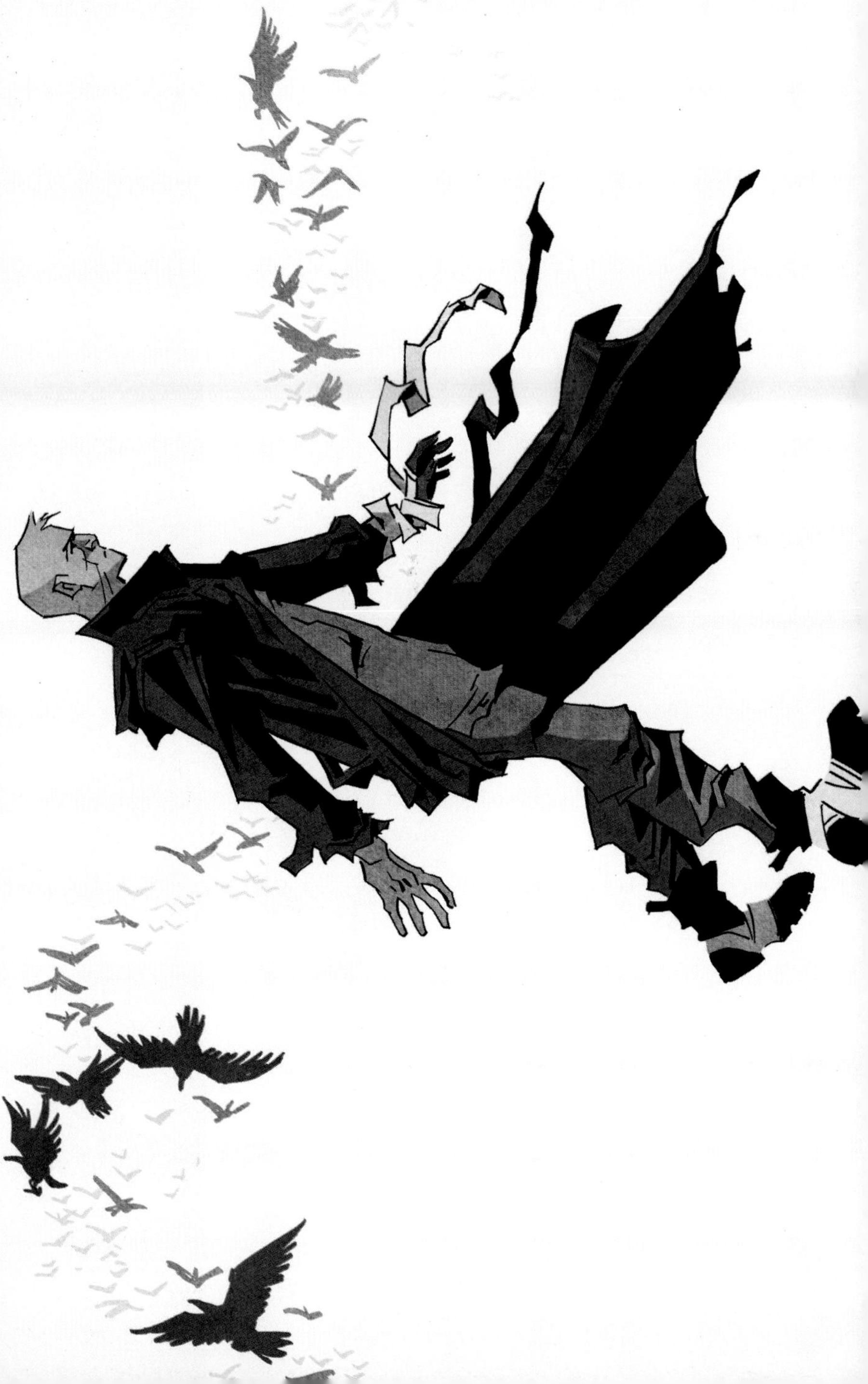

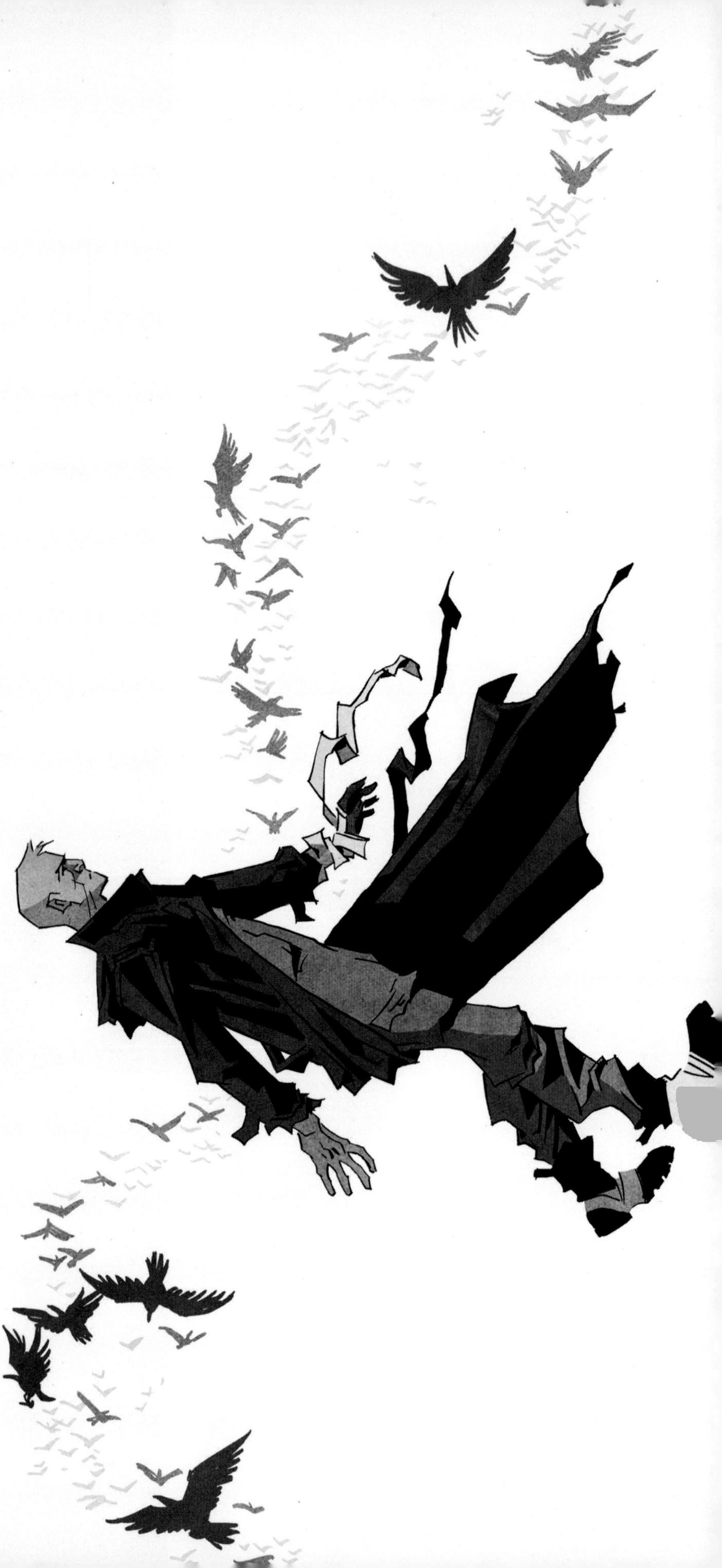

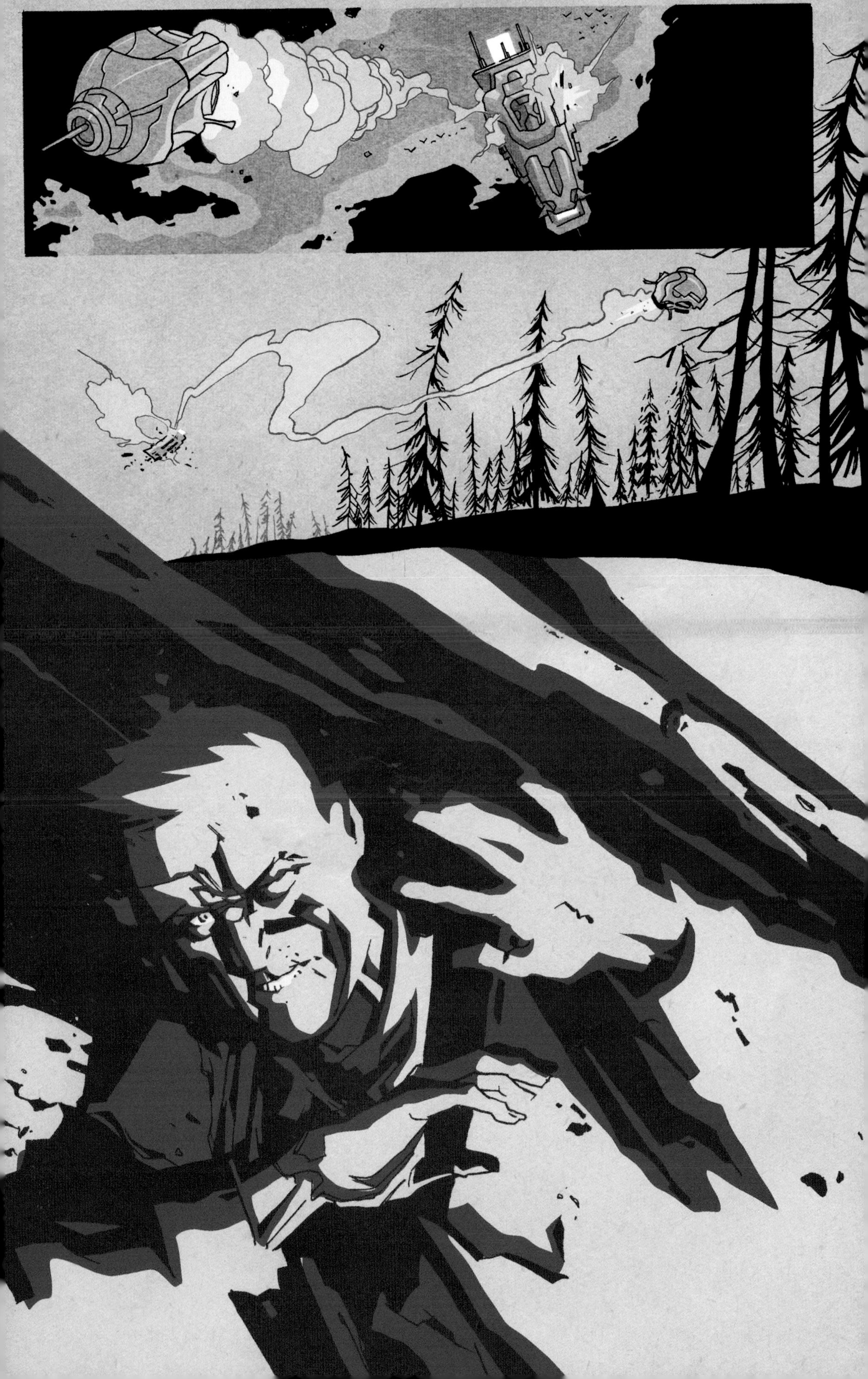

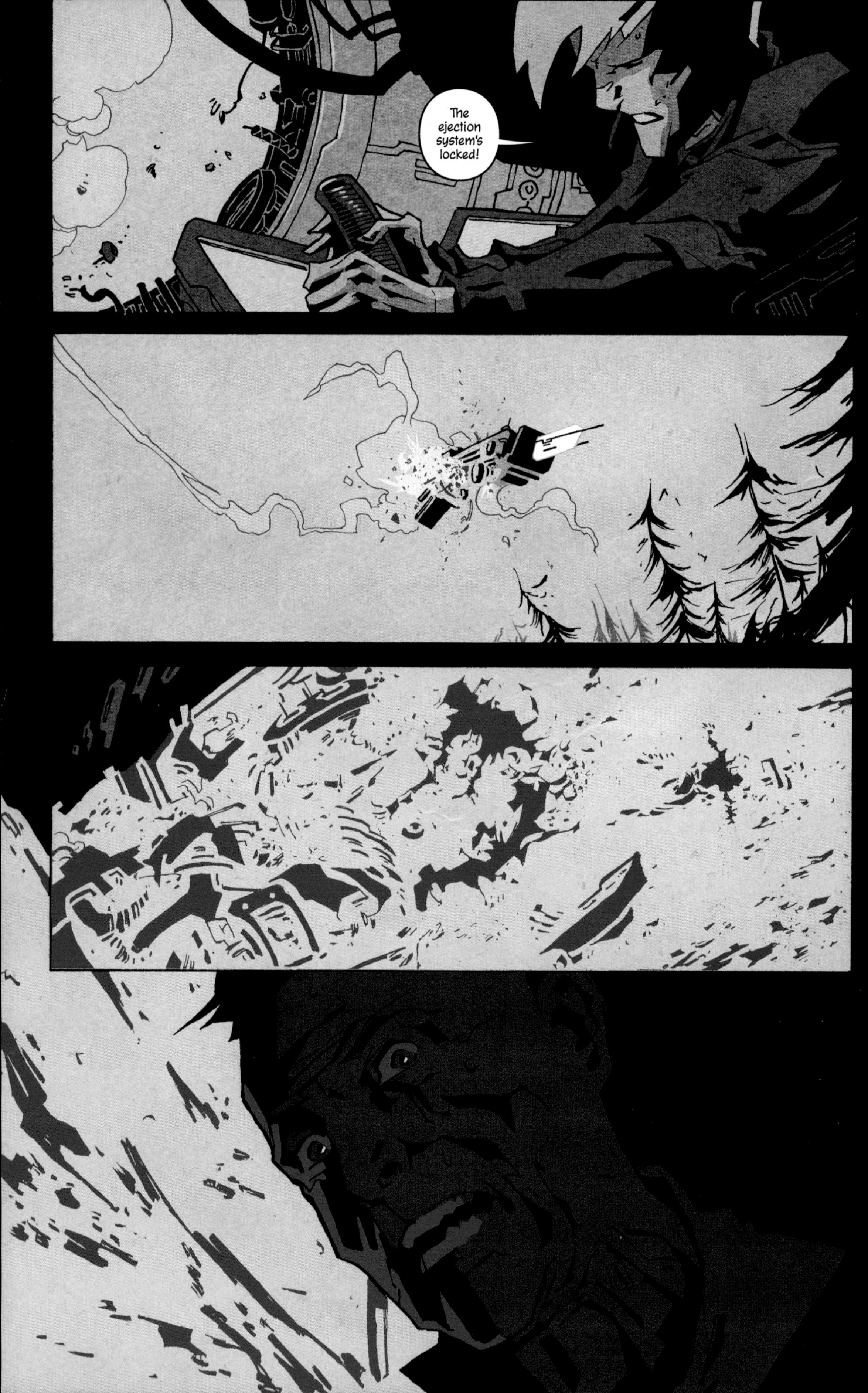
The ejection system's locked!

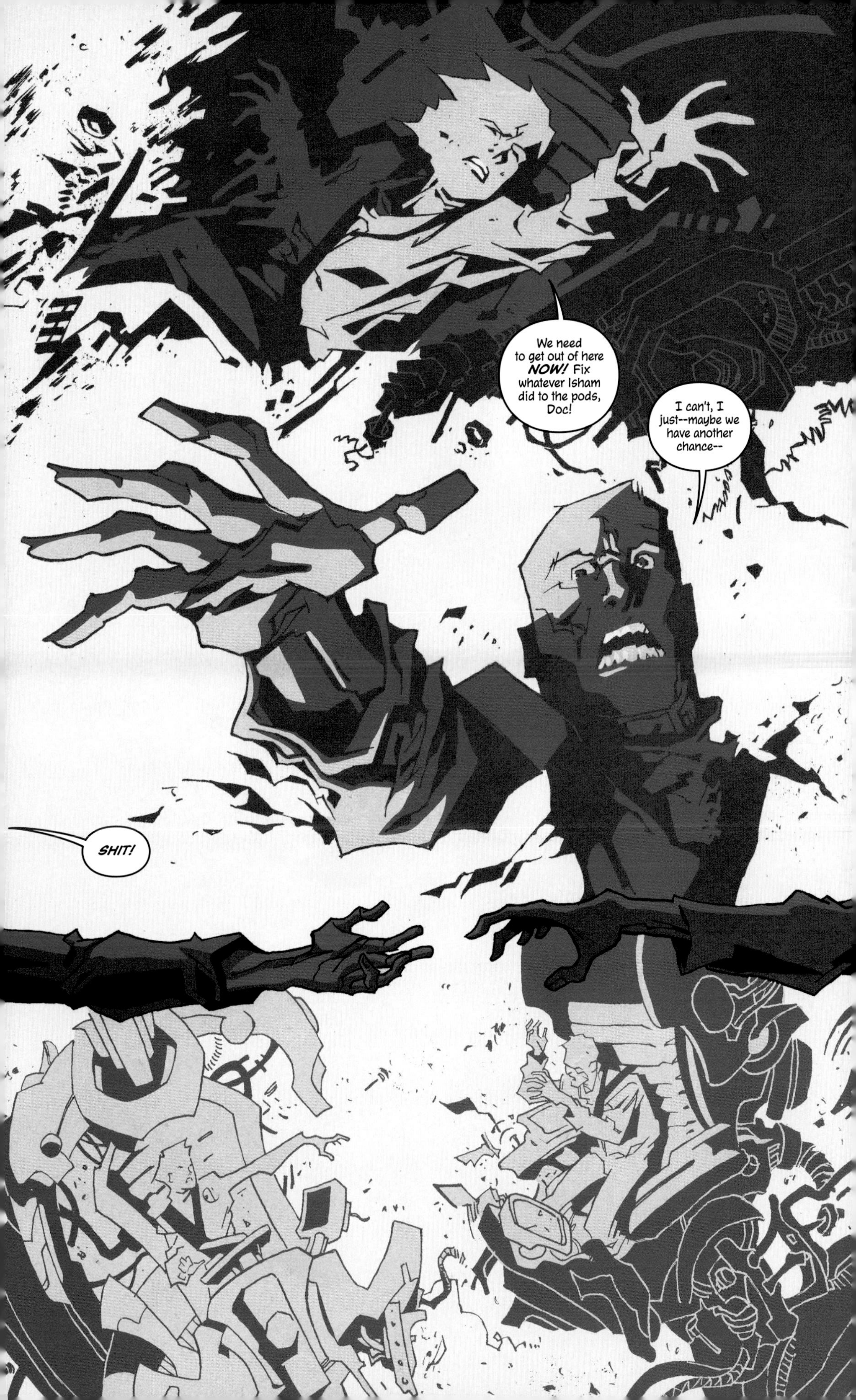
We need to get out of here NOW! Fix whatever Isham did to the pods, Doc!
I can't, I just--maybe we have another chance--
SHIT!

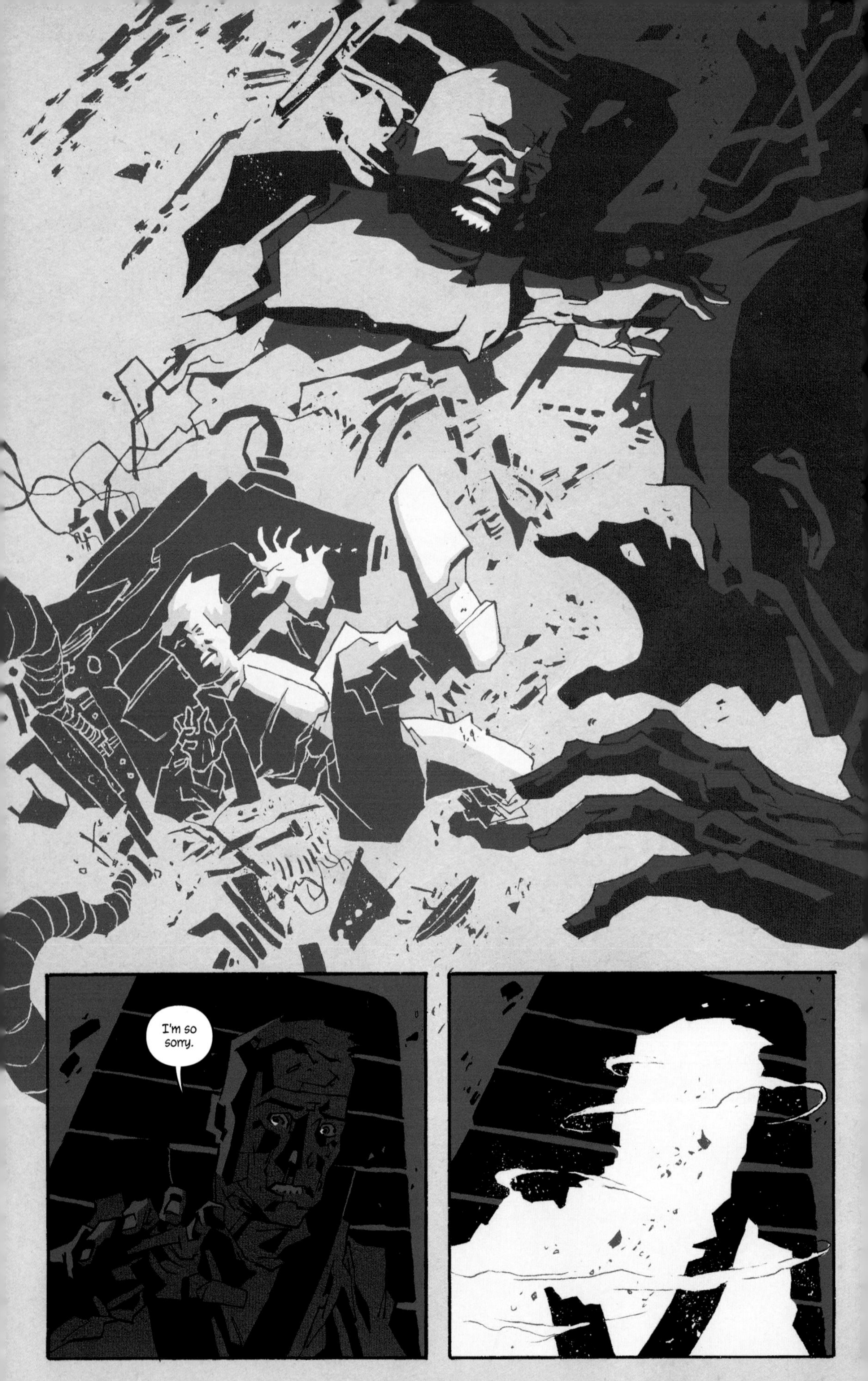
I'm so sorry.

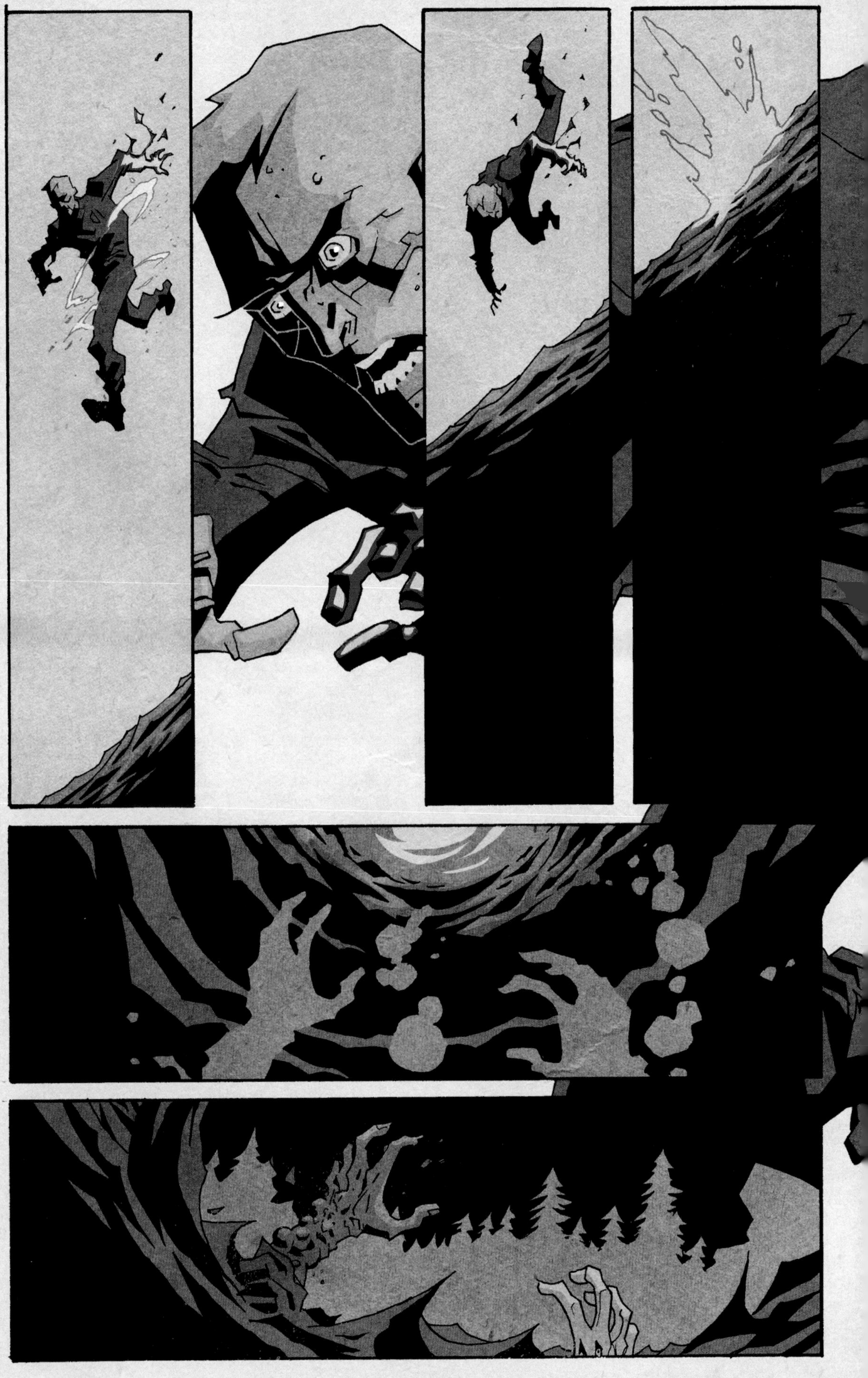

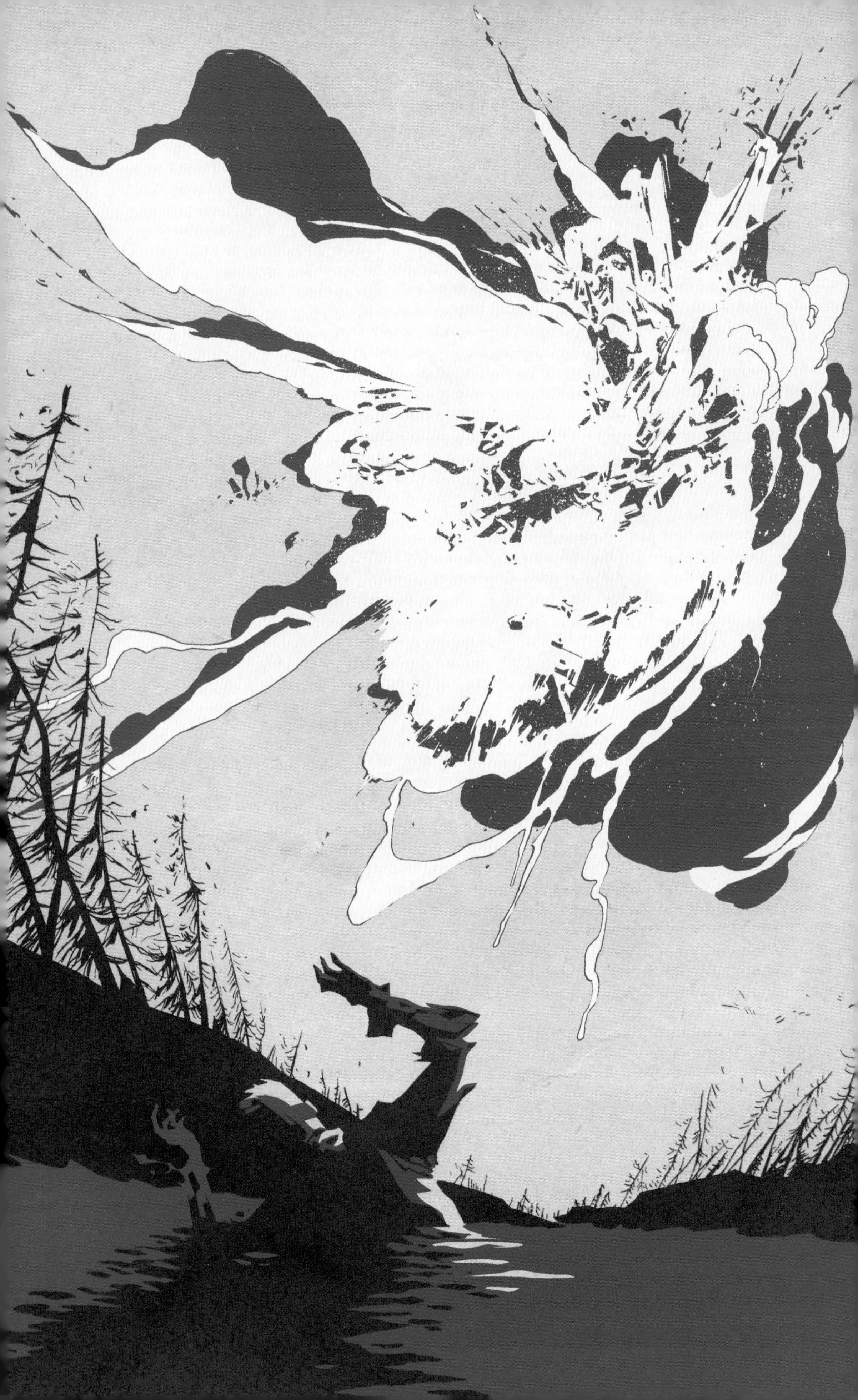

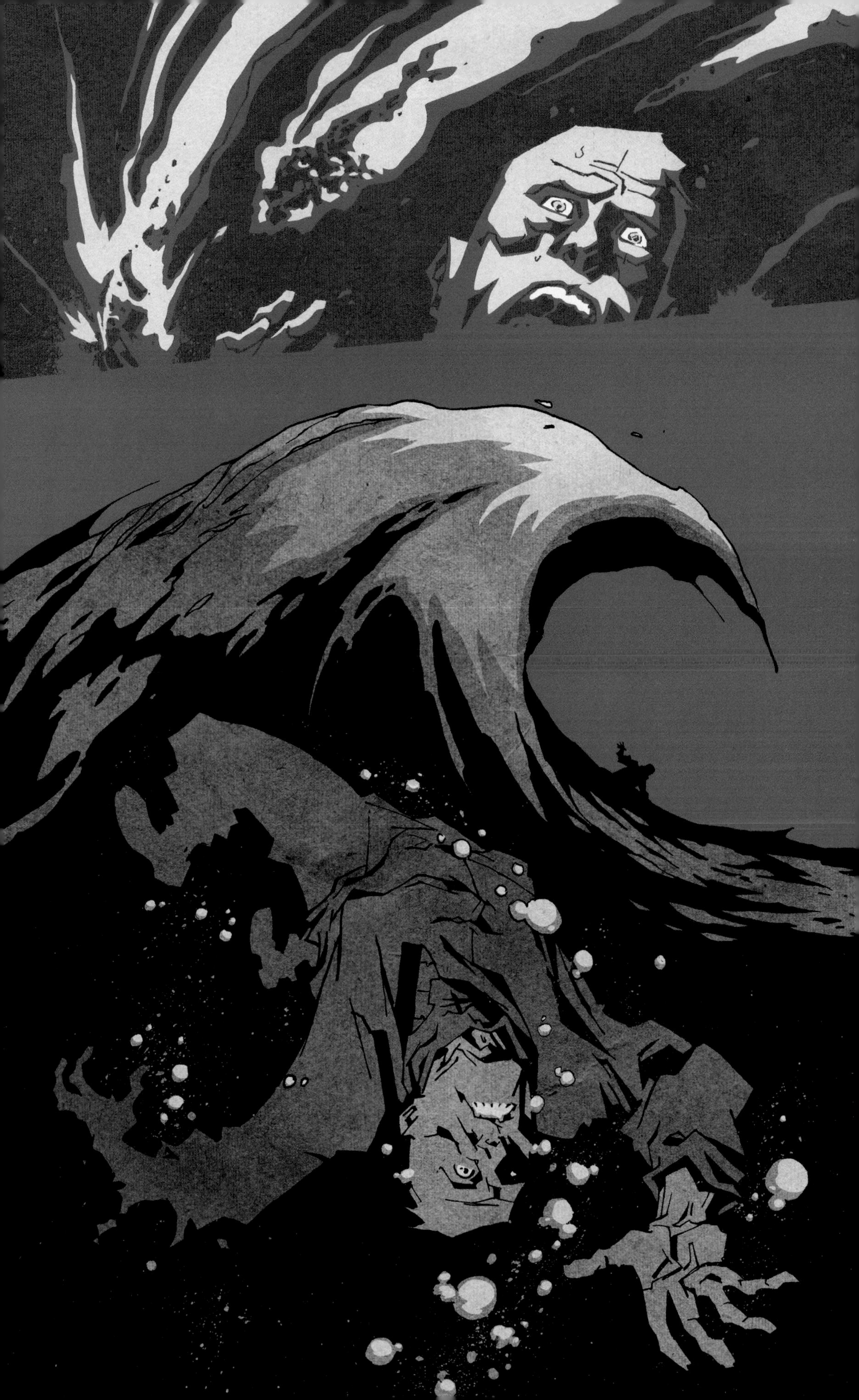

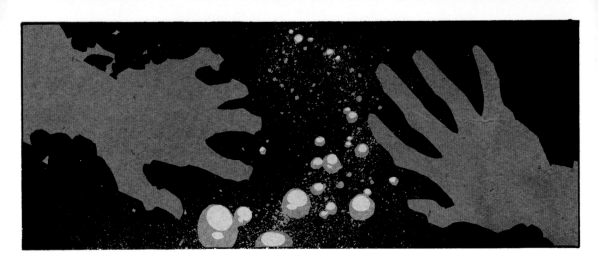

Shipwreck

5. Beacon

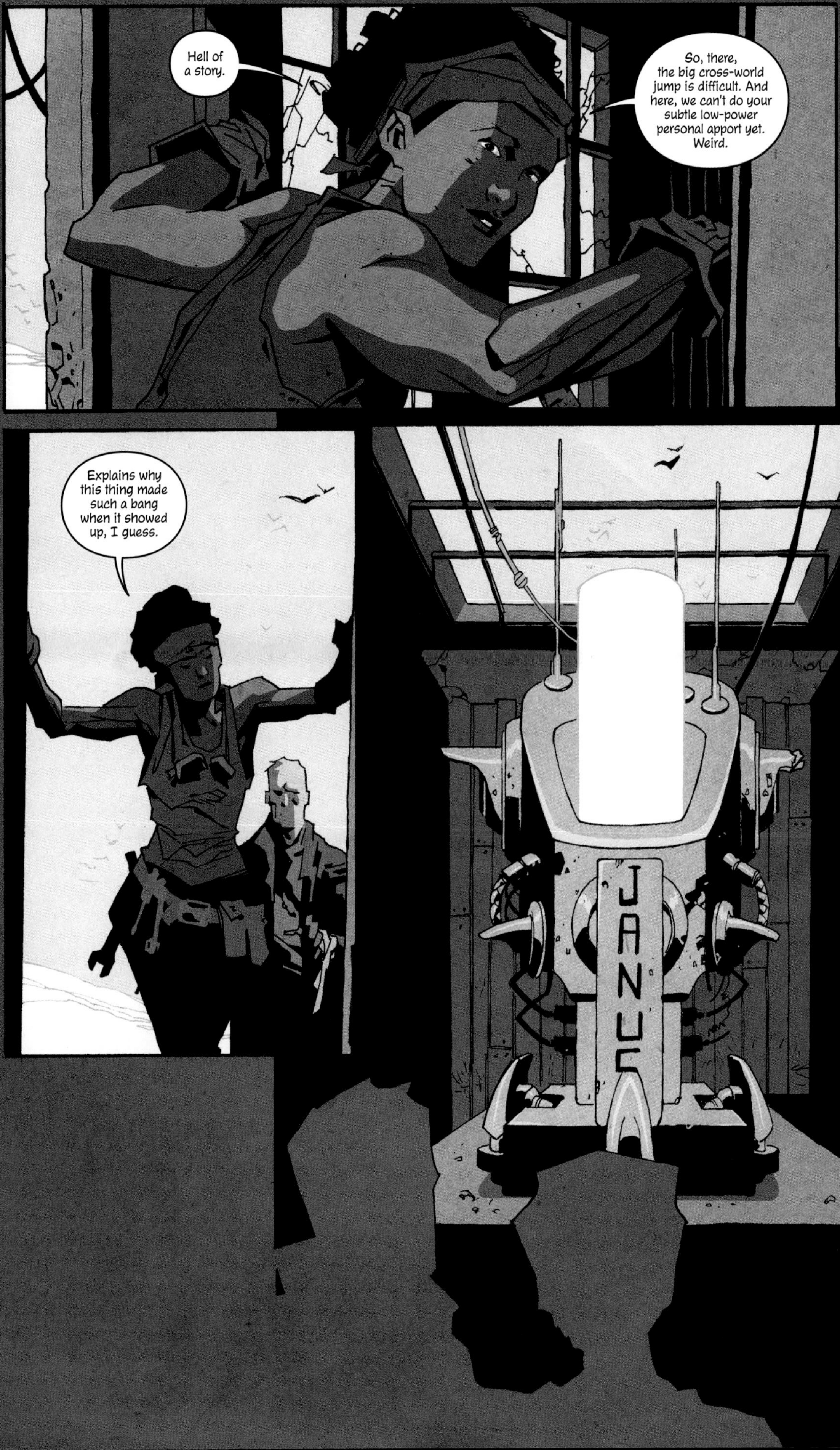
Hell of a story.
So, there, the big cross-world jump is difficult. And here, we can't do your subtle low-power personal apport yet. Weird.
Explains why this thing made such a bang when it showed up, I guess.
JANUS

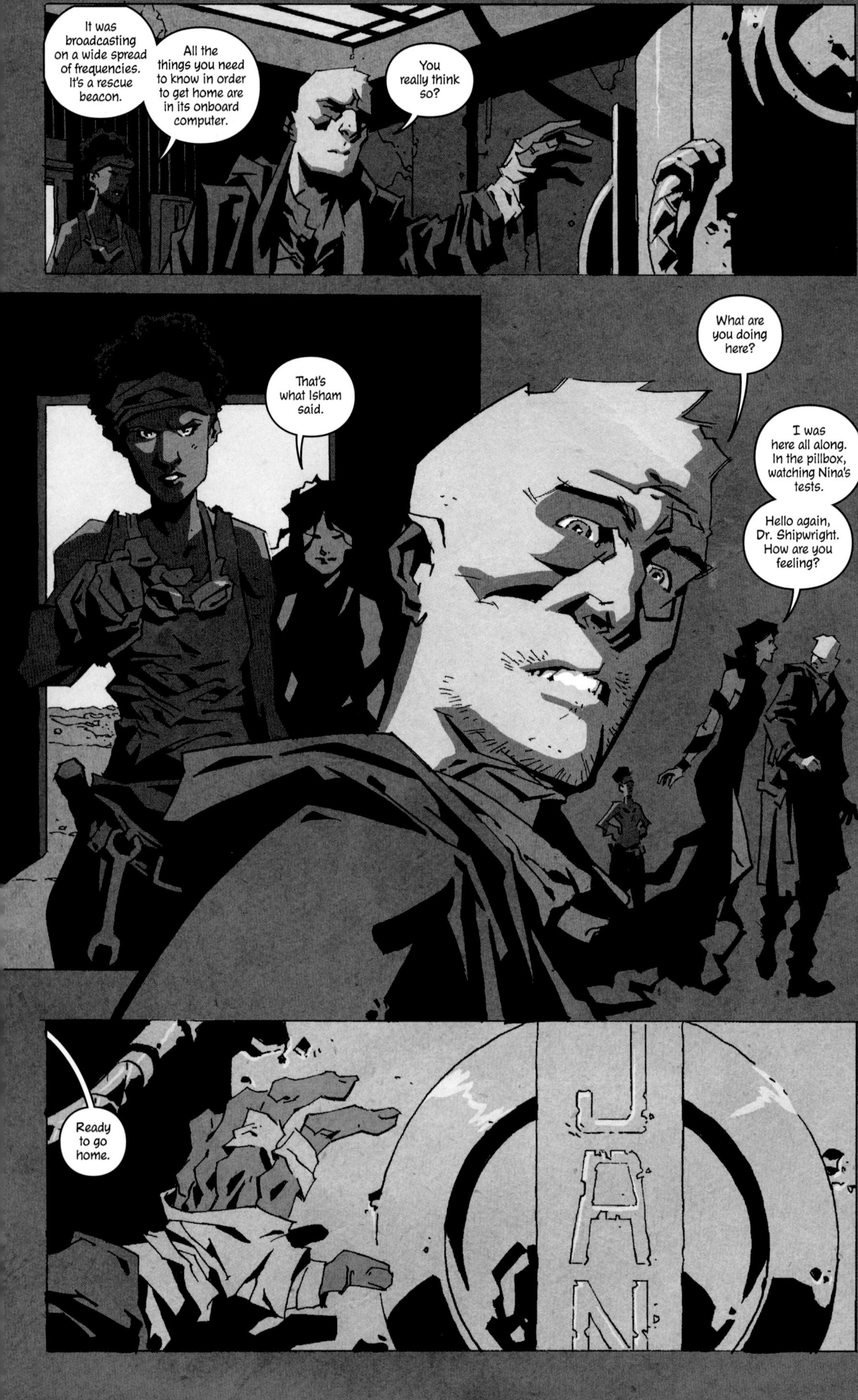

It was broadcasting on a wide spread of frequencies. It's a rescue beacon.
All the things you need to know in order to get home are in its onboard computer.
You really think so?
That's what Isham said.
What are you doing here?
I was here all along. In the pillbox, watching Nina's tests.
Hello again, Dr. Shipwright. How are you feeling?
Ready to go home.

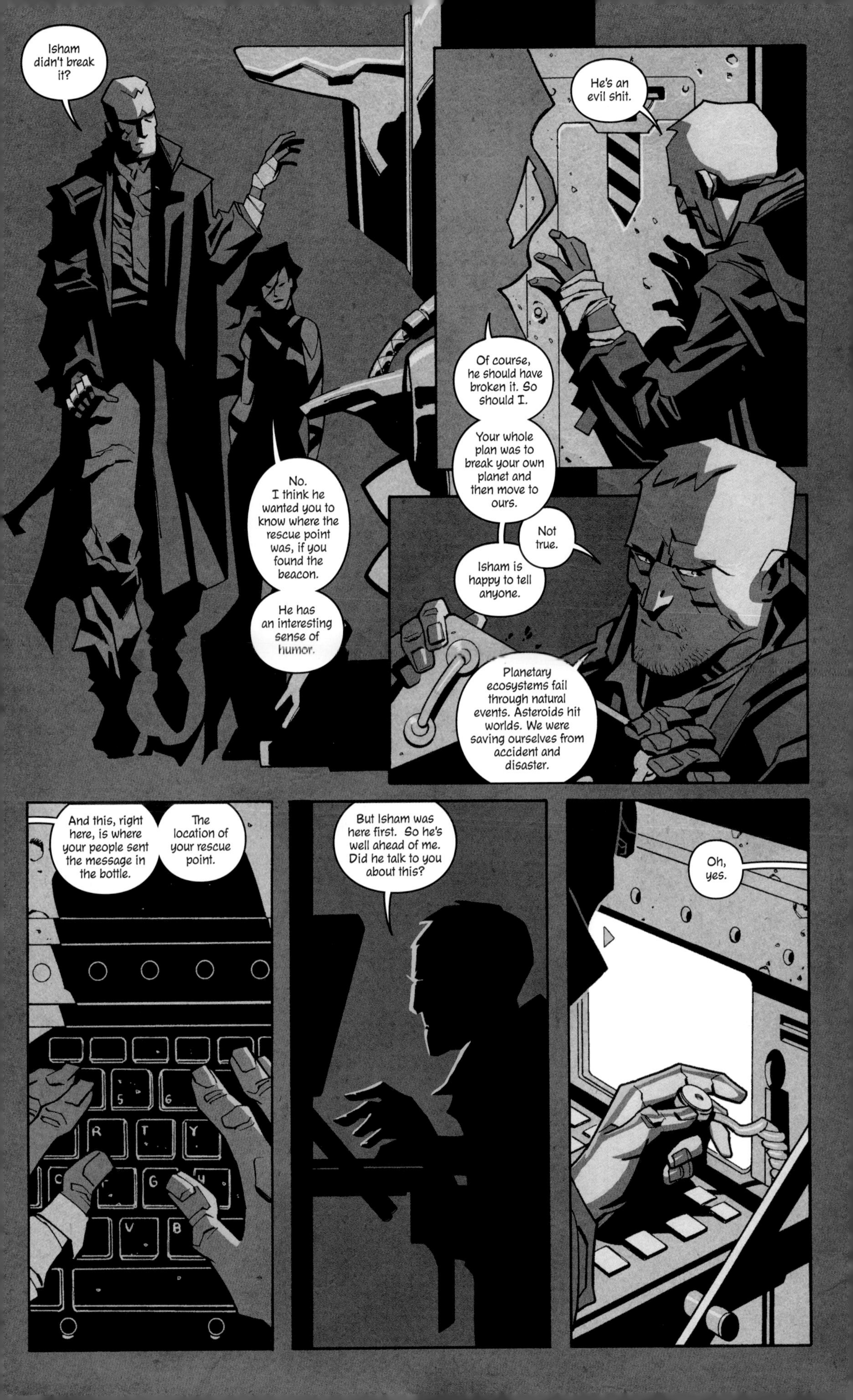
Isham didn't break it?
He's an evil shit.
Of course, he should have broken it. So should I.
Your whole plan was to break your own planet and then move to ours.
No. I think he wanted you to know where the rescue point was, if you found the beacon.
He has an interesting sense of humor.
Not true.
Isham is happy to tell anyone.
Planetary ecosystems fail through natural events. Asteroids hit worlds. We were saving ourselves from accident and disaster.
And this, right here, is where your people sent the message in the bottle.
The location of your rescue point.
But Isham was here first. So he's well ahead of me. Did he talk to you about this?
Oh, yes.

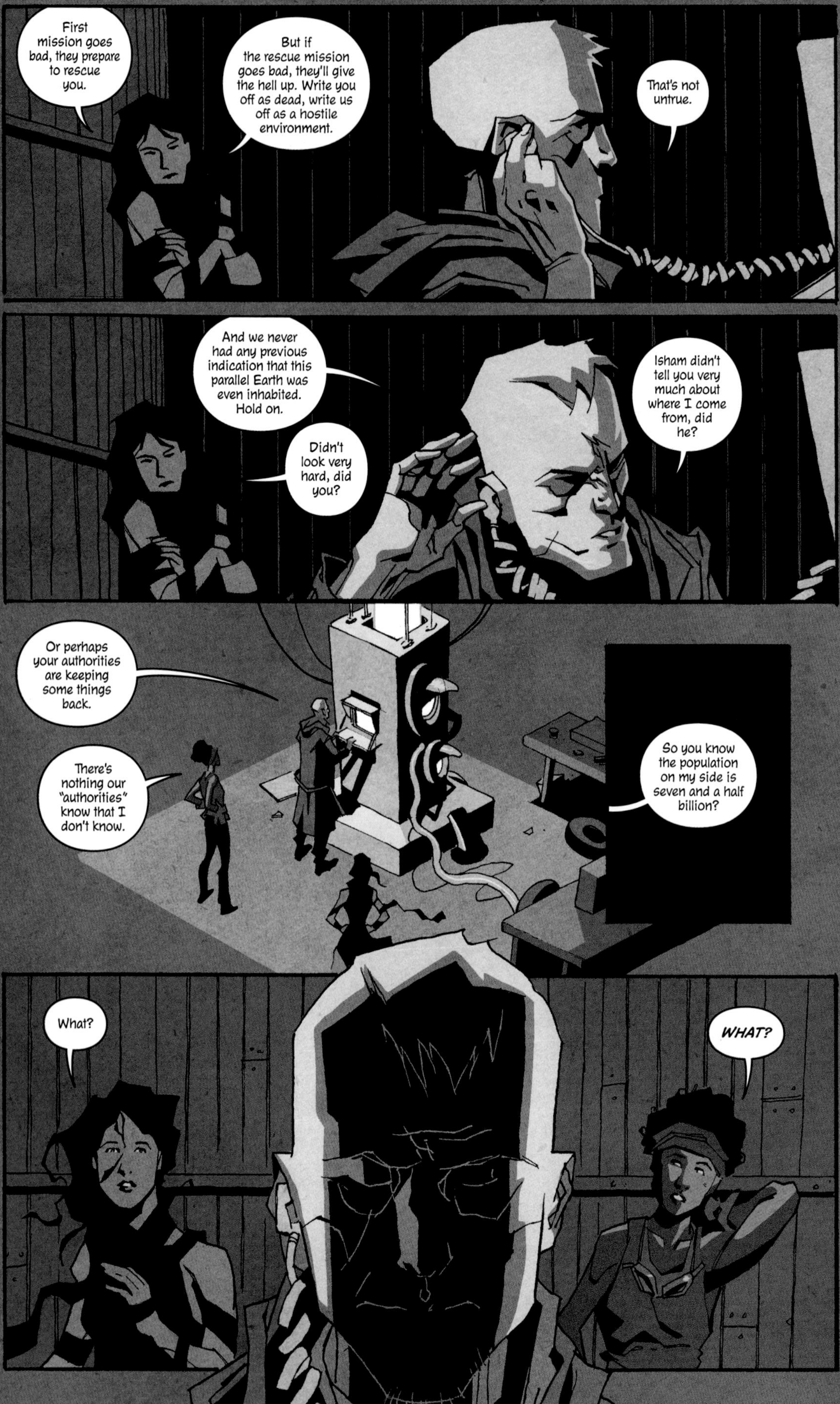
First mission goes bad, they prepare to rescue you.
But if the rescue mission goes bad, they'll give the hell up. Write you off as dead, write us off as a hostile environment.
That's not untrue.
And we never had any previous indication that this parallel Earth was even inhabited. Hold on.
Didn't look very hard, did you?
Isham didn't tell you very much about where I come from, did he?
Or perhaps your authorities are keeping some things back.
There's nothing our "authorities" know that I don't know.
So you know the population on my side is seven and a half billion?
What?
WHAT?

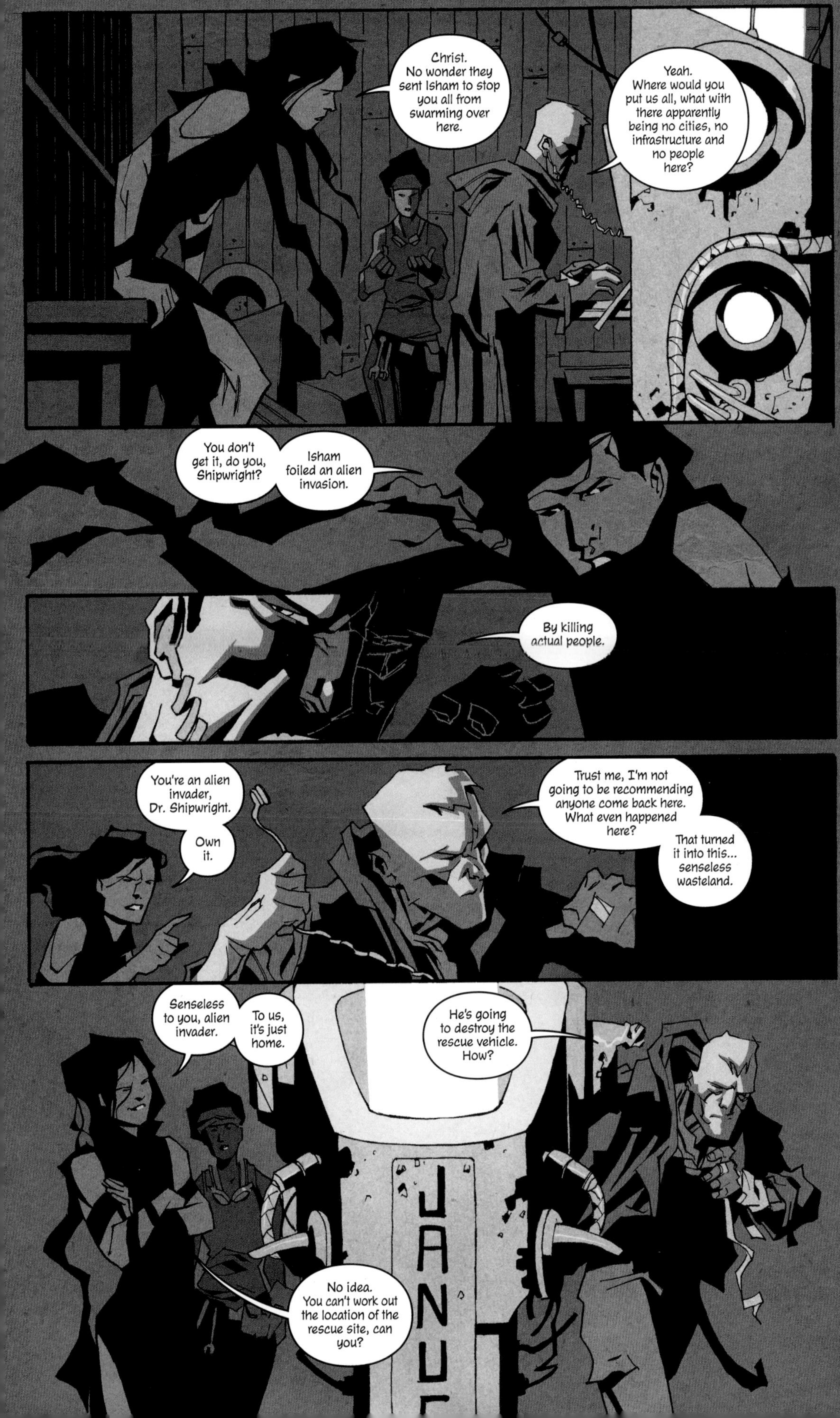
Christ. No wonder they sent Isham to stop you all from swarming over here.
Yeah. Where would you put us all, what with there apparently being no cities, no infrastructure and no people here?
You don't get it, do you, Shipwright?
Isham foiled an alien invasion.
By killing actual people.
You're an alien invader, Dr. Shipwright.
Own it.
Trust me, I'm not going to be recommending anyone come back here. What even happened here?
That turned it into this... senseless wasteland.
Senseless to you, alien invader.
To us, it's just home.
He's going to destroy the rescue vehicle. How?
No idea. You can't work out the location of the rescue site, can you?
JANU

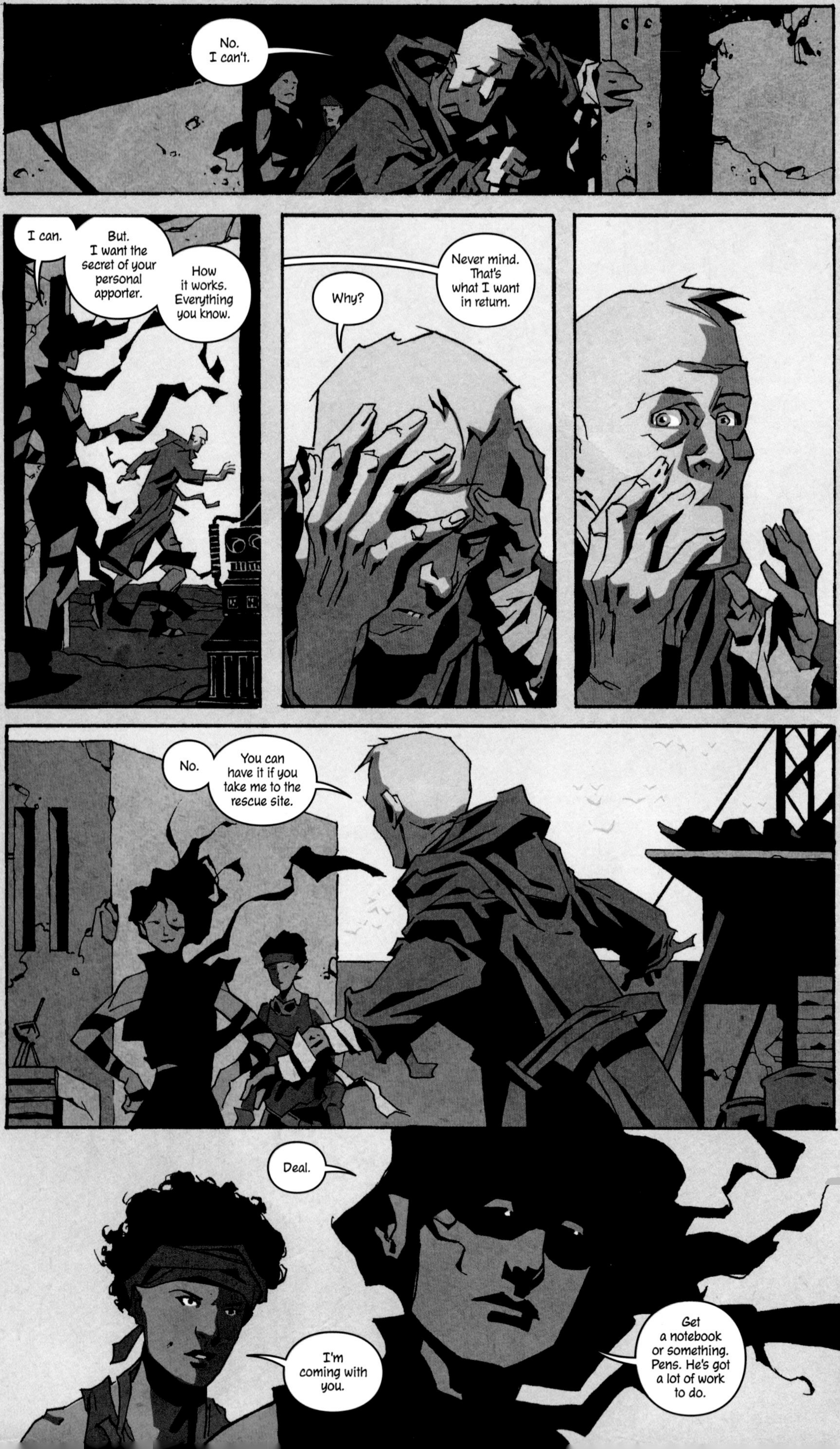
No.
I can't.
I can.
But. I want the secret of your personal apporter.
How it works. Everything you know.
Why?
Never mind. That's what I want in return.
No.
You can have it if you take me to the rescue site.
Deal.
I'm coming with you.
Get a notebook or something. Pens. He's got a lot of work to do.

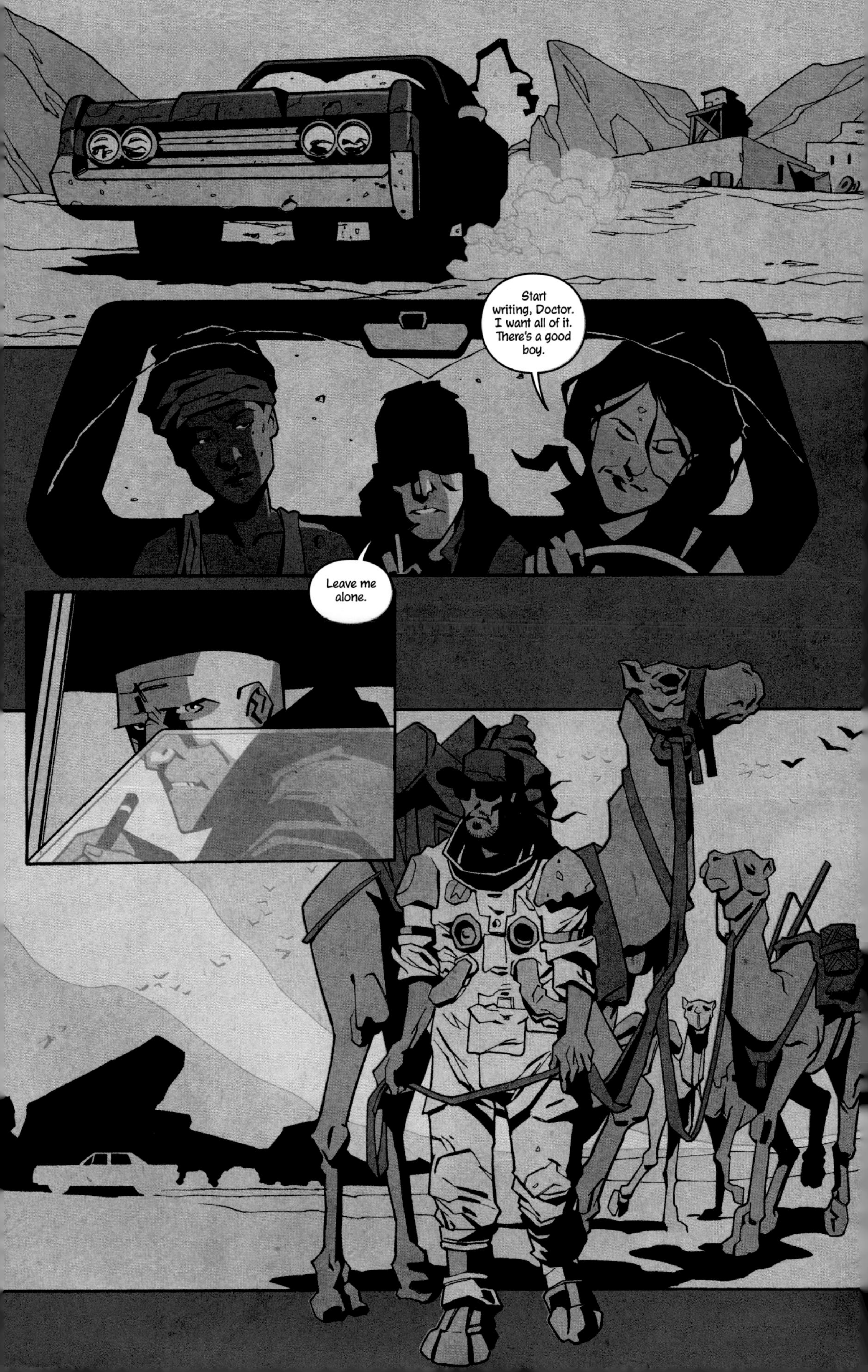
Start writing, Doctor. I want all of it. There's a good boy.
Leave me alone.

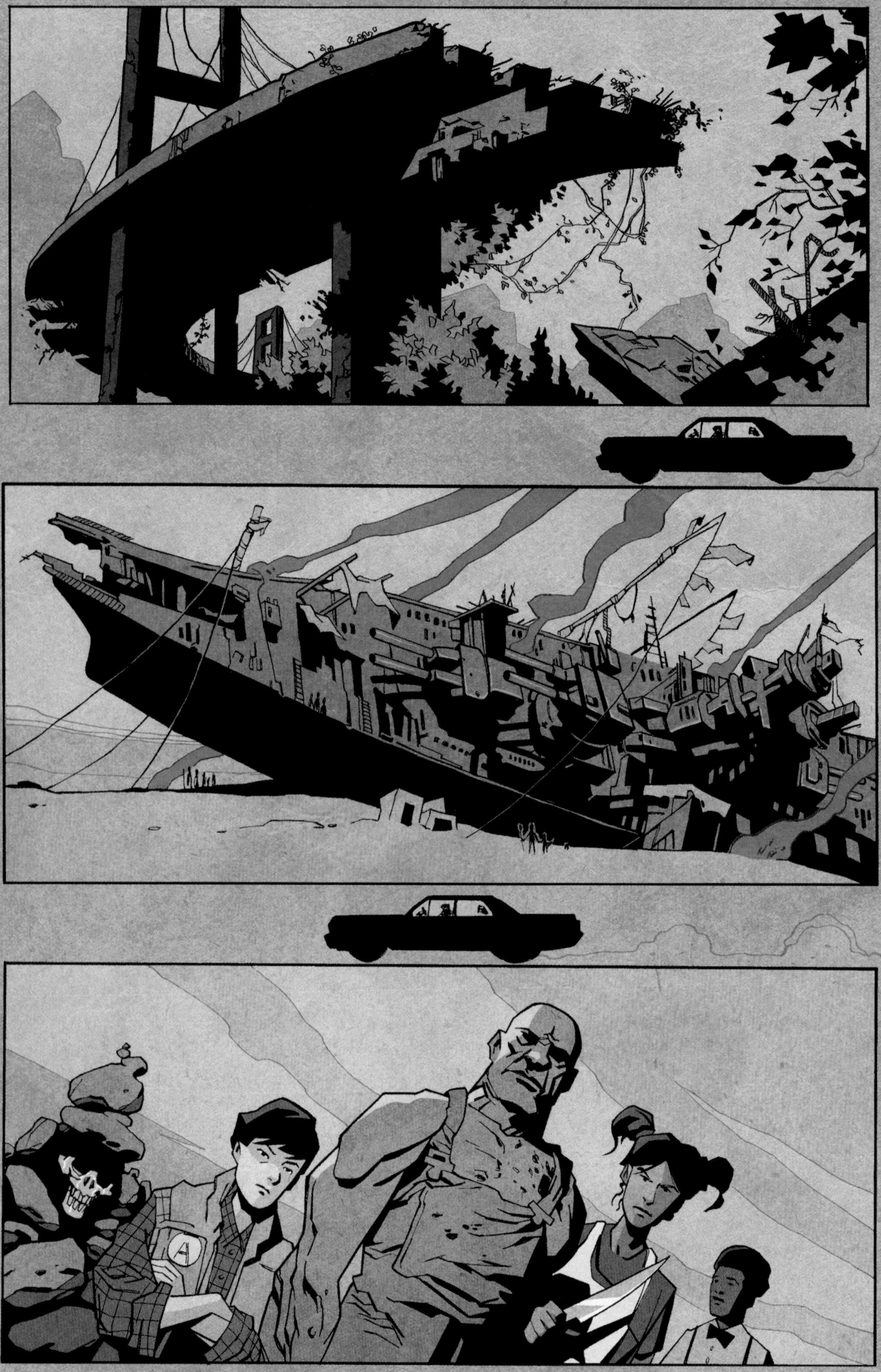

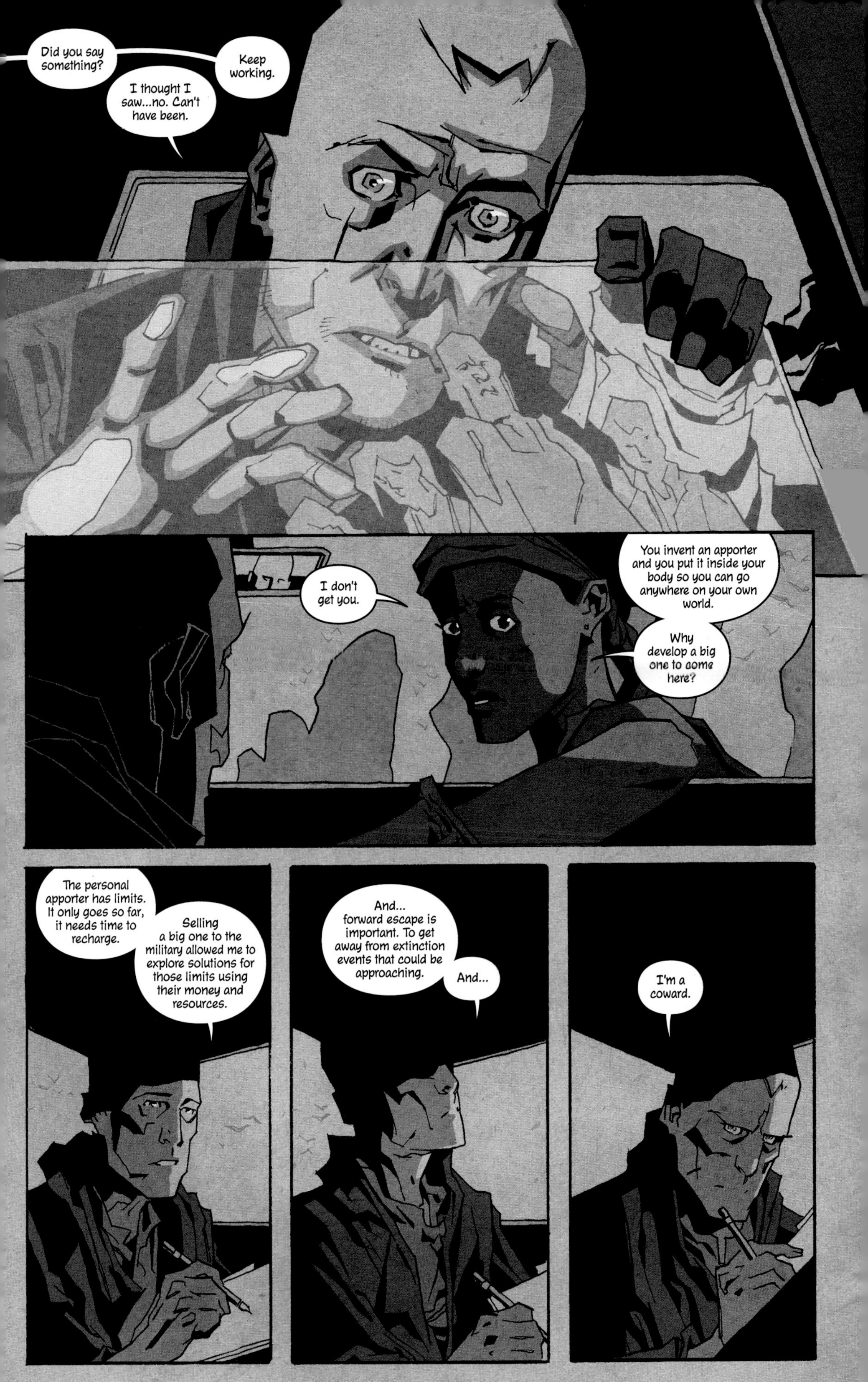
Did you say something?
Keep working.
I thought I saw...no. Can't have been.
I don't get you.
You invent an apporter and you put it inside your body so you can go anywhere on your own world.
Why develop a big one to come here?
The personal apporter has limits. It only goes so far, it needs time to recharge.
Selling a big one to the military allowed me to explore solutions for those limits using their money and resources.
And... forward escape is important. To get away from extinction events that could be approaching.
And...
I'm a coward.

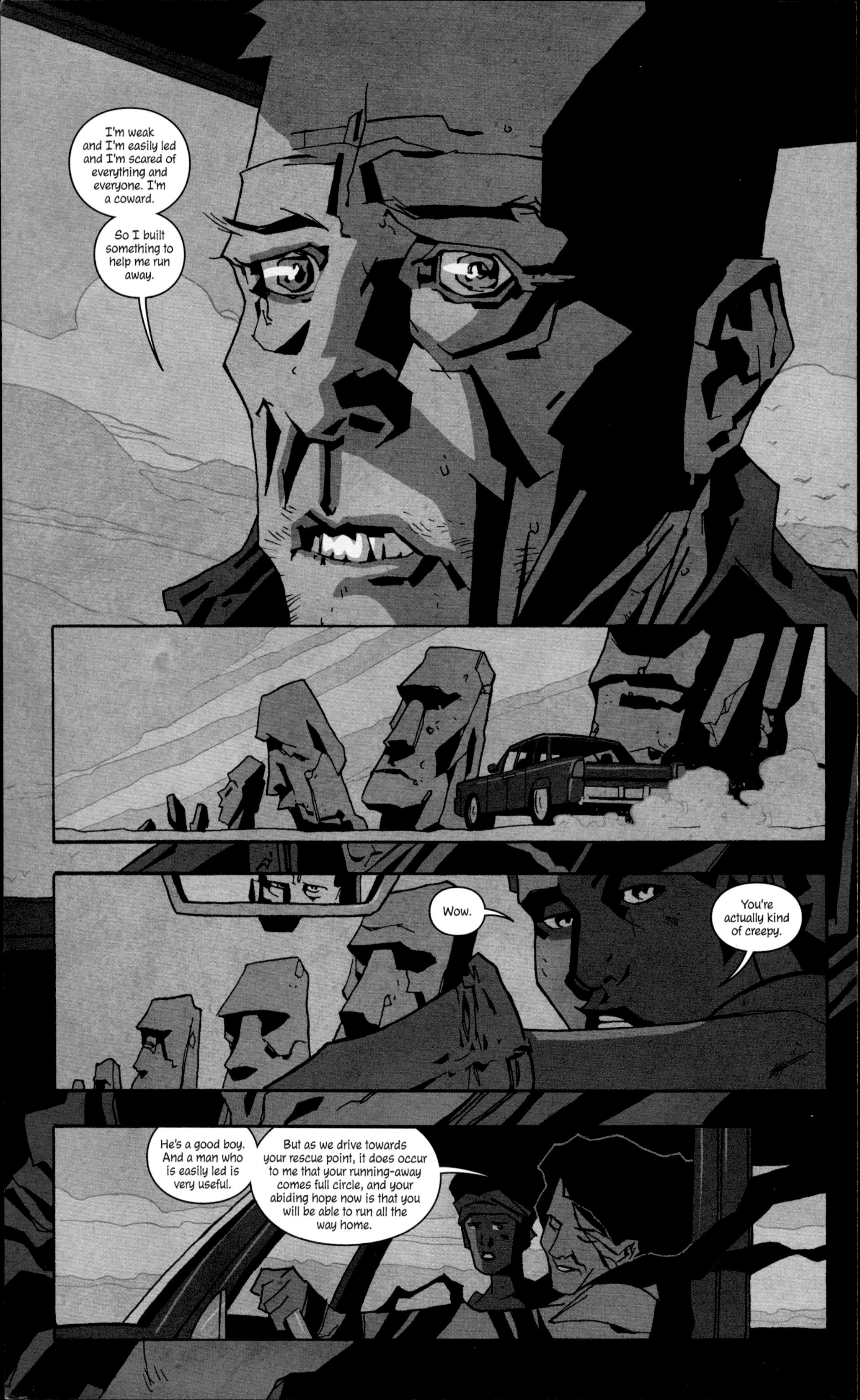
I'm weak and I'm easily led and I'm scared of everything and everyone. I'm a coward.
So I built something to help me run away.
Wow.
You're actually kind of creepy.
He's a good boy. And a man who is easily led is very useful.
But as we drive towards your rescue point, it does occur to me that your running-away comes full circle, and your abiding hope now is that you will be able to run all the way home.

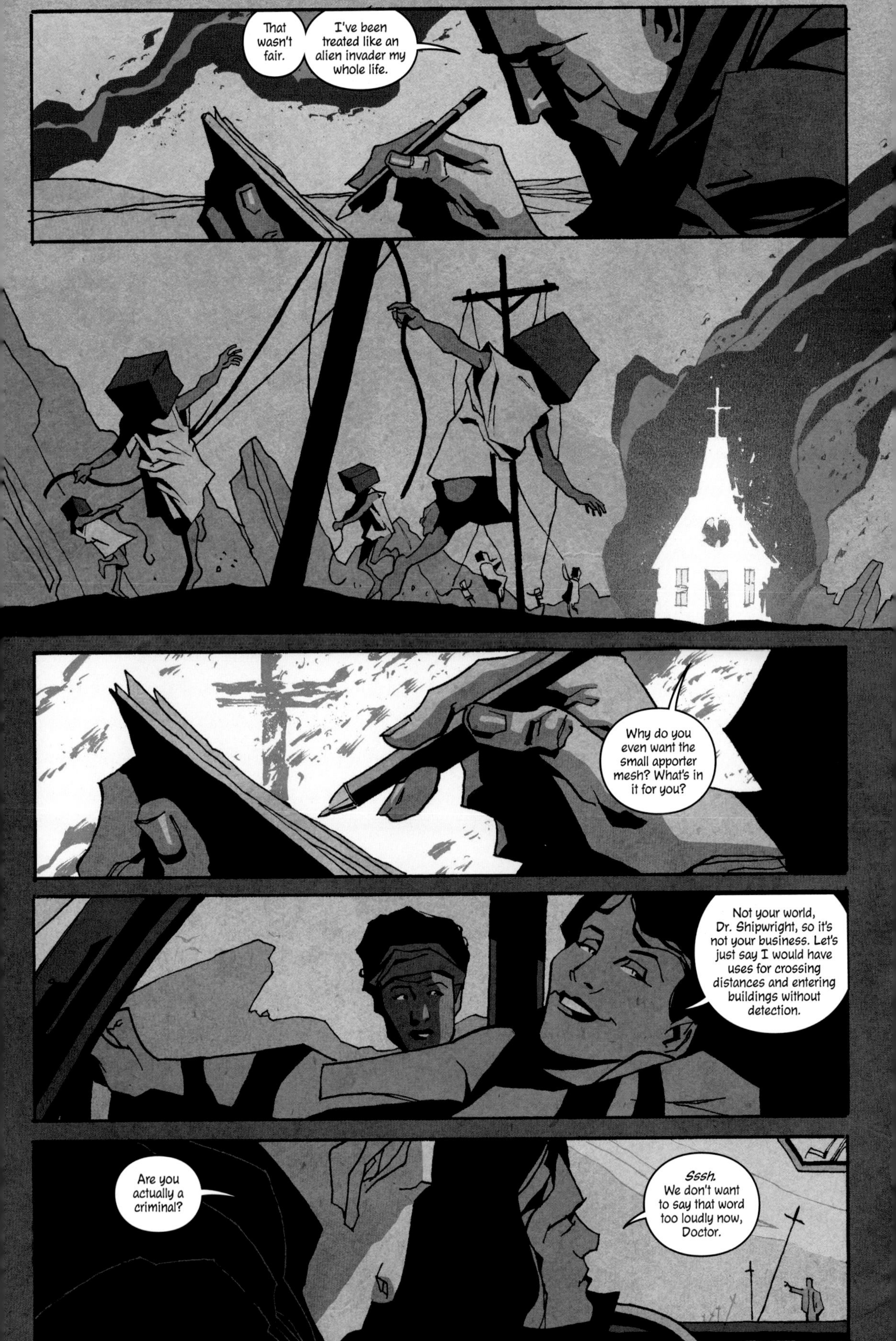
That wasn't fair.
I've been treated like an alien invader my whole life.
Why do you even want the small apporter mesh? What's in it for you?
Not your world, Dr. Shipwright, so it's not your business. Let's just say I would have uses for crossing distances and entering buildings without detection.
Are you actually a criminal?
Sssh. We don't want to say that word too loudly now, Doctor.

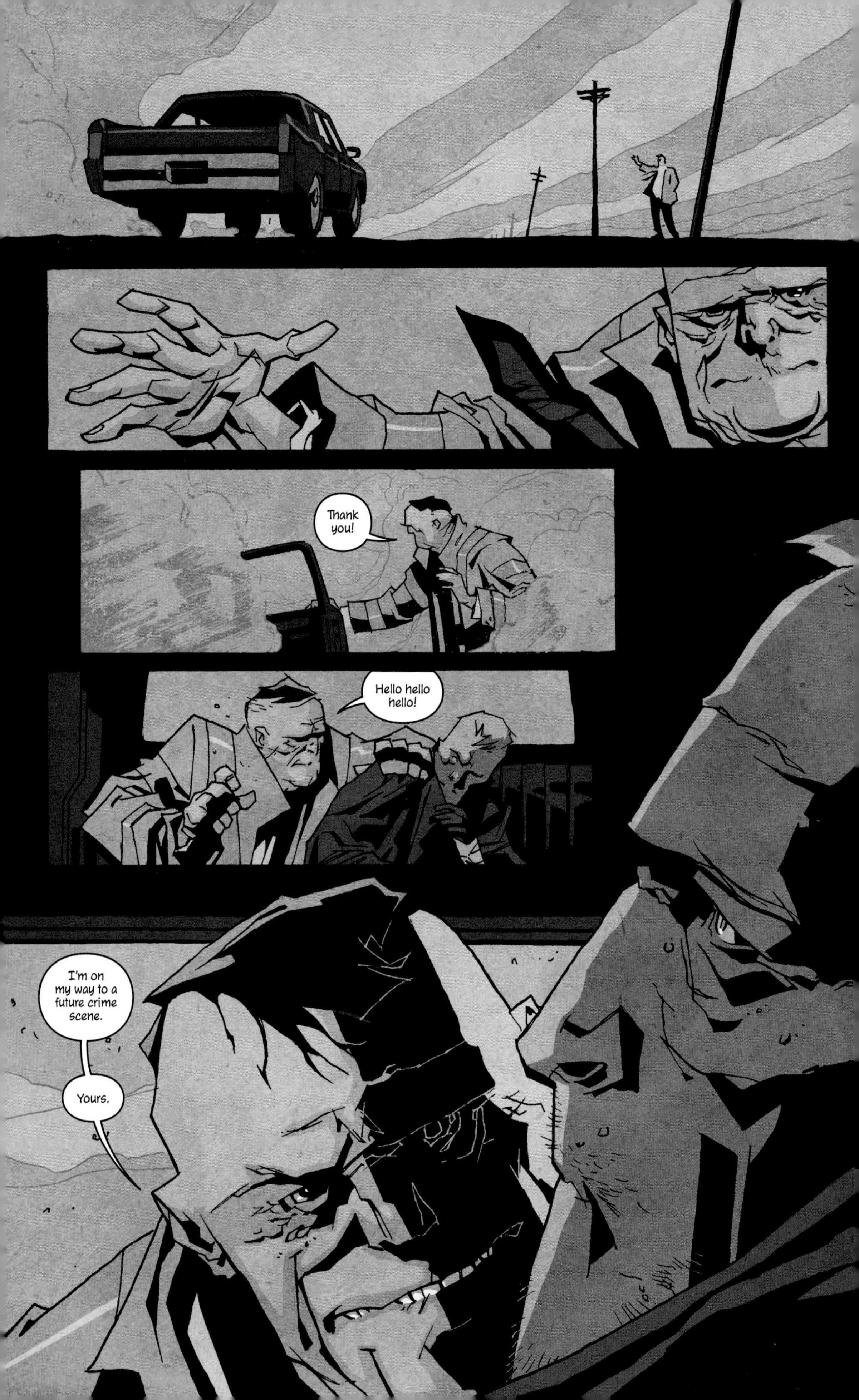
Thank you!
Hello hello hello!
I'm on my way to a future crime scene.
Yours.

6

"SAVED"

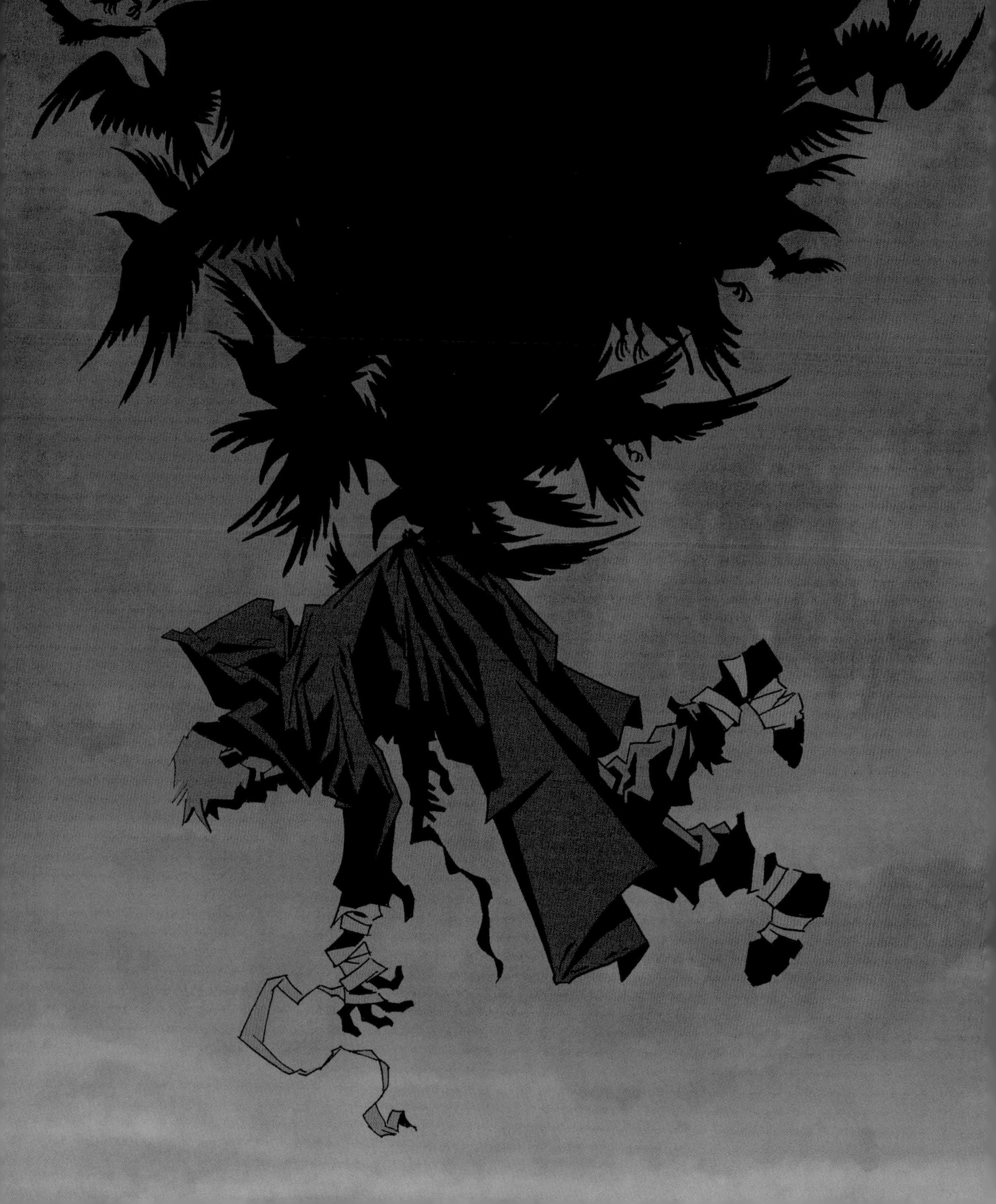

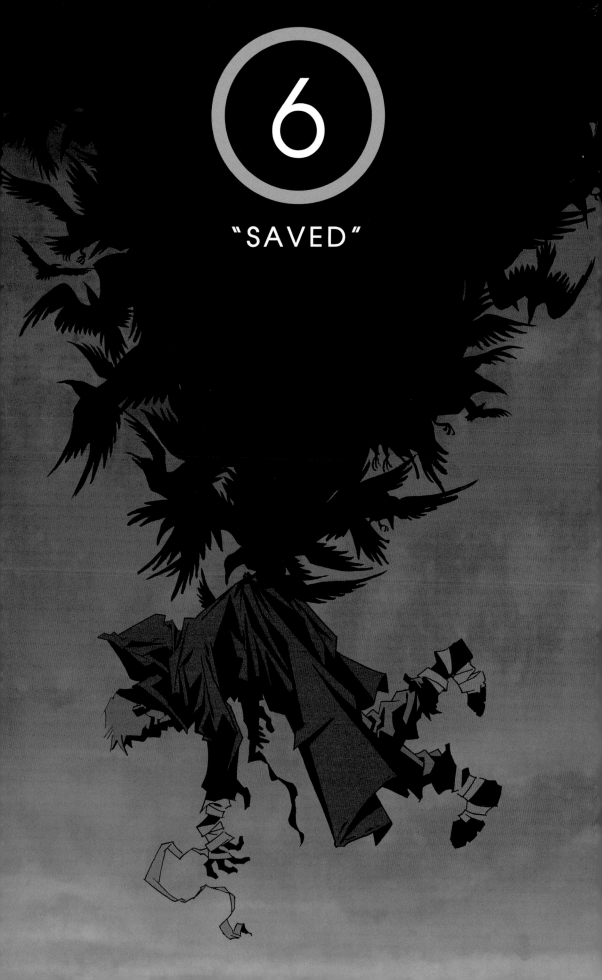

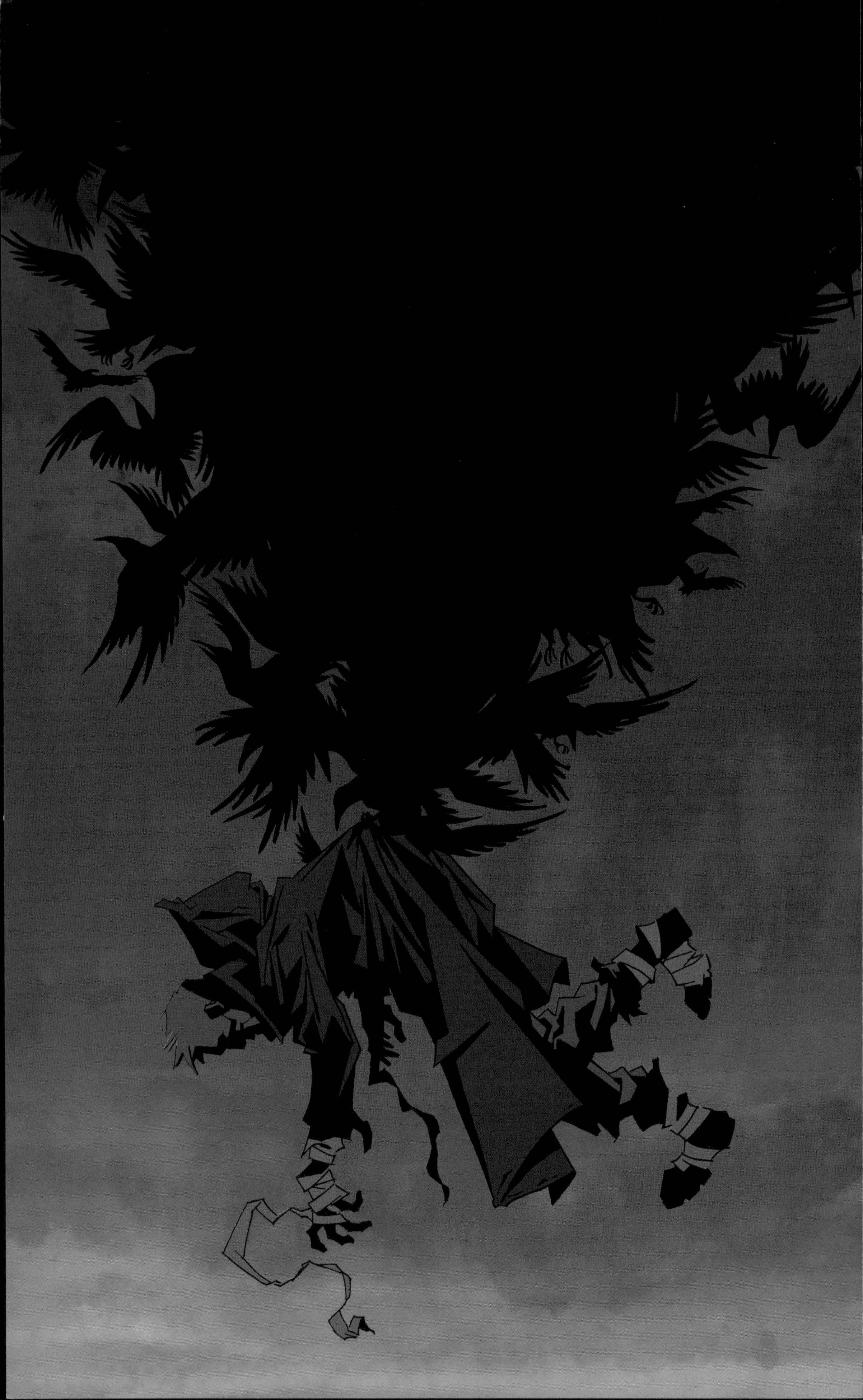

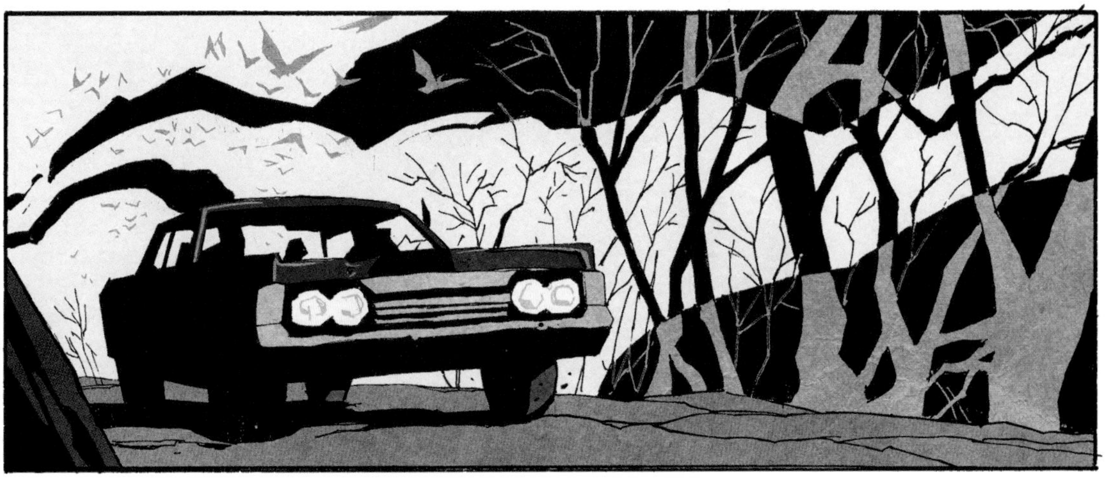

Shipwreck

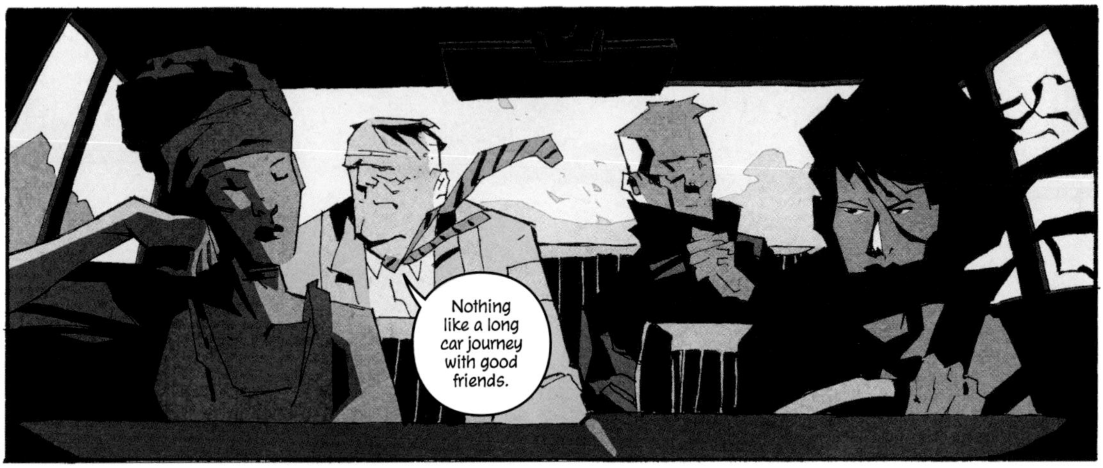
Nothing like a long car journey with good friends.

6. Saved

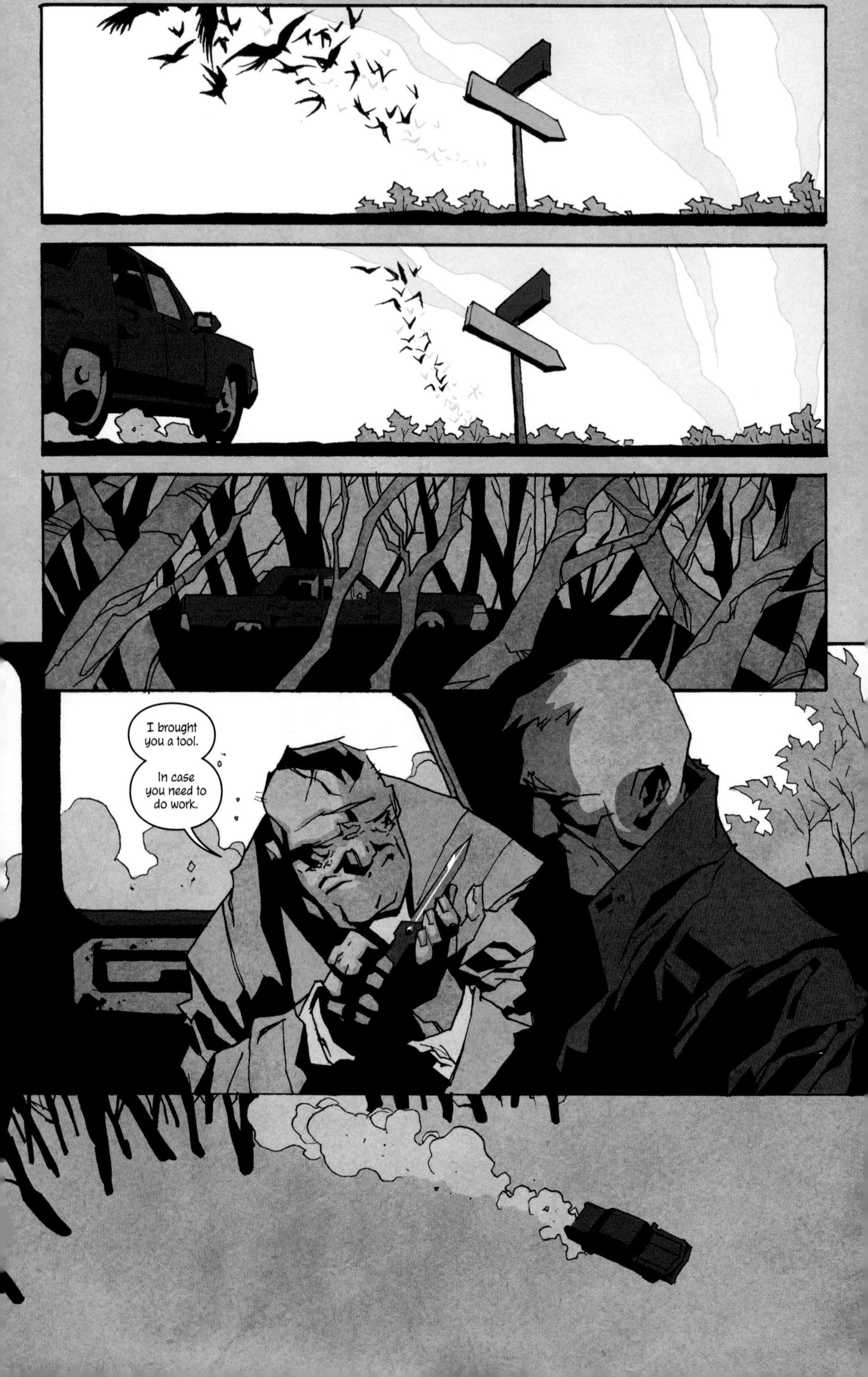
I brought you a tool.
In case you need to do work.

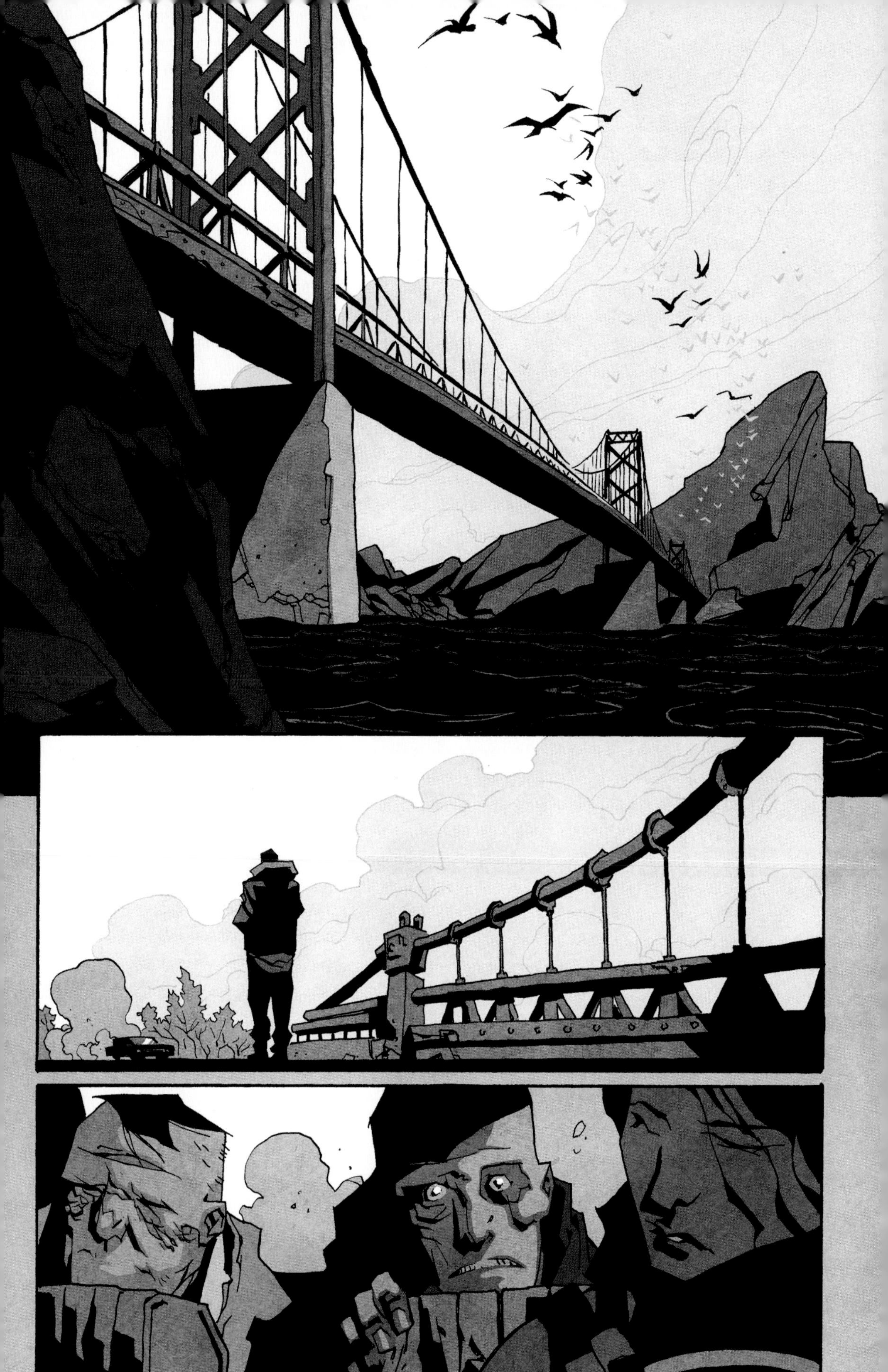

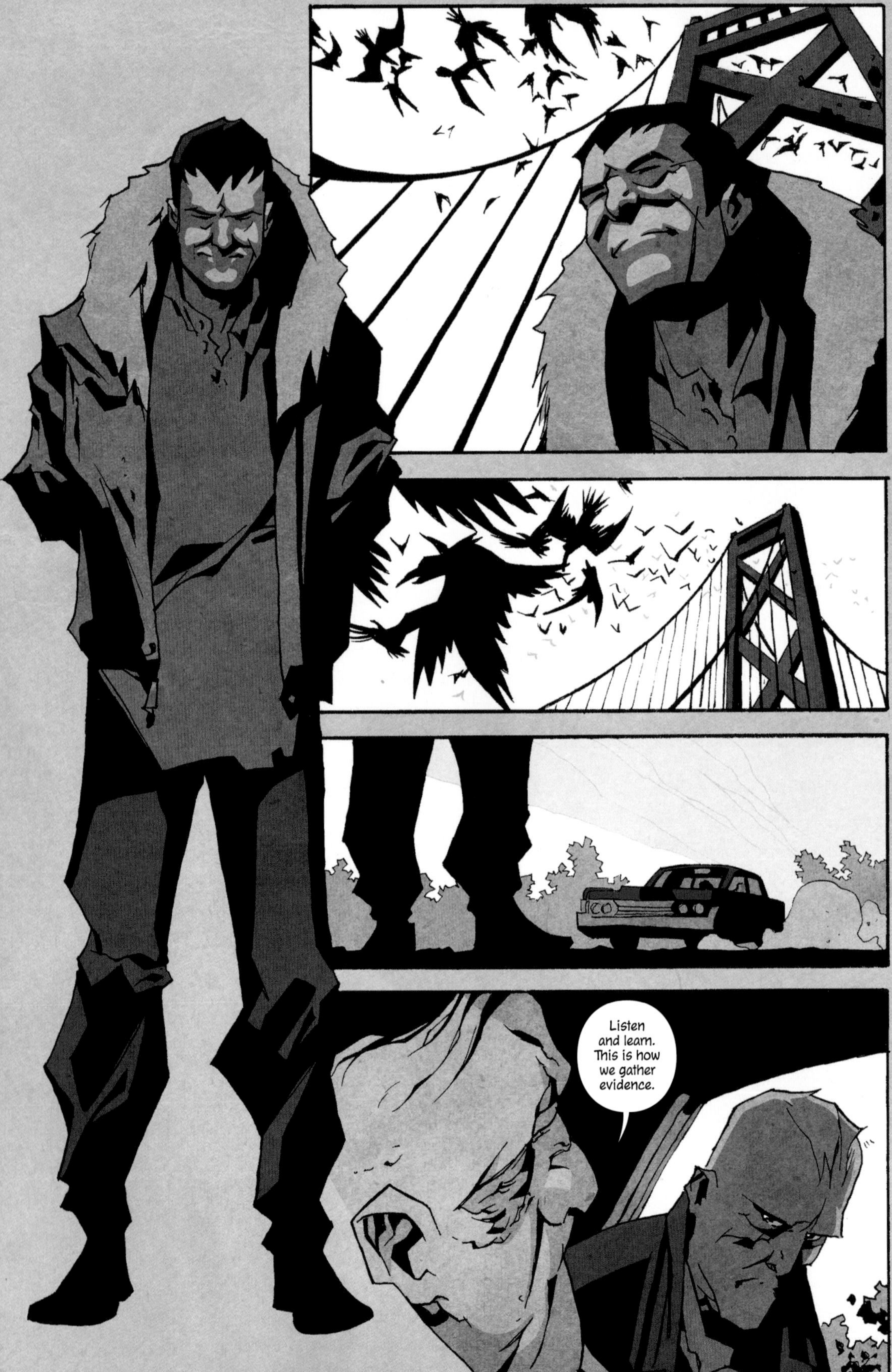
Listen and learn. This is how we gather evidence.

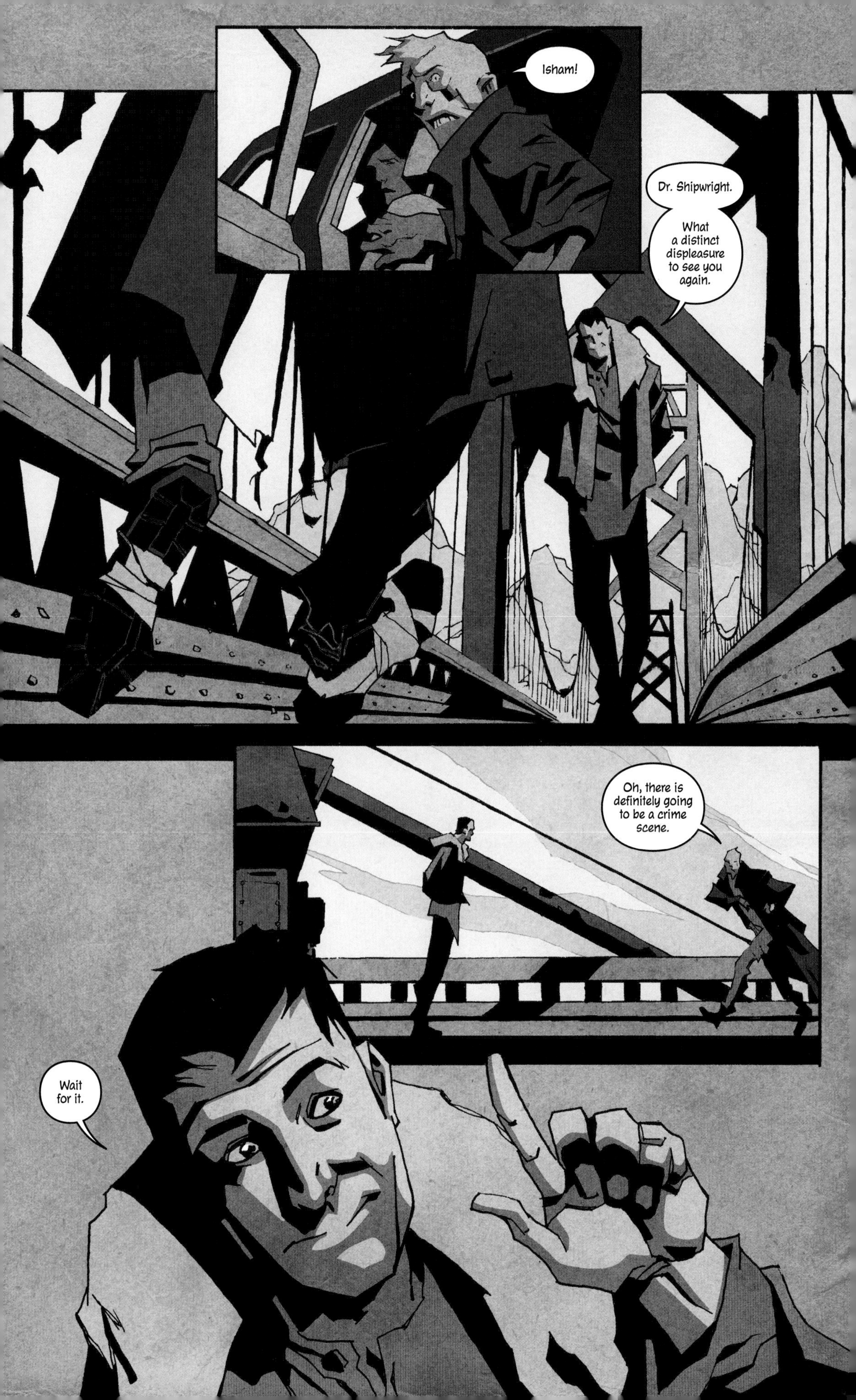
Isham!
Dr. Shipwright.
What a distinct displeasure to see you again.
Oh, there is definitely going to be a crime scene.
Wait for it.

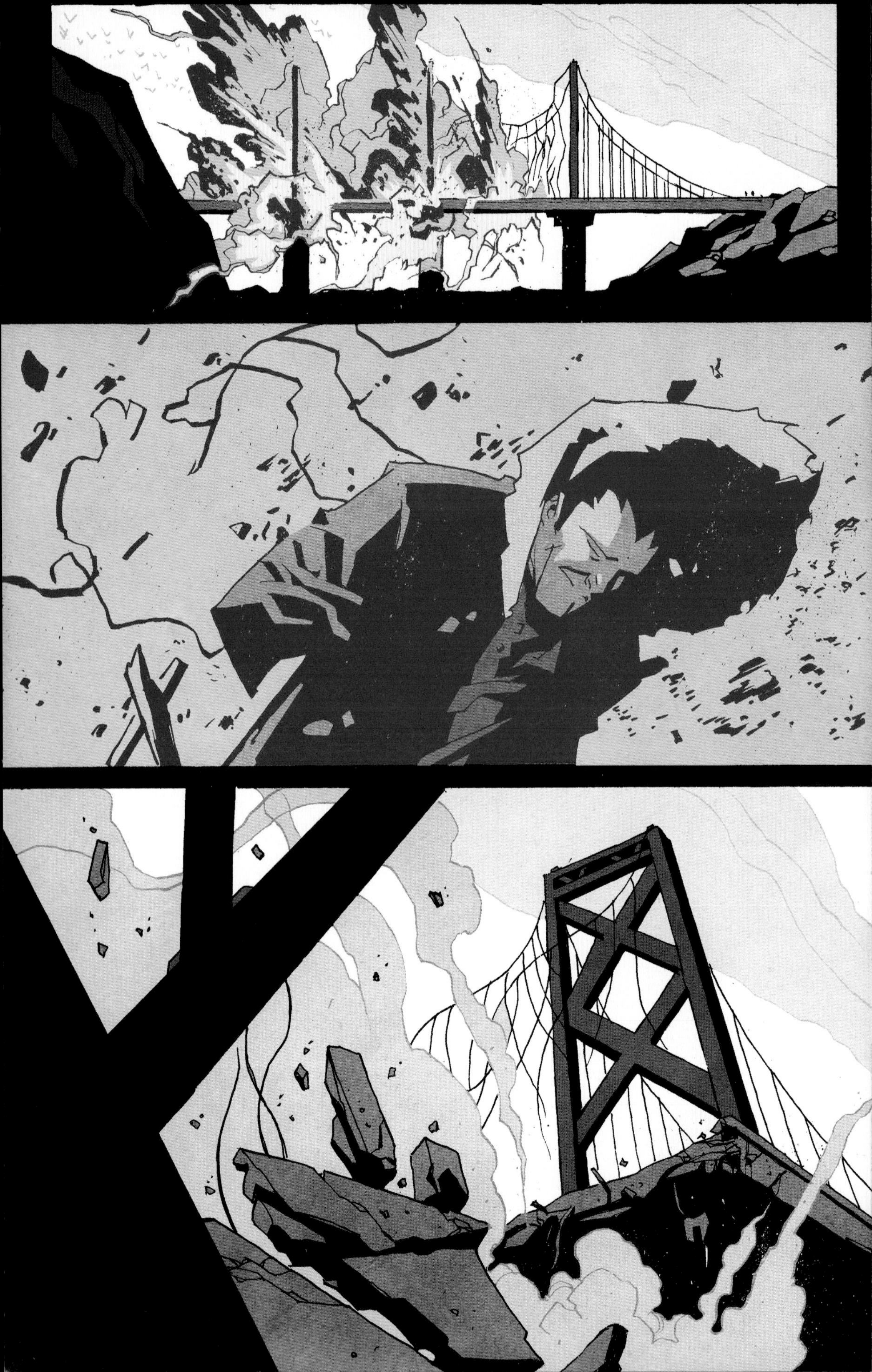

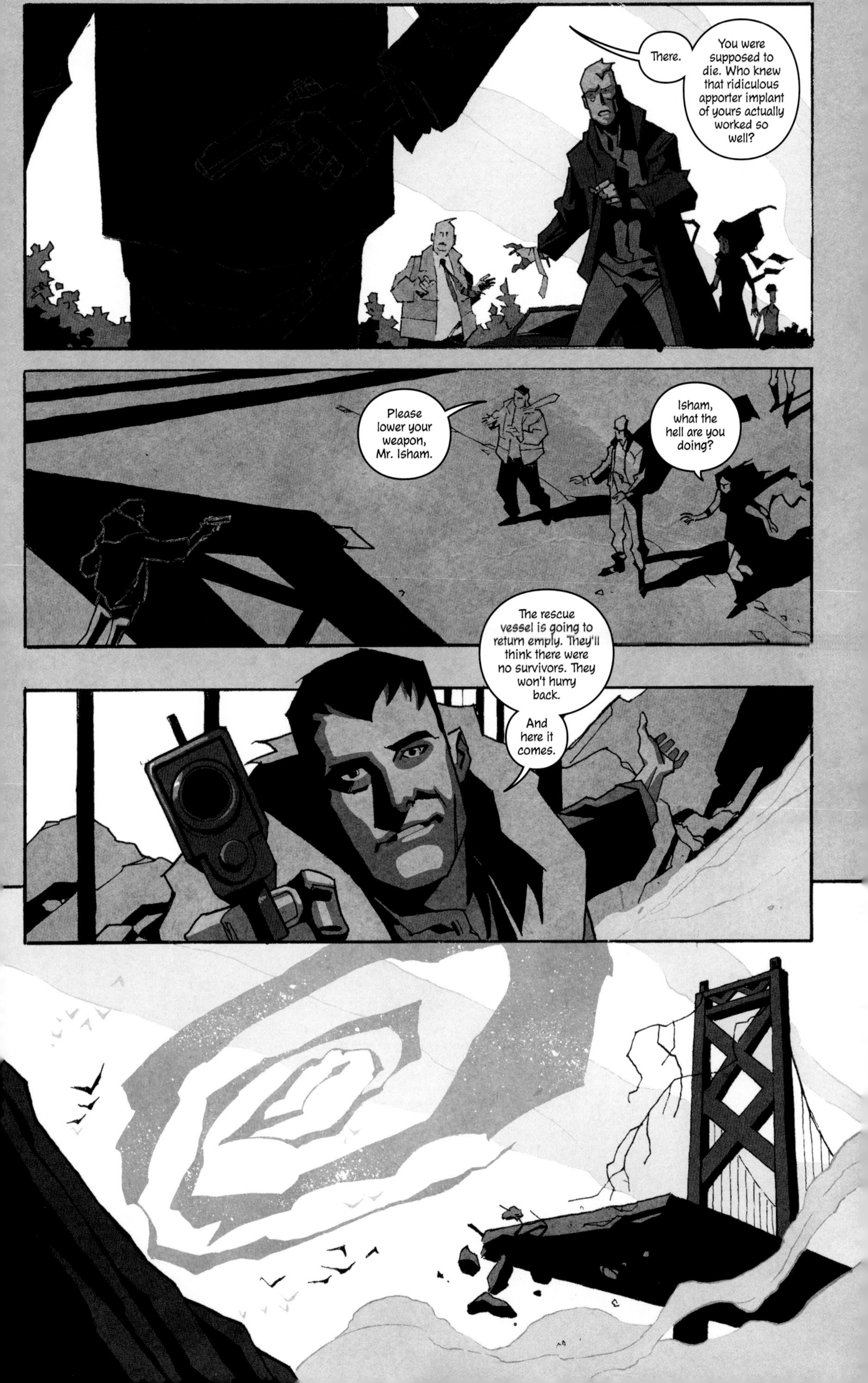
There.
You were supposed to die. Who knew that ridiculous apporter implant of yours actually worked so well?
Please lower your weapon, Mr. Isham.
Isham, what the hell are you doing?
The rescue vessel is going to return empty. They'll think there were no survivors. They won't hurry back.
And here it comes.

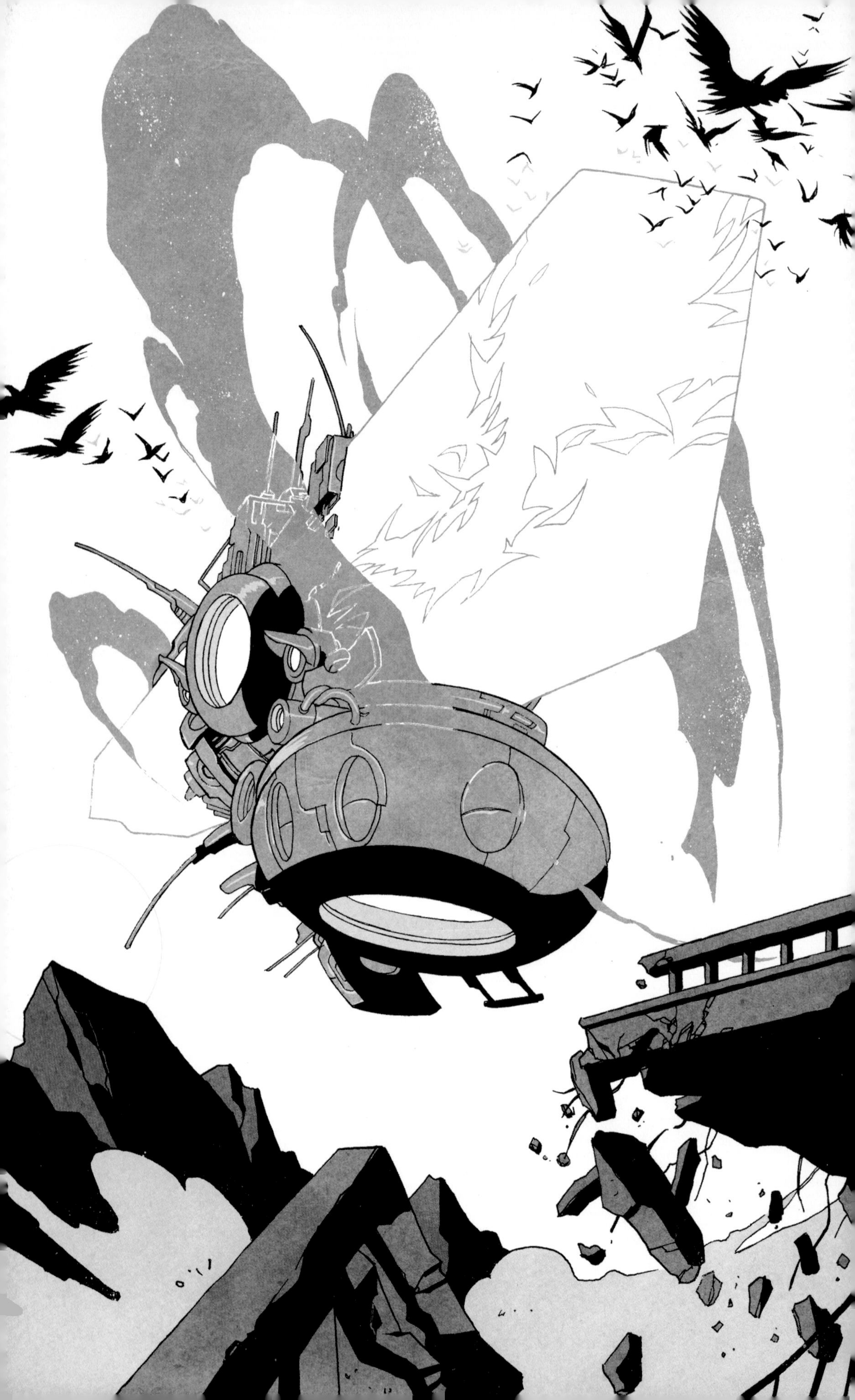

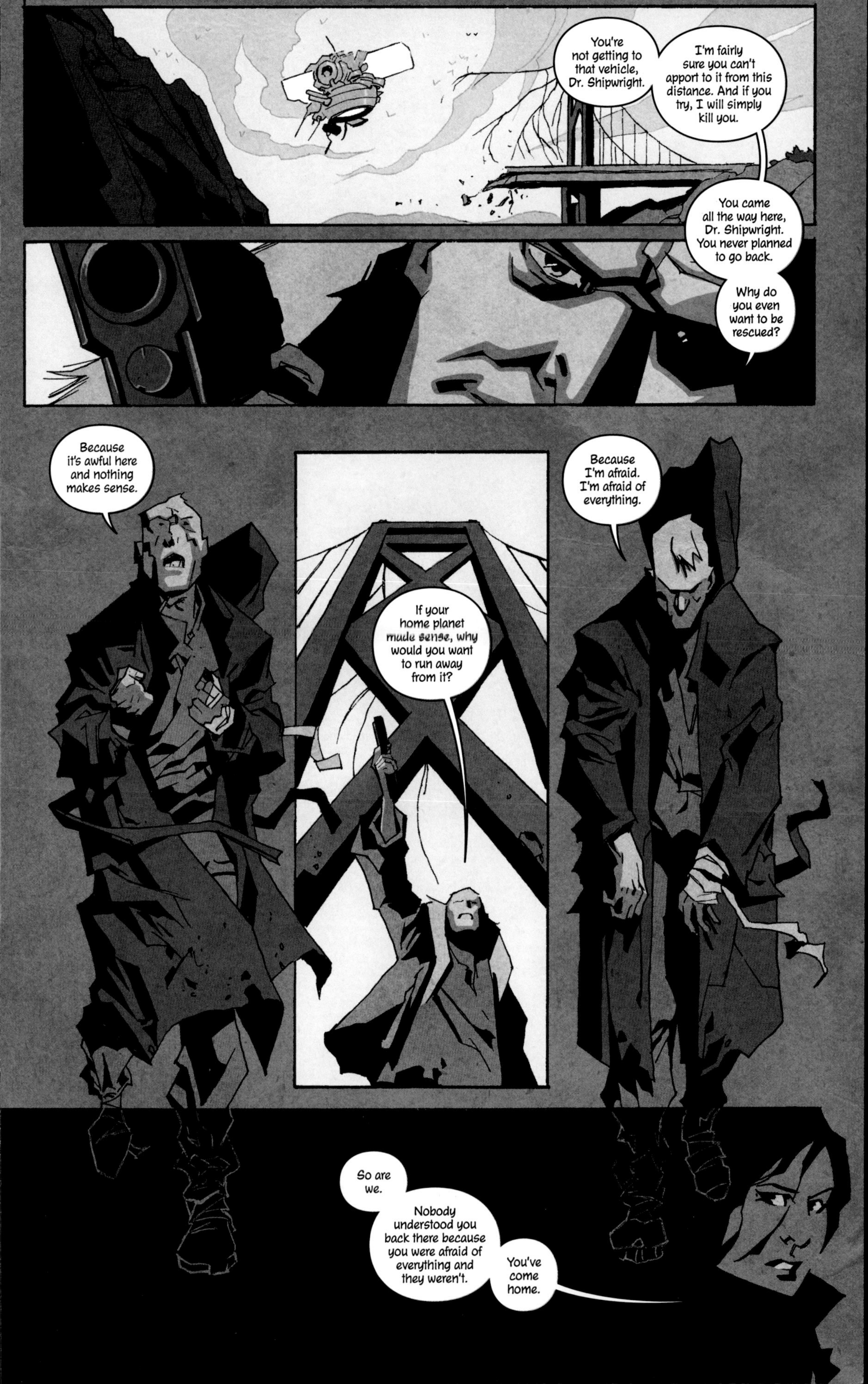
You're not getting to that vehicle, Dr. Shipwright.
I'm fairly sure you can't apport to it from this distance. And if you try, I will simply kill you.
You came all the way here, Dr. Shipwright. You never planned to go back.
Why do you even want to be rescued?
Because it's awful here and nothing makes sense.
If your home planet made sense, why would you want to run away from it?
Because I'm afraid. I'm afraid of everything.
So are we.
Nobody understood you back there because you were afraid of everything and they weren't.
You've come home.

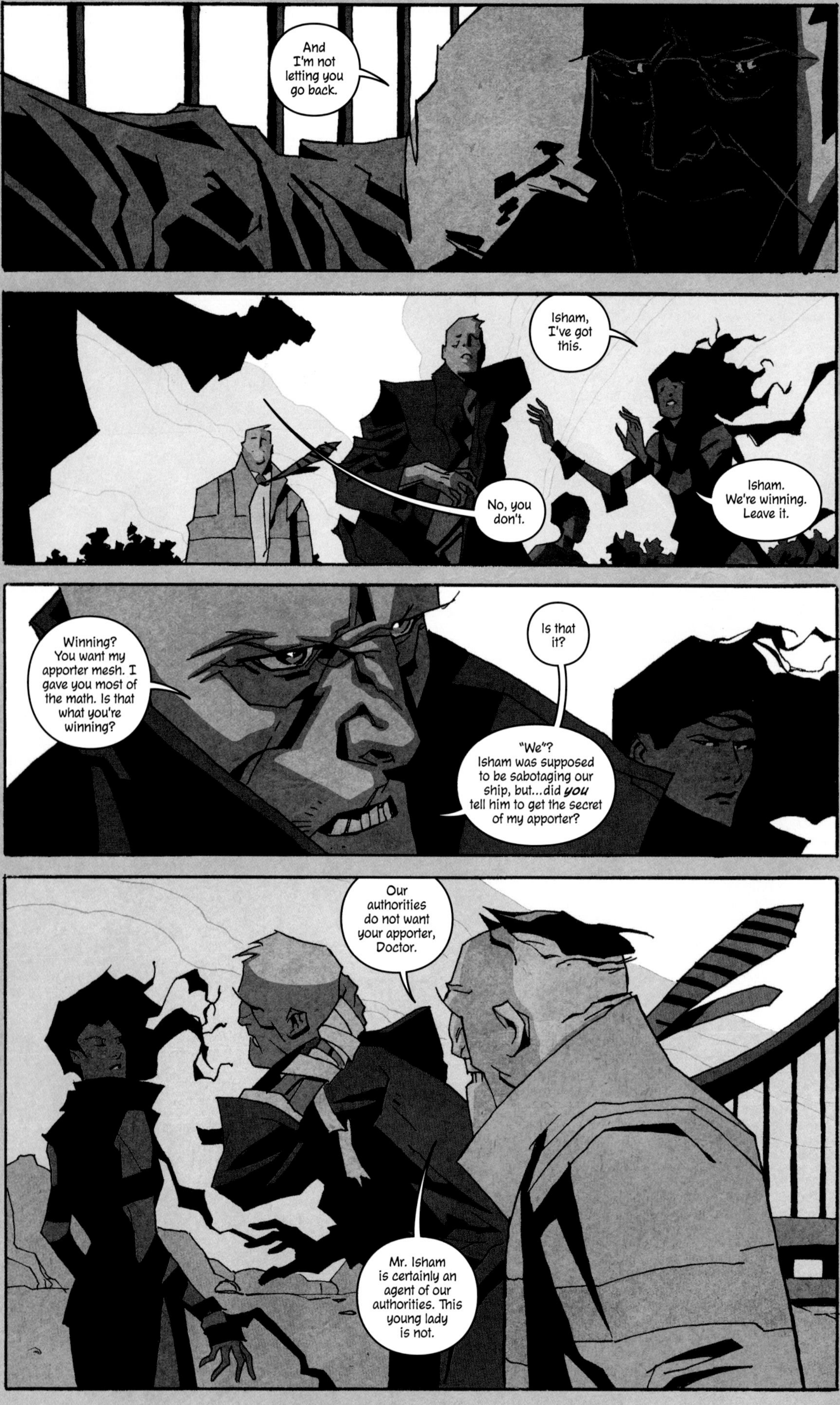
And I'm not letting you go back.
Isham, I've got this.
No, you don't.
Isham. We're winning. Leave it.
Winning? You want my apporter mesh. I gave you most of the math. Is that what you're winning?
Is that it?
"We"? Isham was supposed to be sabotaging our ship, but...did *you* tell him to get the secret of my apporter?
Our authorities do not want your apporter, Doctor.
Mr. Isham is certainly an agent of our authorities. This young lady is not.

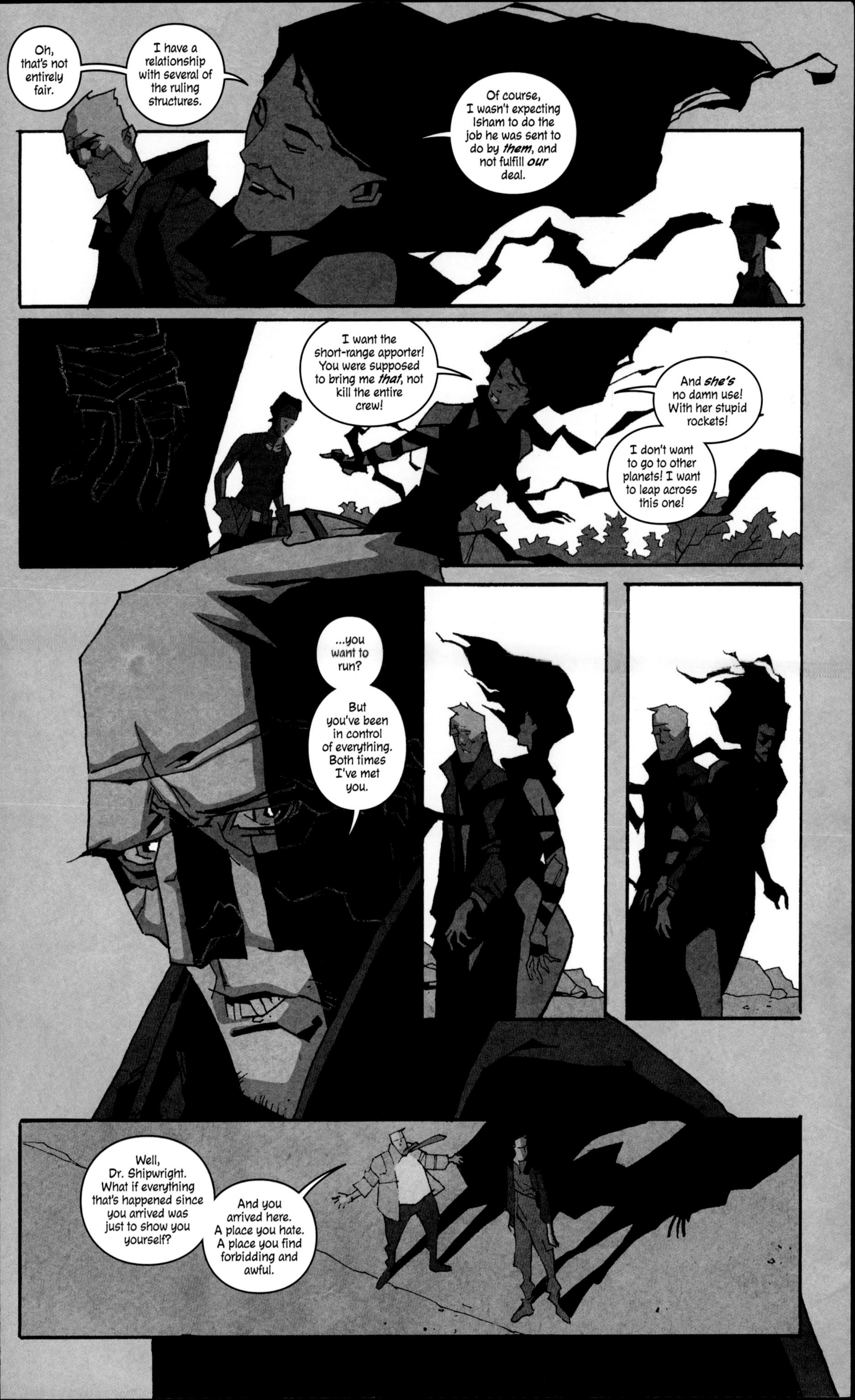
Oh, that's not entirely fair.
I have a relationship with several of the ruling structures.
Of course, I wasn't expecting Isham to do the job he was sent to do by *them*, and not fulfill *our* deal.
I want the short-range apporter! You were supposed to bring me *that*, not kill the entire crew!
And *she's* no damn use! With her stupid rockets!
I don't want to go to other planets! I want to leap across this one!
...you want to run?
But you've been in control of everything. Both times I've met you.
Well, Dr. Shipwright. What if everything that's happened since you arrived was just to show you yourself?
And you arrived here. A place you hate. A place you find forbidding and awful.

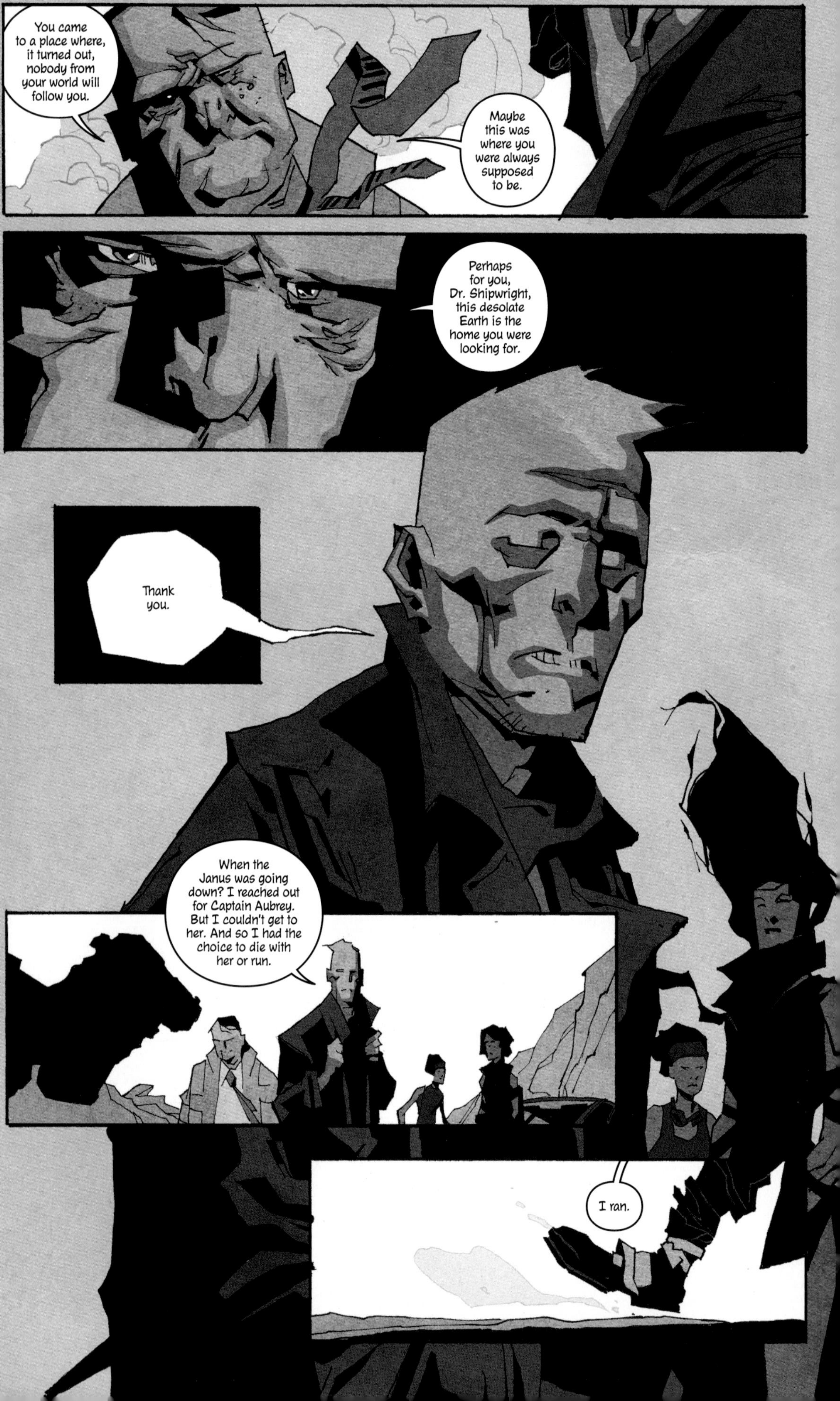
You came to a place where, it turned out, nobody from your world will follow you.
Maybe this was where you were always supposed to be.
Perhaps for you, Dr. Shipwright, this desolate Earth is the home you were looking for.
Thank you.
When the Janus was going down? I reached out for Captain Aubrey. But I couldn't get to her. And so I had the choice to die with her or run.
I ran.

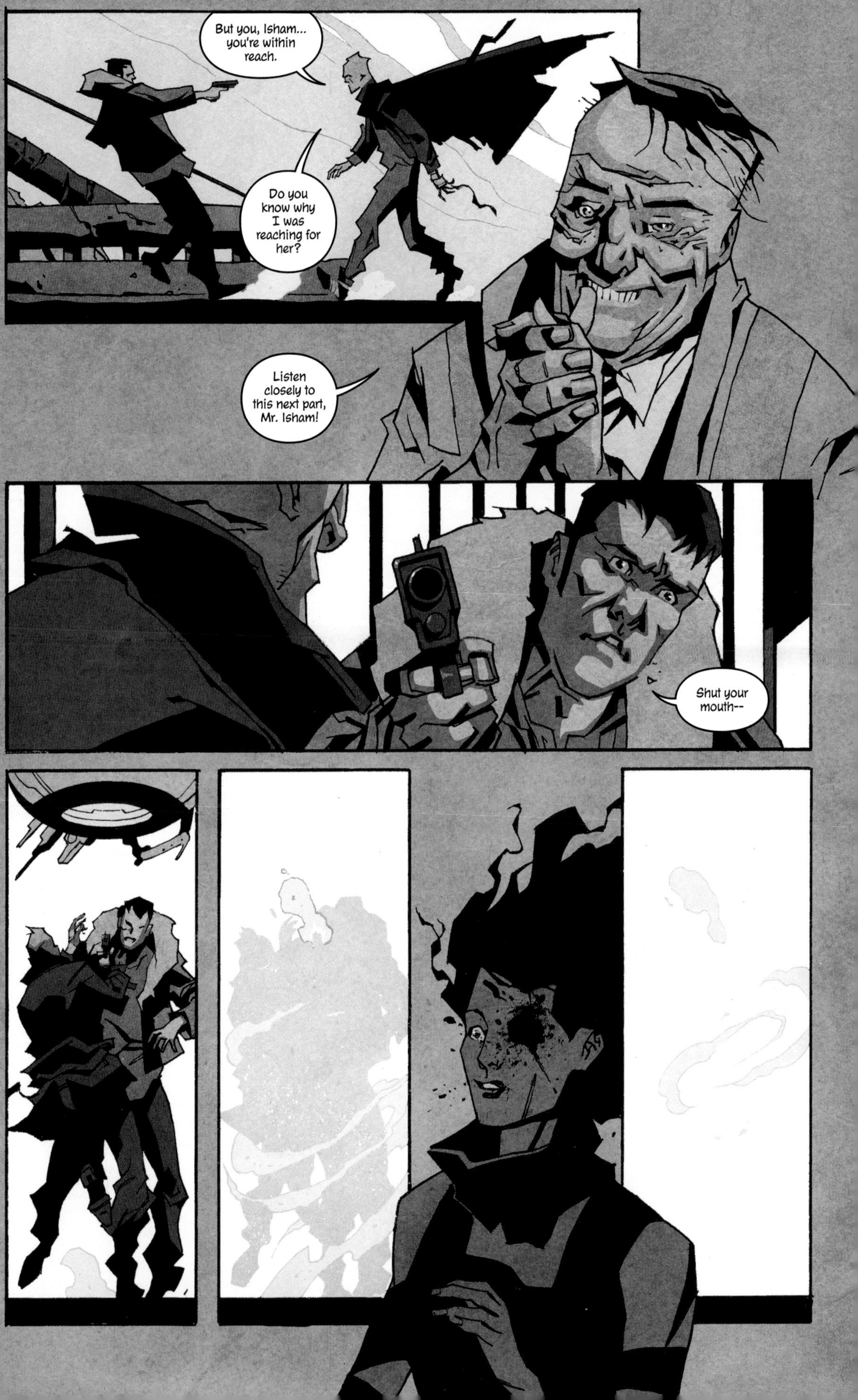

But you, Isham... you're within reach.
Do you know why I was reaching for her?
Listen closely to this next part, Mr. Isham!
Shut your mouth--

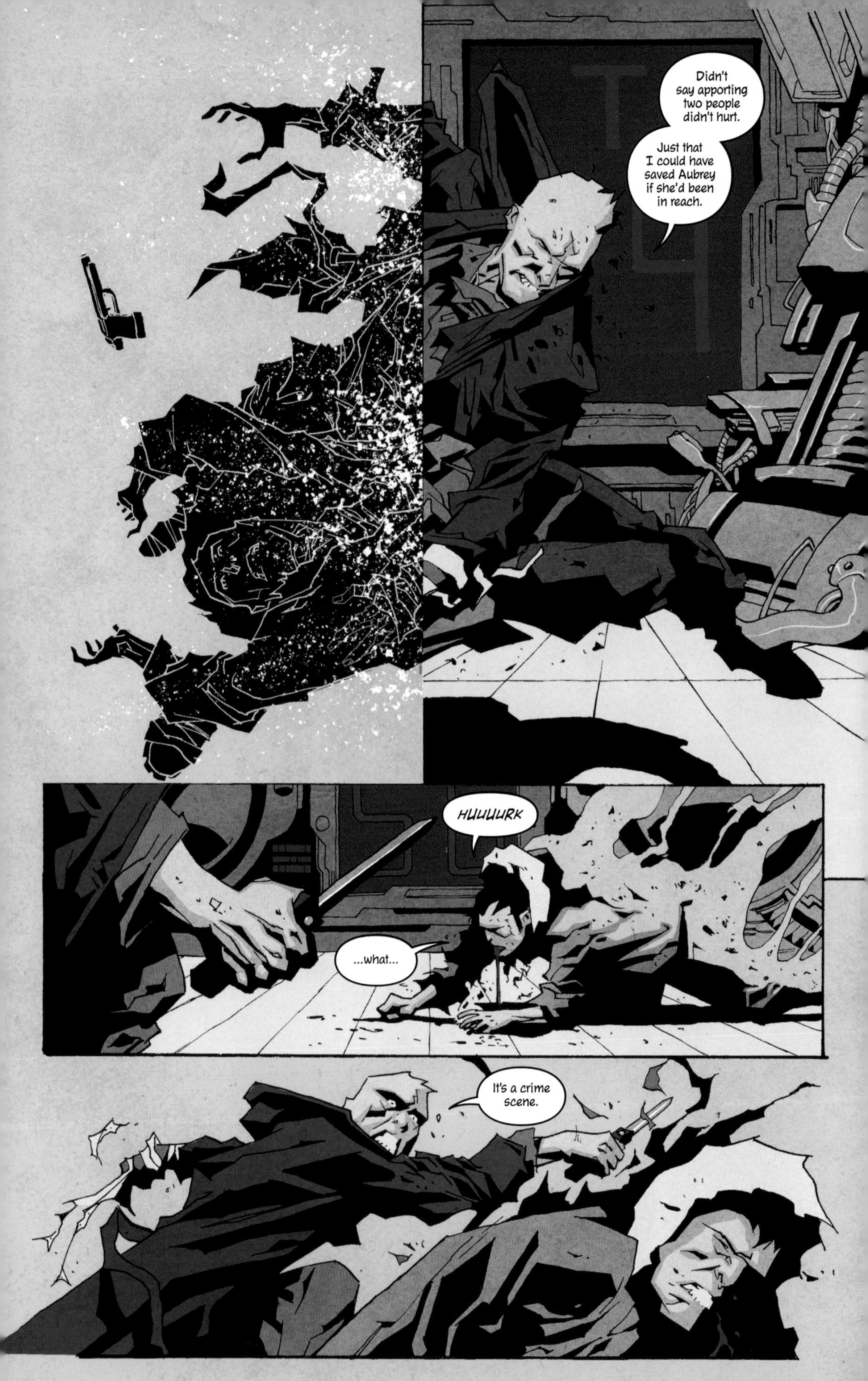
Didn't say apporting two people didn't hurt.
Just that I could have saved Aubrey if she'd been in reach.
HUUUURK
...what...
It's a crime scene.

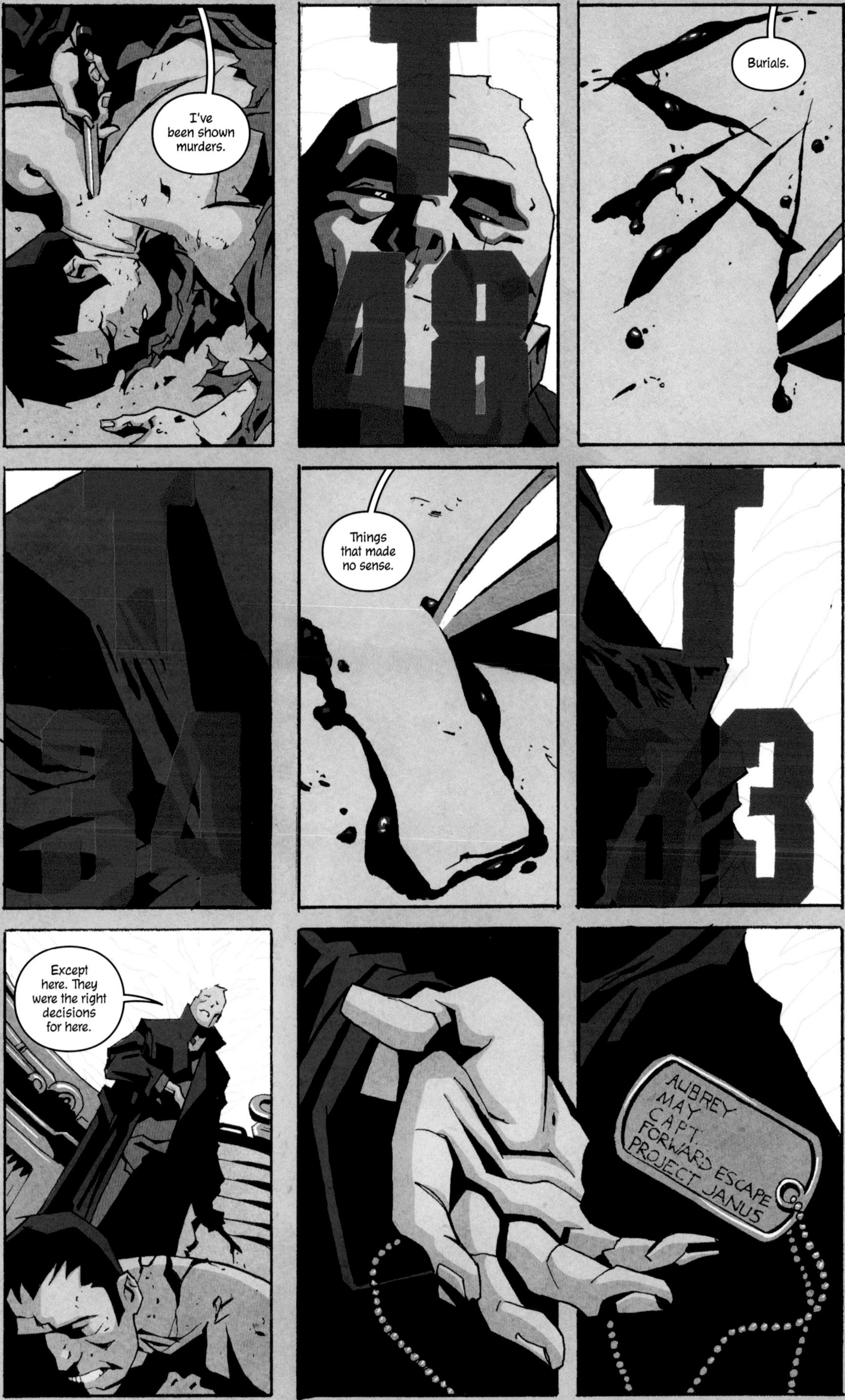
I've been shown murders.
Burials.
Things that made no sense.
Except here. They were the right decisions for here.
AUBREY
MAY
CAPT.
FORWARD ESCAPE
PROJECT JANUS

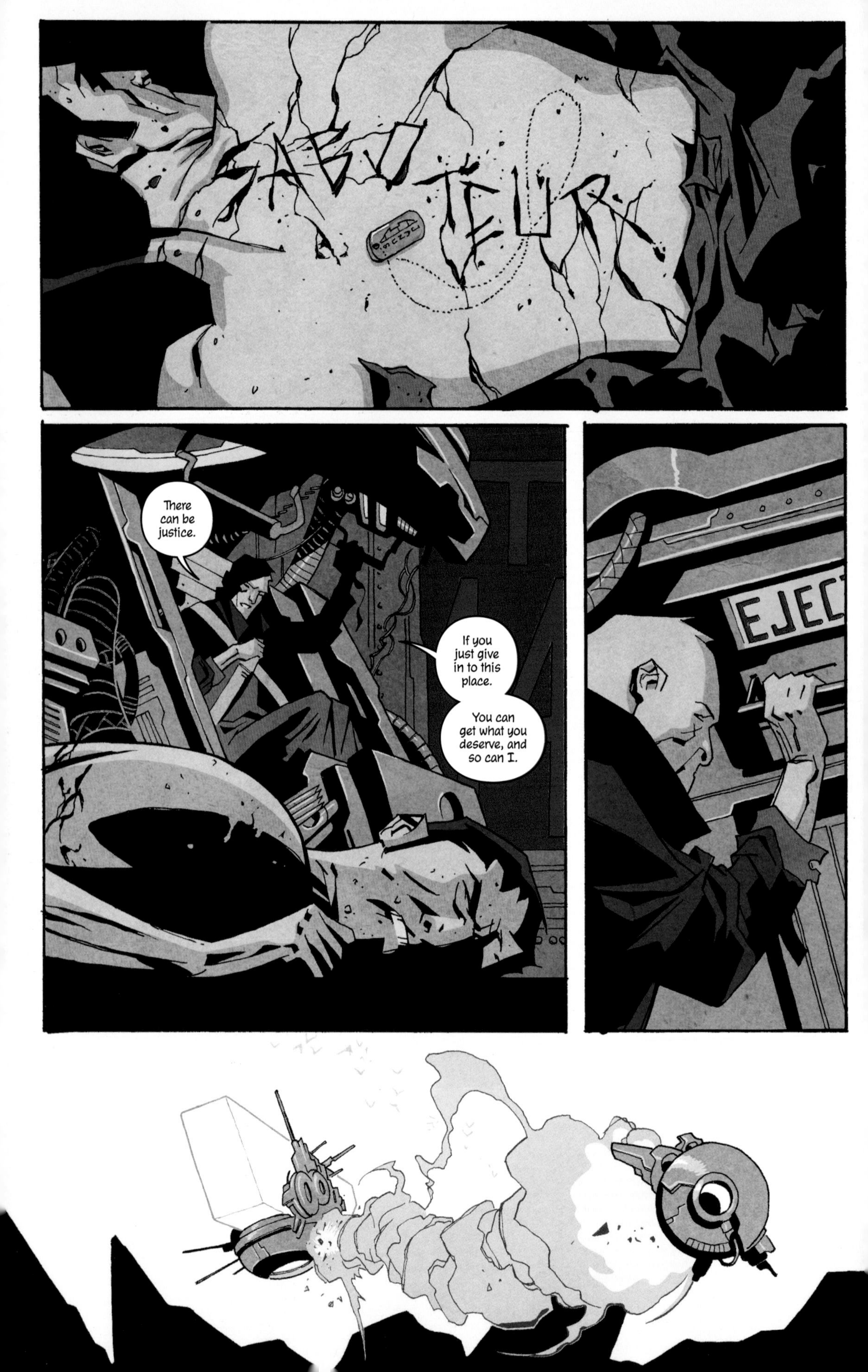
SABOTEUR
There can be justice.
If you just give in to this place.
You can get what you deserve, and so can I.
EJEC

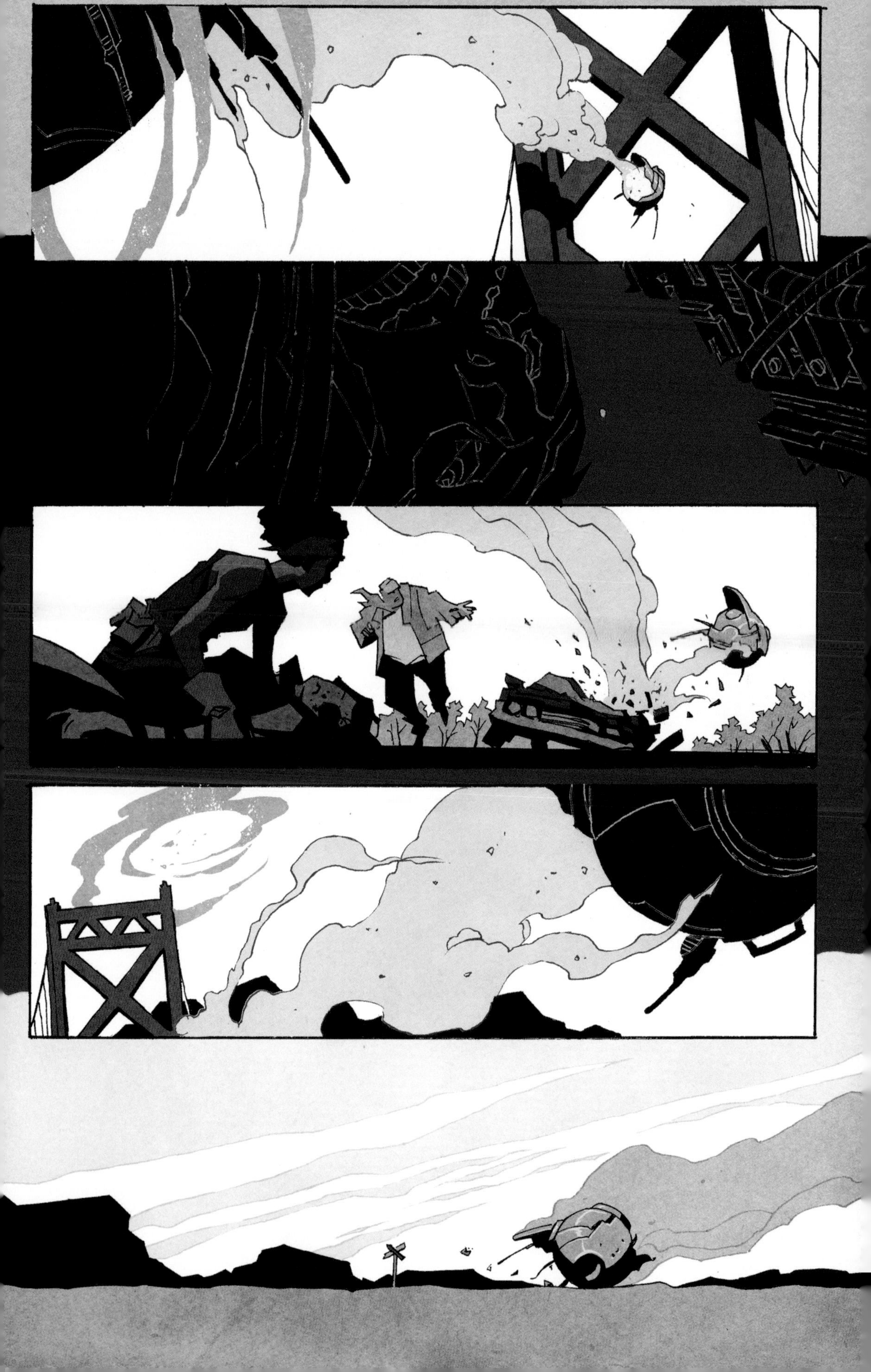

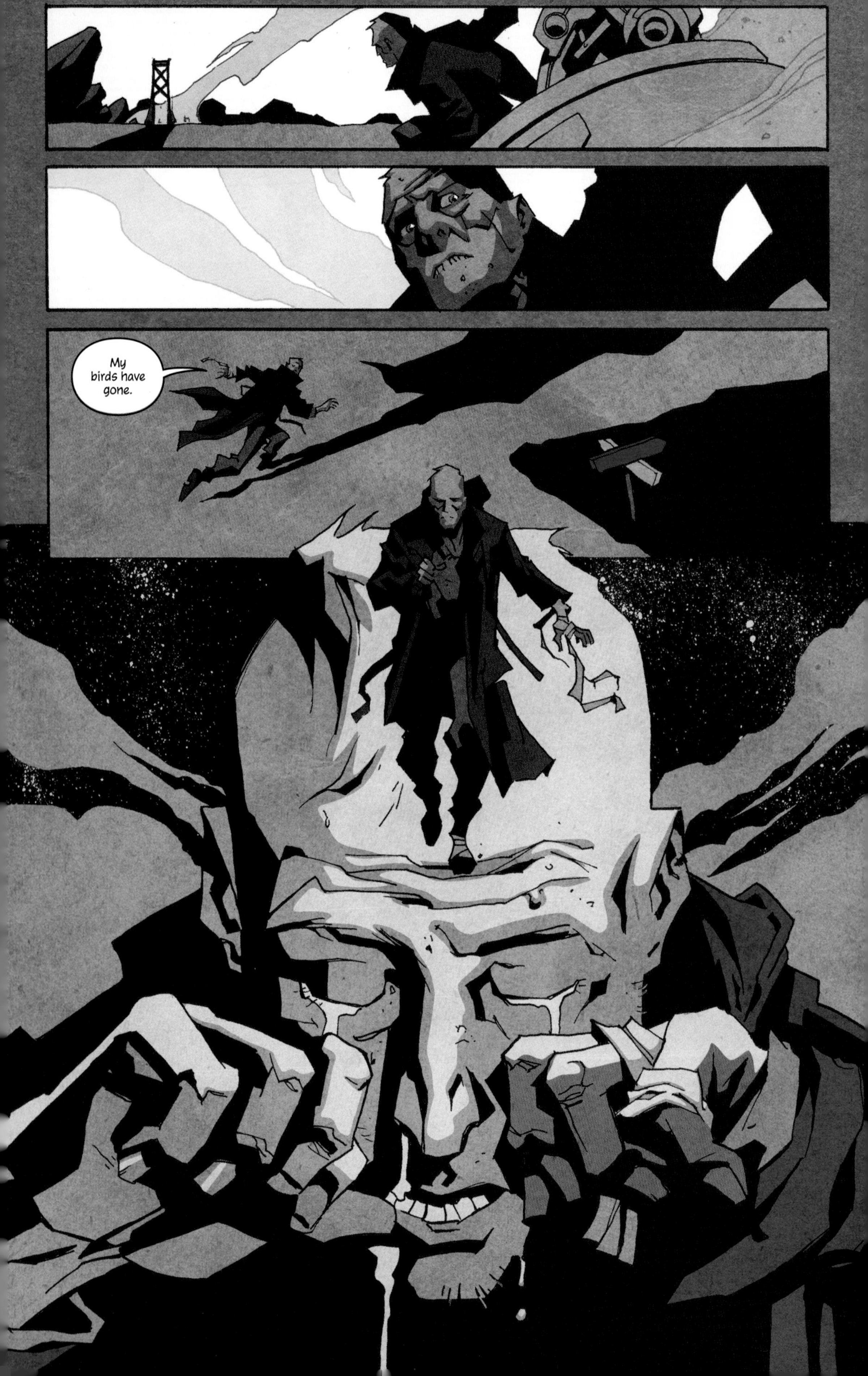
My birds have gone.

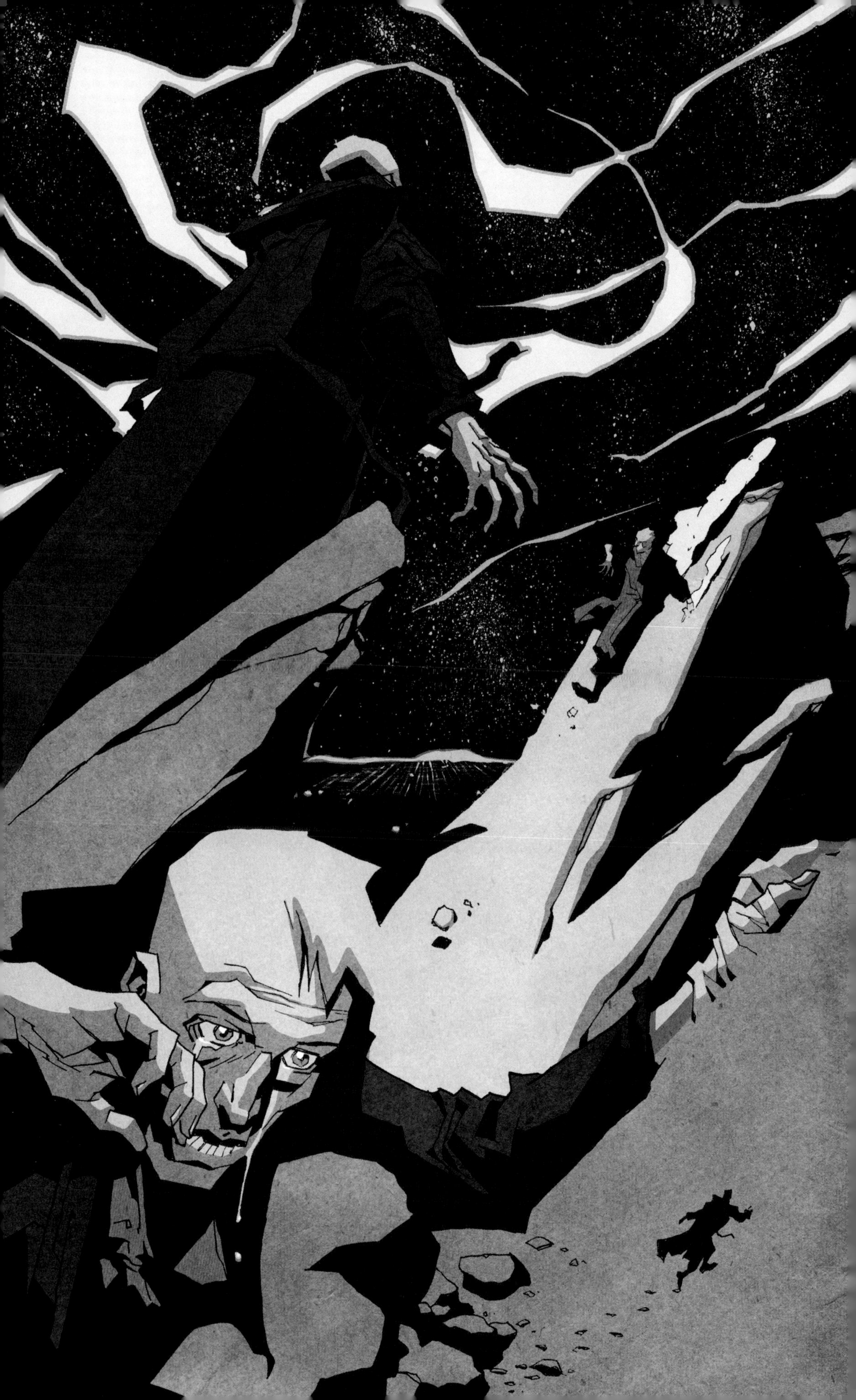

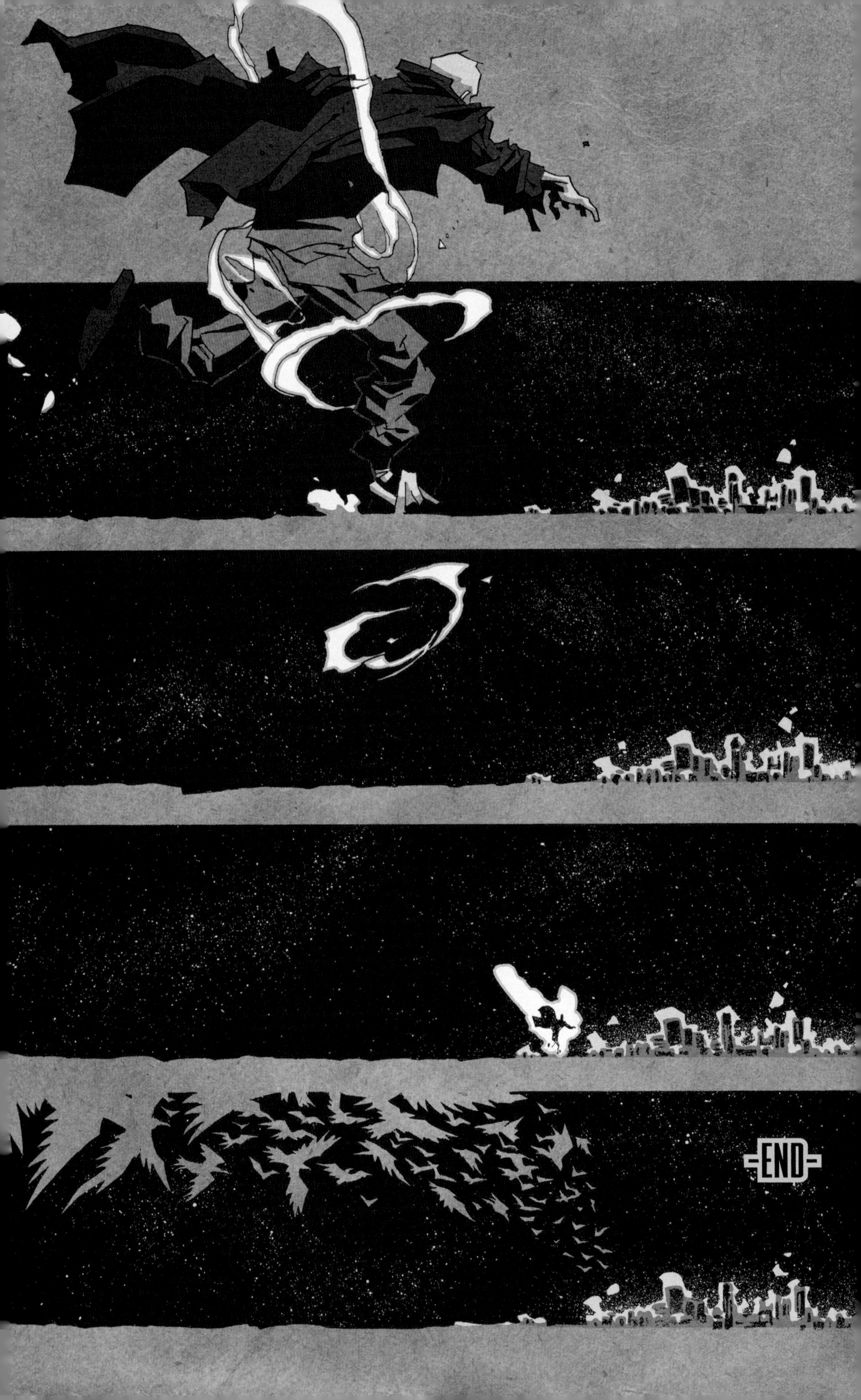
END

SHIPWRECK™

EXTRAS

AFTERSHOCK™

Issue 1
PHIL HESTER w/ **MARK ENGLERT**
Blindbox variant cover

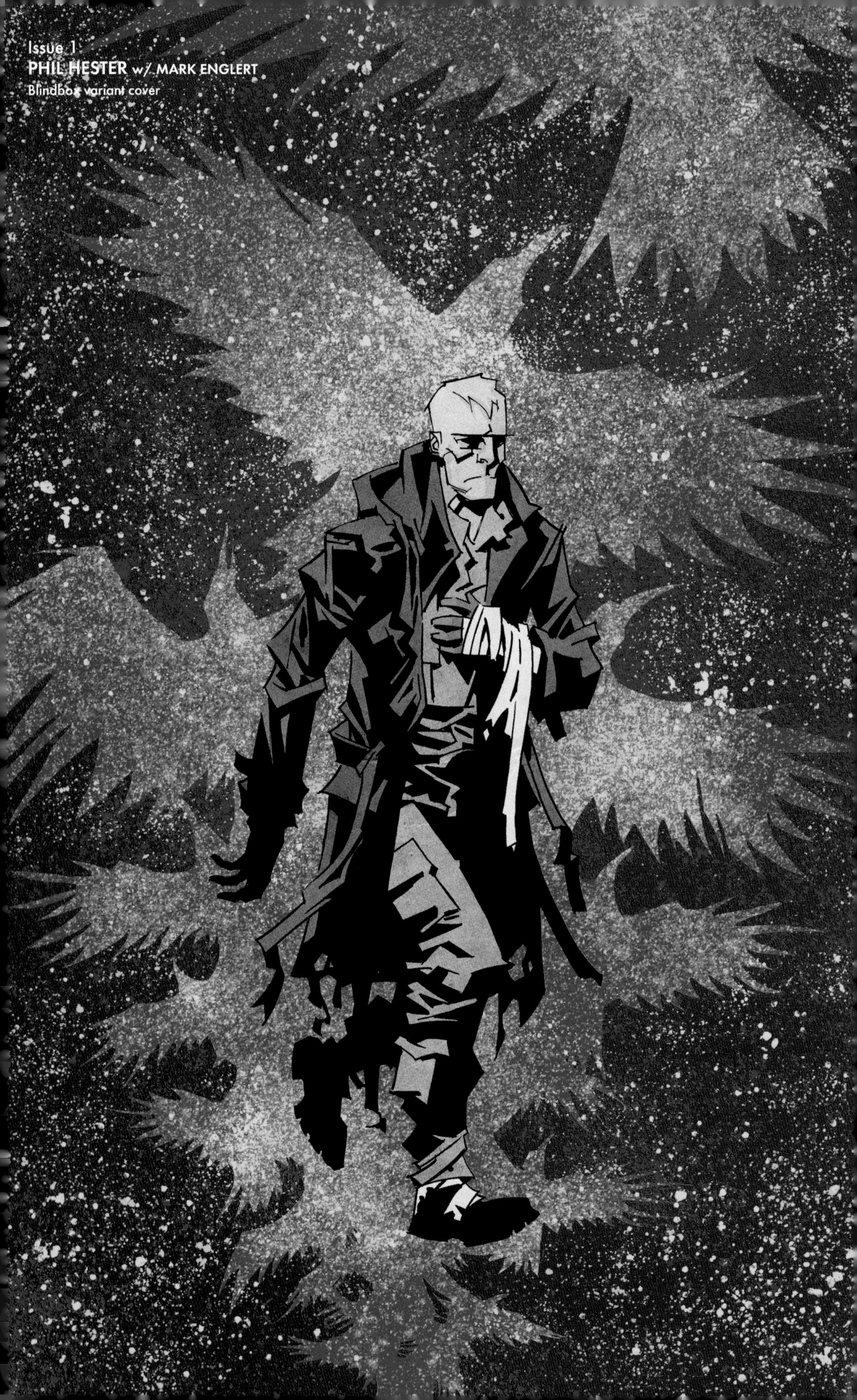

Issue 1
JOHN McCREA
variant cover

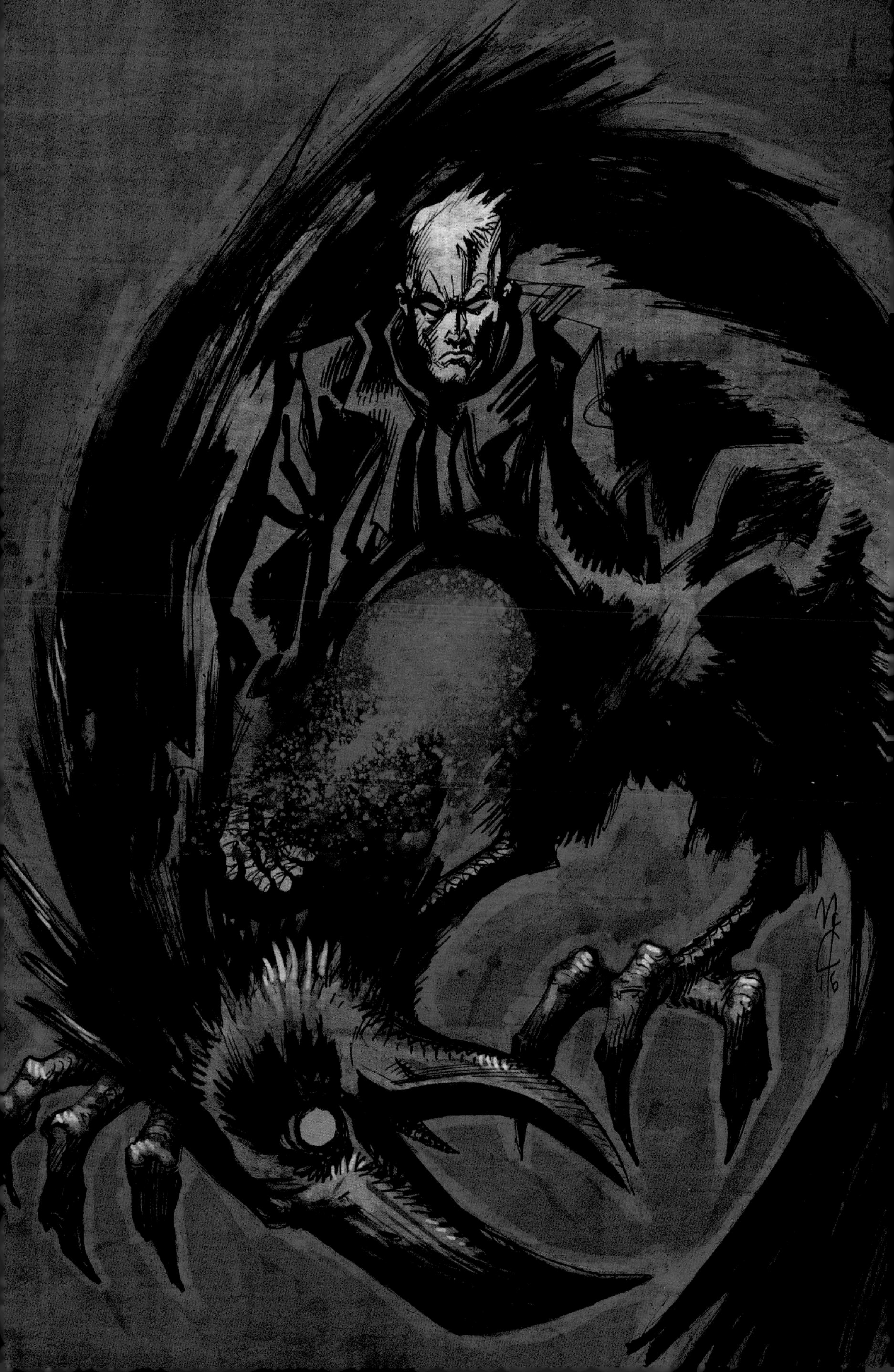

Issue 1
DECLAN SHALVEY w/ JORDIE BELLAIRE
The Comic Mint variant cover

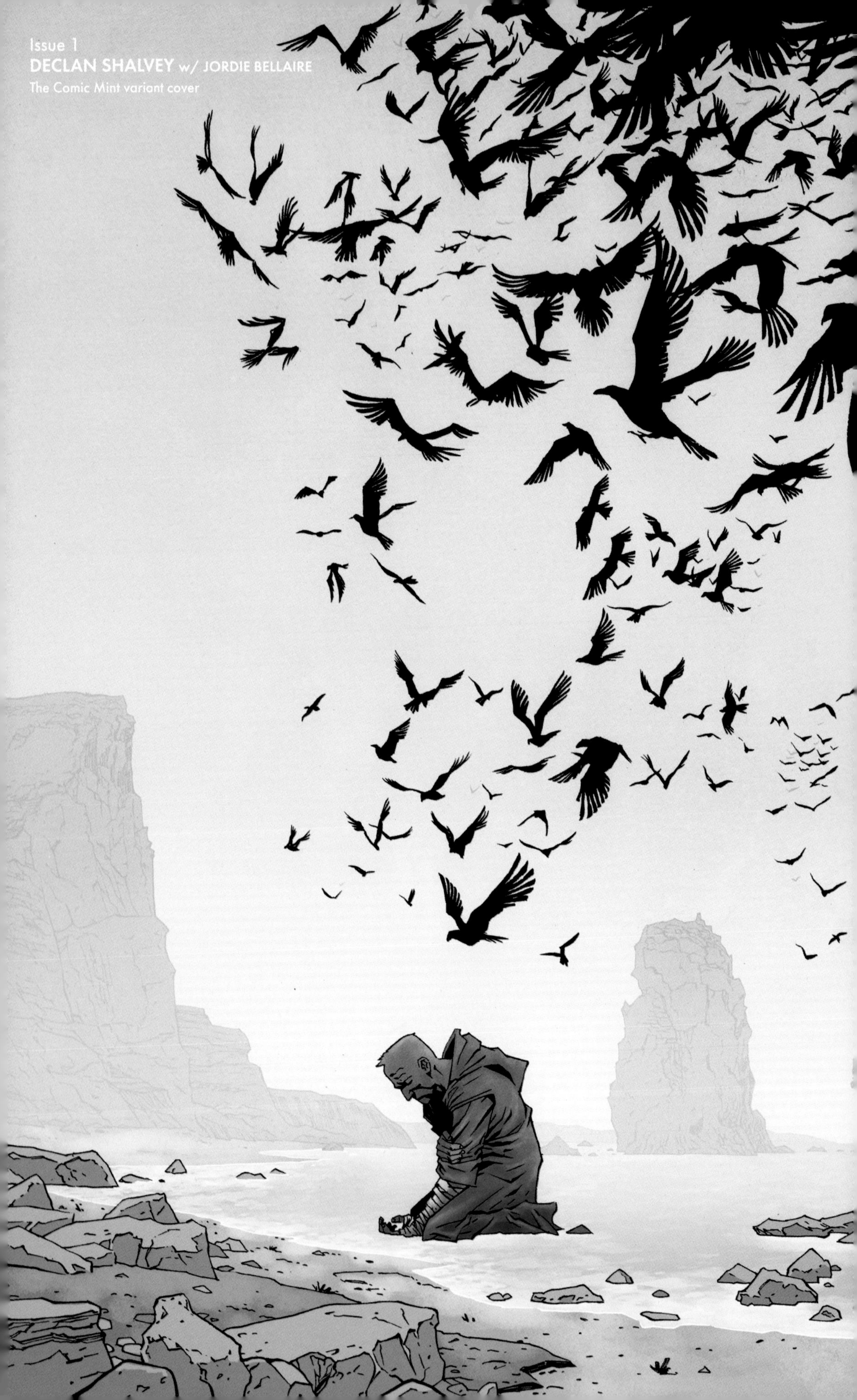

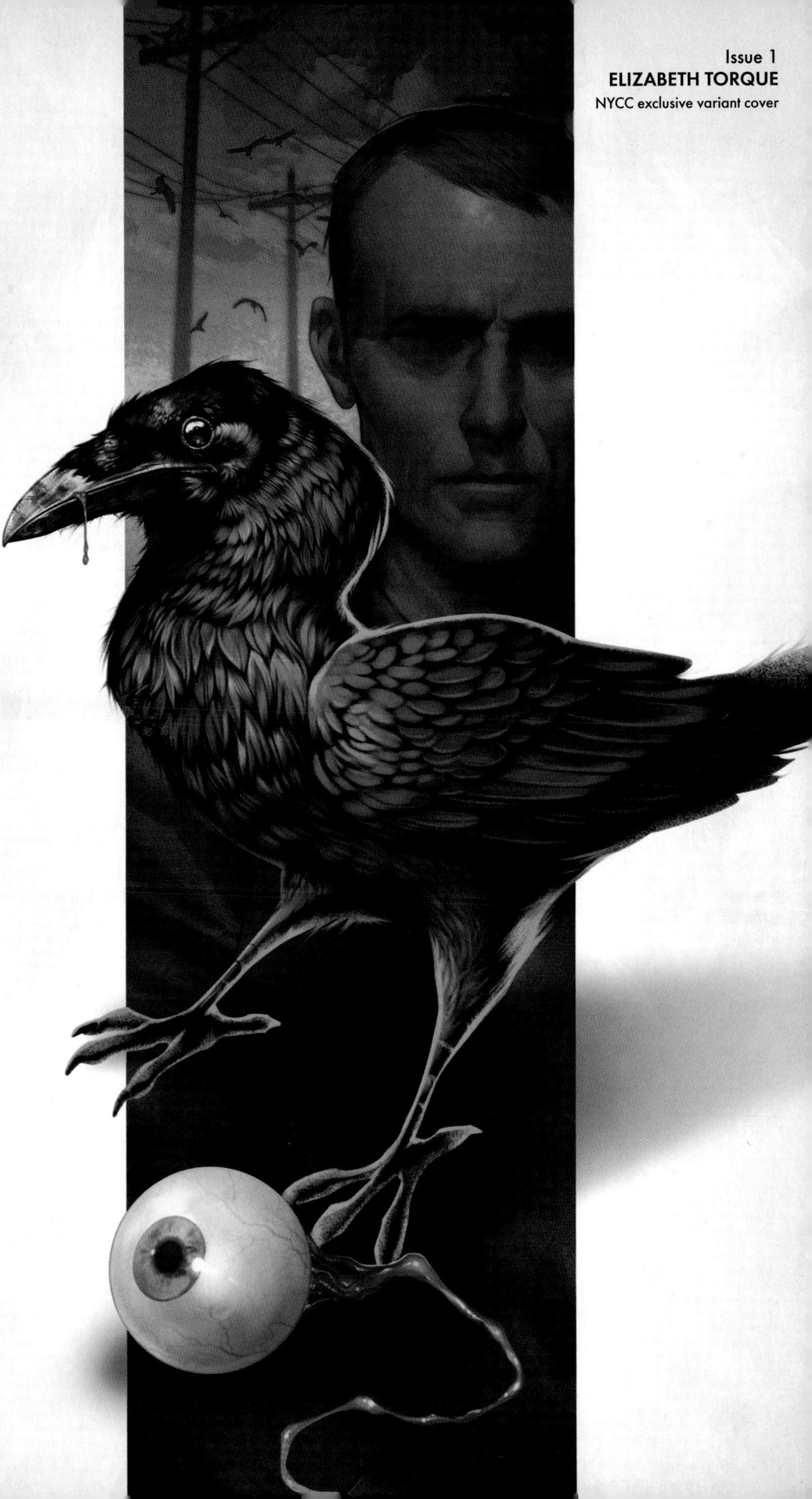

Issue 1
ELIZABETH TORQUE
NYCC exclusive variant cover

sketchbook

character sketches by
PHIL HESTER

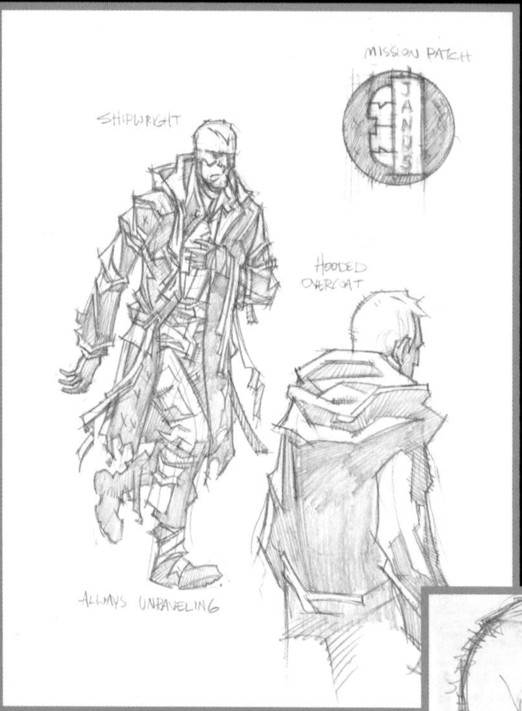
MISSION PATCH
JANUS
SHIPWRIGHT
HOODED OVERCOAT
ALWAYS UNRAVELING

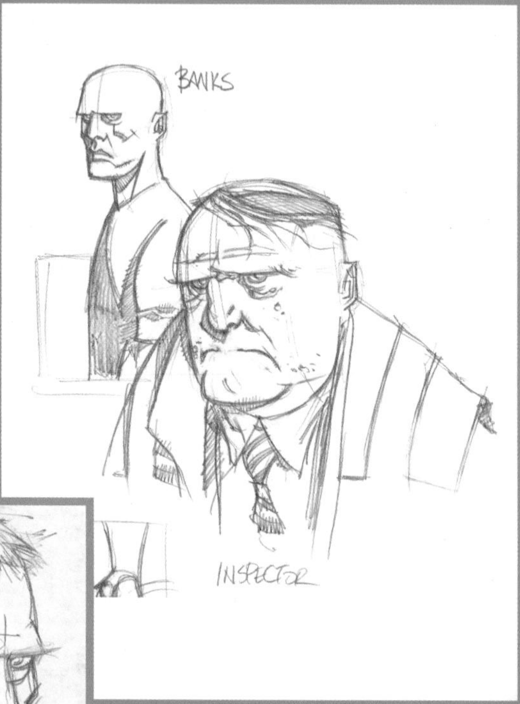
BANKS
INSPECTOR

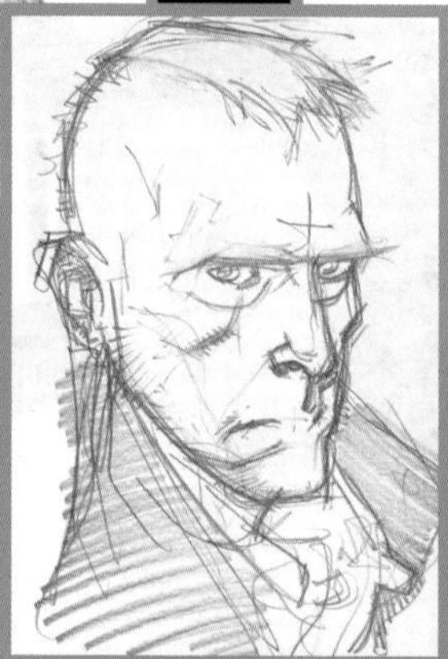

logo tests by JOHN J. HILL

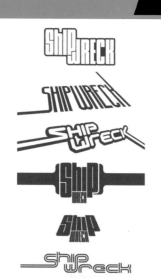

SHIPWRECK™

sketchbook

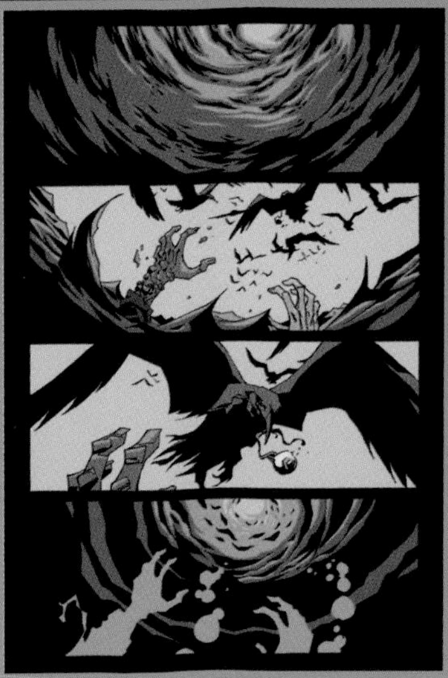

color tests by
MARK ENGLERT

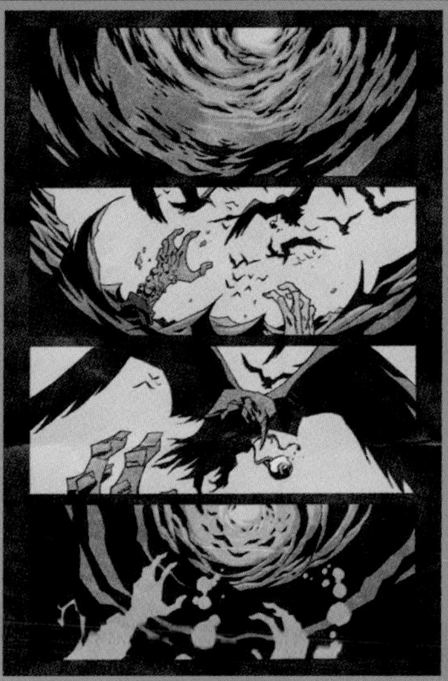

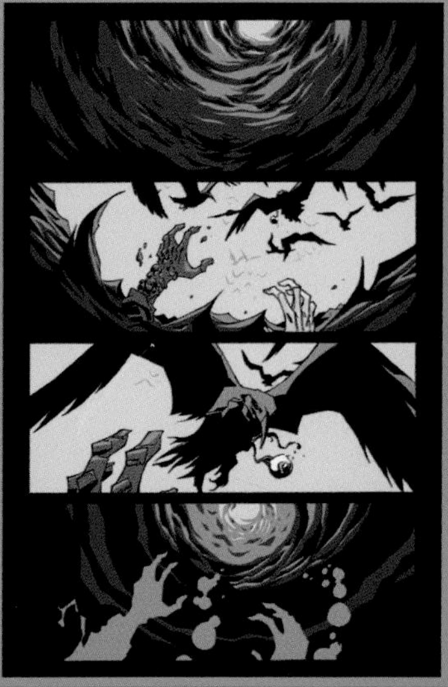

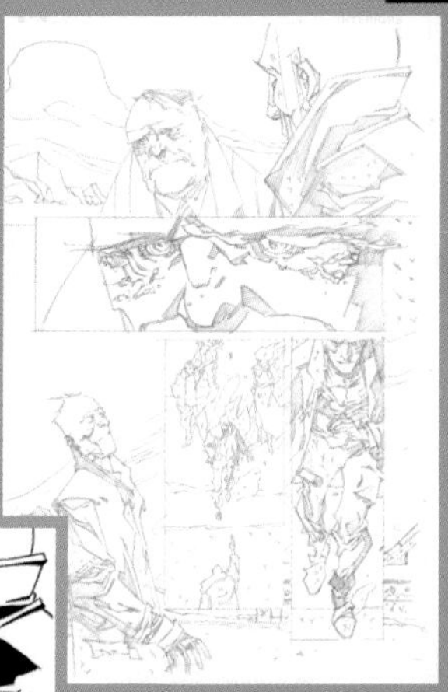

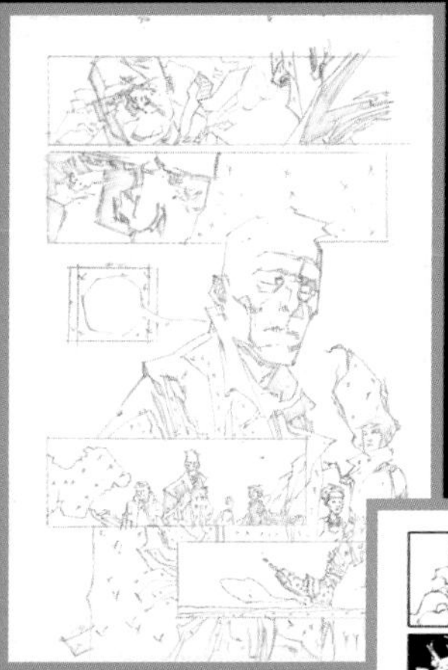

These two versions of page 12 of SHIPWRECK #6 offer an insight into the different ways an artist, in this case Phil Hester, can interpret a script.

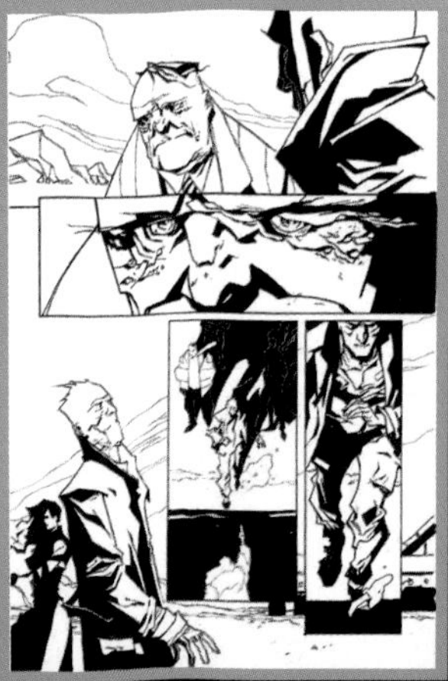

issue #6 pg.12 (unused)
pencils by PHIL HESTER
inks by ERIC GAPSTUR

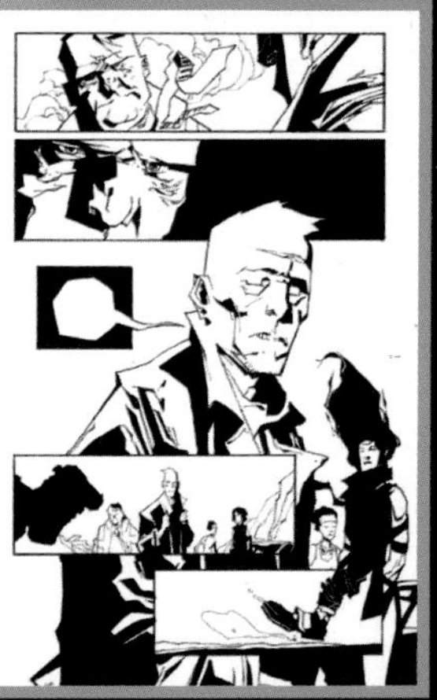

issue #6 pg.12 (final)
pencils by PHIL HESTER
inks by ERIC GAPSTUR

ABOUT THE CREATORS OF

SHIPWRECK

WARREN ELLIS
writer

🐦 @warrenellis

Warren is the award-winning writer of graphic novels like *Transmetropolitan, Fell, Ministry of Space* and *Planetary,* and the author of the NYT-bestselling *Gun Machine* and the "underground classic" novel *Crooked Little Vein.* The movie *Red* is based on his graphic novel of the same name, its sequel having been released in the summer of 2013. *Iron Man 3* is based on his Marvel Comics graphic novel *Iron Man: Extremis.* He's also written extensively for Vice, Wired UK and Reuters on technological and cultural matters. Warren Ellis is currently working on a non-fiction book about the future of the city for Farrar Giroux Straus. His newest publication is the digital short-story single *Dead Pig Collector* from FSG Originals. His next book will be the novella *Normal,* also from FSG, out in print in November 2018.

A documentary about his work, *Captured Ghosts,* was released in 2012. Recognitions include the NUIG Literary and Debating Society's President's Medal for service to freedom of speech, the Eagle Award's Roll Of Honour for lifetime achievement in the field of comics & graphic novels, the Grand Prix de l'Imaginaire 2010, the Sidewise Award for Alternate History and the International Horror Guild Award for illustrated narrative. He is a Patron of the British Humanist Association, an Associate of the Institute of Atemporal Studies and the literary editor of *Edict* magazine. Warren Ellis lives outside London, on the south-east coast of England, in case he needs to make a quick getaway.

(photo by Ellen J Rogers)

PHIL HESTER
artist

🐦 @philhester

Phil has been writing and drawing comics for nearly three decades, beginning while still a student at the University of Iowa. He broke into the mainstream with a long run as artist of DC's *Swamp Thing* with writer Mark Millar. He also wrote and drew the Eisner Award nominated series *The Wretch.* Phil drew Kevin Smith's revival of DC's *Green Arrow.* He wrote the original graphic novels *The Coffin* and *Deep Sleeper* with artist Mike Huddleston. At Image Comics, he created *Firebreather* with artist Andy Kuhn.

His work, as both artist and writer, has been featured in hundreds of comics from nearly every American publisher, and includes runs on such titles as *The Darkness, Wonder Woman, Ant-Man, Ultimate Marvel Team-Up, Nightwing, Invincible Universe, Batman Beyond, The Flash: Season Zero, Deathstroke* and *Mythic.*

ERIC GAPSTUR inker

🐦 @ericgapstur

Eric has been creating comics professionally since 2011, most notably inking Phil Hester on such titles as *Legends of the Dark Knight, Adventures of Superman* and *Batman Beyond 2.0.* Additionally, Eric is pencilling *Flash: Season Zero* and now, ANIMOSITY: EVOLUTION for AfterShock. He lives in Eastern Iowa with his wife, Michelle and son, Liam.

MARK ENGLERT colorist

🐦 @markenglert

Mark Englert was born in 1979. The first movie he ever saw on opening day was *Star Trek: The Motion Picture* and he slept through the whole thing. Since then, he grew up a little, saw a lot more movies, watched way too much TV, spent countless hours reading comic books when he wasn't busy playing video games. He has been steadily working as an illustrator since 1999, coloring comics, doing concept work at Microsoft and drawing posters for almost every major movie studio . His future plans include continuing to work on comics, illustrating a lot more posters and to one day stay awake for an entire viewing of *Star Trek: The Motion Picture.*

MARSHALL DILLON letterer

🐦 @marshalldillon

A comic book industry veteran, Marshall got his start in 1994, in the midst of the indy comic boom. Over the years, he's been everything from an independent self-published writer to an associate publisher working on properties like *G.I. Joe, Voltron* and *Street Fighter.* He's done just about everything except draw a comic book, and worked for just about every publisher except the "big two." Primarily a father and letterer these days, he also dabbles in old-school paper & dice RPG game design. You can catch up with Marshall at firstdraftpress.net.